TAKE THE
RICH OFF
WELFARE

Published in the United States by South End Press, Cambridge, Massachusetts. Any properly footnoted quotation of up to 500 sequential words may be used without permission, as long as the total number of words quoted does not exceed 2,000. For longer quotations or for a greater number of total words, please write for permission to South End Press.

Cover design by Ellen P. Shapiro
Cover illustration by Alan Gordon
Page design and production by the South End Press collective
All cartoons courtesy of Kirk Anderson

Printed on recycled, acid-free paper by union labor

LIBRARY OF CONGRESS CATALOGING-IN-PUBLICATION DATA

Zepezauer, Mark.

Take the rich off welfare / by Mark Zepezauer. — New exp. ed.
p. cm.

Includes bibliographical references and index.

ISBN 0-89608-706-9 (pbk. : alk. paper)
ISBN 0-89608-707-7 (cloth : alk. paper)

1. Waste in government spending—United States. 2. Government spending policy—United States. 3. Fiscal policy—United States.
I. Title.
HJ7537.Z46 2004
339.5'22'0973—dc22   2004000630

South End Press
7 Brookline Street, #1
Cambridge, MA 02139
www.southendpress.org
southend@southendpress.org

10 09 08 07 06 05 04   2 3 4 5

TAKE THE
RICH OFF
WELFARE

New, Expanded Edition

by Mark Zepezauer

Cartoons by Kirk Anderson

South End Press
Cambridge, Massachusetts

TABLE OF CONTENTS

About the Author

Author/cartoonist Mark Zepezauer was raised amidst the idyllic semiconductor farms of Silicon Valley, the son of immigrants from Milwaukee and Chicago. After graduating from UC Santa Cruz, he worked for several newspapers in that community, creating the cartoon panel "US History Backwards." In 1989 he produced a limited edition art book, *The Nixon Saga*, now found in more than two museum collections. He moved to Arizona in 1993, publishing the *Tucson Comic News*, a monthly compendium of political cartoons and commentary, until 2000. He is the author of *The CIA's Greatest Hits* (1994), *Take the Rich Off Welfare* (1996), and *Boomerang! How Our Covert Wars Have Created Enemies Across the Middle East and Brought Terror to America* (2003). Zepezauer lives in Tucson with his splendid wife, two miraculous babies, and four recalcitrant cats.

Acknowledgements

Many thanks to my infant son Forrest for learning to sleep more than a few hours at a stretch. That's been a big help, bud. His big sister Iris has also done much better at learning to play quietly by herself while Daddy is working, instead of climbing up in his lap and banging on the keyboard. And you would not be holding this volume without the million incalculable efforts of their mom, my dear wife Nan, to maintain some semblance of order in the household. To her I dedicate this book.

The first edition of this book was written in collaboration with Arthur Naiman and published as a Real Story book by Odonian Press in September, 1996. Arthur's spirit remains an integral part of the book, and many of the best jokes are still his. Much as I'd like to take credit for the title of the book, it apparently originated with Senator Fred Harris of Oklahoma in his 1976 campaign for the Democratic presidential nomination. (Too bad he didn't win.) Author Michael Parenti used a similar slogan in a 1978 Congressional campaign (for more about him, go to michaelparenti.org).

Everyone at South End Press has been wonderful, and you should go right back to the store and buy some of their other books. Asha Tall has been gracious and patient in the face of my many missed deadlines, and her careful reading has greatly improved the text. Many thanks also to Loie Hayes, Anthony Arnove, Joey Fox, Jill Petty, Tina Beyene, Alexander Dwinell, Elizabeth Maki, and Martha Osgood. I would thank the proofreaders, too, but I don't know their names. Insert them here [Erich Strom and Cindy Milstein], folks.

A number of others have contributed in some way to the progress of this book, and thanks must go to Mom and Dad, Marvin and Carroll, the Enchilada Faceplants, and David Blaisdell; a small army of think tankers including Janice Shields, Bob McIntyre, Chuck Collins, Gawain Kripke, Russell Mokhiber, John Pike, Bill Wagner and others too numerous to mention; the helpful and patient reference staff of the Tucson Public Library; plus Matt Somers, Chaz Bufe, Greg Bates, Chuck and Laurie; echinacea and goldenseal, Google, George Seldes and the Pixies.

Any mistakes are of course my own, unless I'm mistaken. You can send hate mail or fan mail to me at comicnews@earthlink.net, but mention the book in the subject line or you're likely to be deleted as spam.

Introduction

Wealthfare—the money government gives away to corporations and wealthy individuals—costs us more than $815 billion a year. That's:

- 47% of what it costs to run the US government (which is about $1.73 trillion a year, not counting entitlement trust funds like Social Security and Medicare)[1]
- enough money to eliminate the federal debt in just over eight years (the total is now $6.6 trillion, accumulated over 200-plus years)[2]
- more than four times what we spend on welfare for the poor (currently around $193 billion a year; see Appendix A for a breakdown)

For a summary of what goes into that $815 billion figure, turn back to the Table of Contents, which lists the estimated annual cost of the various subsidies, handouts, tax breaks, loopholes, ripoffs, and scams this book describes.

I've calculated these amounts as precisely as possible, but they change every year, and data is often hard to obtain, so they are, of course, estimates. If they seem high to you, cut them all by 50%—or 75%; welfare for the rich would still cost more than welfare for the poor.

In fact, $815 billion is definitely an underestimate. Limitations of time and space forced me to leave out many major categories of wealthfare. Most of these could be books in themselves: state and local wealthfare (my figure includes just federal giveaways), Medicare waste and fraud, automobile subsidies (much of which are state and local spending), the effects of Federal Reserve policies, the NAFTA and GATT treaties, foreign aid, deregulation of various industries, fraudulent charitable deductions, the easy treatment given white-collar criminals, and on and on.

I discuss some of them in the chapter called "What's Been Left Out," which begins on p. 133. (Only the military chapter is longer, which gives you an idea of how much wealthfare isn't included in the estimate.)

Even within categories I do cite figures for, there are often additional wealthfare expenses I haven't been able to nail down. So there's no doubt that $815 billion greatly understates the amount of money American taxpayers lose each year on welfare for the rich.

IT'S GETTING WORSE

When the first edition of this book was published in 1996, the figure for total wealthfare was $448 billion a year.[3] By 1999, that number had grown to $603 billion. The 2003 estimate of $815 billion shows an 82% increase in just seven years (or 69% if you adjust for inflation).[4]

In contrast, spending for the poor rose only $63 billion (from the 1996 figure of $130 billion); taking inflation into account, that's a 41% increase. But in fact, spending that exclusively benefits the poor dropped by 10% in constant dollars. The only reason there was any increase at all is the vastly higher cost of Medicaid, which also serves some people who aren't poor.

In the intervening years, there's been a lot more discussion of wealthfare—and very little reform. In 1997, then-Representative John Kasich (R-OH) brought together a coalition of groups from both the right and the left to oppose a dozen especially dreadful corporate welfare programs. They managed to agree on the need to eliminate $11 billion—spread out over five years (in other words, about $2.2 billion a year, or less than half of one percent of what actually needed to be cut).[5] Six years later, some of the programs they targeted have been cut back considerably, but every one of them still survives.

On the positive side, there have been small victories. Some especially odious nuclear boondoggles were canceled. The McNugget subsidy (an agricultural marketing program exploited by huge firms like McDonald's) was scaled back by 90%. Reformers have occasionally managed to keep things from getting worse. But overall, we've lost ground.

At this writing, both houses of Congress have passed a new generation of atrocious nuclear giveaways (though the two bills have yet to be reconciled and sent to the White House). The 2002 farm bill added another $73 billion in new subsidies. Despite then-bipartisan fervor for balancing budgets, the 1998 highway bill contained nearly 1,500 pork-barrel projects, costing over $9 billion.[6] Cutting the tax rate for long-term capital gains to 15% has more than doubled the amount of revenue lost to the US Treasury. The income cap on payroll taxes is now costing us 60% more than in 1996 (because the rich have gotten so much richer in the meantime).[7]

Even when activists have worked for years to kill off indefensible programs, the funding has often shifted to less-scrutinized parts of the budget. According to Jim Riccio, who works on nuclear issues for Public Citizen, "All those victories we've been getting have turned into lessons learned for industry and [federal] agencies, so they can make sure [such] victories never happen again."[8]

Back when the Democrats controlled the Congress, their districts pulled in about $35 million more a year in goodies from Uncle Sam than GOP districts did. The Republicans complained mightily about that, but then the Dem's districts did tend to have more poor people in them, who were presumably in need of federal assistance. But by 2001, after seven years of GOP control, the well-heeled Republican districts were taking in, on average, $612 million more than those served by Democrats. That's a 1748% increase.[9]

THE RICH ARE STEALING FROM THE POOR

Before we go on, I'd like to clarify something. I'm not saying there's anything wrong with being rich, in and of itself. Many wealthy people earned their money by producing a product or a service the public liked and wanted to buy, or by helping a company do that. (The Grateful Dead are one example—their concerts became so popular that they had to run lotteries to decide who got to buy tickets.)

Speaking personally, I don't think that some people should inherit vast fortunes tax-free while others spend their whole lives scrambling to get by. And I believe that no one should live in luxury while others are starving. (That's not as hard to fix as you might think. A wealth tax of just 4% on the 200 richest people on earth would guarantee everyone enough to eat.)[10]

But this book isn't about those issues. All it says is that it's not fair for people to get rich—and stay rich—by defrauding people who are poorer than them. As you'll soon see, stealing from the poor—actually, from anybody who isn't rich—has become standard operating procedure in this country. In fact, the US government today functions mostly as a huge Robin-Hood-in-reverse.

BUT DOESN'T IT HELP THE ECONOMY?

It is sometimes argued that corporate welfare benefits society as a whole by recirculating money back into the economy. Of course, that's even more true of welfare for the poor, which benefits grocery stores, supermarkets, clothing stores, landlords, doctors, dentists, etc. Furthermore, many welfare programs pay for themselves many times over in future savings on health care, prisons, and welfare payments. (For example, according to conservative estimates, $1 invested in Head Start saves $3 in future costs to society.)[11] Corporate welfare, on the other hand, tends to finance industries that pollute our air, water and soil, so we end up paying for them twice—with our money and with our health.

Subsidizing certain businesses or industries is not only unfair to competitors who aren't subsidized, but it also stifles the incentive of the subsidized businesses to innovate and develop new products (which might not be eligible for subsidies), ultimately making them less competitive.

Welfare for the rich fosters corruption, both in business and in government. And it's not uncommon for two wealthfare programs to conflict—as when the Interior Department subsidizes irrigation water for agribusinesses and the Agriculture Department pays those same companies not to grow crops with that water. (What do the companies do? Why, sell the water back to local governments at a profit, of course. What else? See the section called "The Waters of Babylon" on pp. 91–92.)

In any case, it's not as if the money currently spent on wealthfare would suddenly evaporate if we weren't handing it over to the rich. It would go into the economy some other way and would almost certainly have a more beneficial effect. (For more on this, see the section "What about the Jobs We'd Lose?" on p. 64, in the chapter on military waste and fraud.)

Wealthfare has one final cost: the creative talents of many bright lawyers, accountants, and financial advisors are spent figuring out how to squeeze the maximum benefit from our labyrinthine tax code. If they weren't wasting their time on that, they could be doing something genuinely useful, which would make the economy more productive for all of us.

LOOPHOLES ARE WORTH MORE THAN HANDOUTS

Welfare for the rich takes five basic forms. The first two are tax breaks and direct subsidies. The former are more insidious, for a couple of reasons. First, while subsidies typically have to be appropriated by Congress and signed into law by the president each year, tax breaks usually get little scrutiny, and since they don't have to be renewed annually, they last until they're repealed by some future tax law.

Second, while subsidies are usually for fixed amounts of money, the amount the government loses on a tax loophole depends on how many taxpayers take advantage of it each year, and to what extent. This means tax breaks are basically open-ended—there's no way the government can control, or even accurately predict, what they're going to cost. Furthermore, they're less controversial for politicians because everybody likes tax cuts; it's just that the tax cuts I talk about in this book go only to certain groups.

To understand how money is spent in Washington, we have to make a distinction between budgets and bills. When the White House submits a budget to Congress every February, it's basically a suggestion. Then the Congressmembers pass their own budget, which is basically a set of spending guidelines for them to rely on (more or less loosely) as they pass their appropriations bills over the rest of the year. Theoretically, they've passed all those bills by October 1, reconciled between the House and Senate versions, and sent them to the president for signature.

If Congressmembers want to throw money at, say, nuclear power, they could budget for that every year and include it as an item in an appropriations bill. The other method is to write a tax break for nuclear power plant operators and get that passed and signed. Then it stands every year until it's repealed. Some tax breaks do come with a deadline, as with the "sunset" gimmicks in the latest tax bill that expire in 2006 or 2008 or 2010, unless some future Congress extends them. But something like the Oil Depletion Allowance (see Chapter 18) is more or less immortal.

Over half of the $815 billion wealthfare figure comes from various tax breaks and loopholes. If you think that eliminating them amounts to raising taxes, that's fine; just be clear that you're saying the rich deserve to get more than $400 billion a year in tax breaks that aren't available to poorer people. The Earned Income Tax Credit (EITC) is included in the section on welfare for the poor. Legislators created the EITC out of the recognition that people who are working hard still can't make ends meet. Okay, so this is a handout necessary for survival. I've still included it in the section on welfare for the poor, and most people think of it that way. By the same token, tax breaks for the wealthy are government handouts, and they should be counted as that—welfare for the rich. Handouts are handouts. The only difference is that the rich don't need them.

Back in 1940, US corporations paid roughly half of the federal government's general revenues.[12] Over the intervening years, business taxes have been steadily declining (except for a little blip in 1986). In fiscal year 1999, corporate tax payments dropped 2.5% and corporate profits rose 8.9%. Citizens for Tax Justice reported in 2002 that corporate tax payments were near record lows as a percentage of GDP (gross domestic product).[13] Today, corporations pay just 7.4%.[14] So if "fiscally responsible" candidates want to balance the budget and lower individual taxes, it's easy. All they have to do is tax corporations at the same rate as they did back when what was good for General Motors was good for the country.

The taxes corporations avoid paying have to be raised from individuals. Not all individuals, of course—that would be un-American. Thanks to a series of tax "reforms" that began in 1977, the rate paid by the richest Americans has been cut nearly in half, while Social Security taxes—which are paid overwhelmingly by ordinary wage earners, and not paid at all on income over $87,000—have steadily risen.[15]

Now, I'm certainly no fan of the IRS, and I don't enjoy paying taxes any more than anybody else. (I'd probably enjoy it a bit more if I knew that more of it was going to fund worthwhile things like teachers and parks and hospitals.) But since corporations and wealthy individuals derive most of the benefit from what the government does, I think they should pay their fair share of taxes. They say they're in favor of free enterprise—let's pretend they mean it, and take them off the dole.

FIRE SALES, OVERRUNS, AND LAZY COPS

The other three forms of welfare for the rich are more subtle than handouts or tax breaks. One is when Uncle Sam sells off properties belonging to We the People at a fraction of their true market value. You can find examples of this sort of boondoggle in the chapters on timber and mining subsidies. The magnificent trees in your national forests are being sold off to private interests for pennies on the dollar. But if you think that's bad, try the chapter on media subsidies and you'll find out how much Uncle Sam charges radio and TV broadcasters for your public airwaves: nothing.

The flip side of the "fire sale" scam is when Uncle Sam shells out many times more than market value for goods and services from favored contractors. These cost overruns defraud the taxpayer, and seem to continue no matter who is elected (or appointed) to office. There are plenty of examples of this just a few pages away—in the section on waste, fraud, and abuse in military spending. You've probably heard about the $640 toilet seat, but believe me, it gets much worse than that.

The fifth and final form of wealthfare might not sound like welfare at all, but it's a major aspect of how government policies favor the rich: the lax enforcement of white-collar crime. Because this sort of "public assistance" is so difficult to quantify, it's discussed in the chapter called "What's Been Left Out" (p. 133).

THE RICH KEEP GETTING RICHER

Changes in the tax laws have contributed to a widening gap between rich and poor. Between 1983 and 1998, 91% of the increase in Americans' wealth went to the top 20% of the US population, and 53% of it went to the top 1% of the population (those families whose net worth is $3.35 million or more).[16]

Income disparity in the United States is now the widest it's been since the crash of 1929, and it continues to grow. The top 1% of the population now owns more than the bottom 95%. In other words, the 2.9 million Americans who are worth $3.35 million or more have as much money and property as the 276,769,922 poorest Americans. (And those are 1998 figures, the last year for which data is available. The disparity is even worse today, given the tax cuts and job losses of the past three years.)[17]

Wherever you look on the economic ladder, the rich are getting richer. The wealthiest 20% have gotten wealthier while the other 80% of the people have gotten poorer. Within the top 20%, the top 5% have gotten richer than the other 15%. Within the top 5%, the top 1% have gotten richer than the other 4%. Within the top 1%, the top quarter have gotten richer than the other three-quarters.[18] And so it goes, right up to the 400 richest Americans. Their average net worth in 2000 was 13 times higher than in 1982.[19]

Inequality increased rapidly in the 1980s and continued to increase—though more slowly—in the 1990s. Median family income did increase slightly in the last decade, but only in 1999 did it catch up to where it was ten years earlier.[20] The poverty rate has also declined to its 1989 figure, but the number of children living in extreme poverty (in families whose income is less than half the official poverty level) has gone up.[21] (The poverty threshold is currently set at an annual income of $14,255 for a family of three, or $17,960 for a family of four.)

THIS IS HOW THE BOOK IS ORGANIZED

There are three main sections. Part One covers a number of tax breaks available to wealthy individuals. Part Two outlines a number of general business loopholes, and Part Three delves into specific cookie jars available to specific industries. In each part, I've started with the biggest kinds of wealthfare and worked my way down to the smallest (which aren't all that small). That way, if you don't make it all the way through that part, you'll still have covered the most important ripoffs and scams. (But then you'll miss some of the most extraordinary ones; for an example, see the section on Taxol, which begins on p. 132.) Let me give you an example from each part.

Horse write-offs

The original idea behind the tax deduction for horse expenses was that horses were essential to the functioning of a farm, like pigs and cattle. Although that's no longer true for most of the horses in this country, this deduction has been expanded into a major tax shelter. As *The Wall Street Journal* put it, "Some of the people breeding horses now... can barely tell a horse from a donkey, but [they] recognize a nice tax shelter." And they aren't too subtle about it either, as you can see from some of the names given racehorses in recent years: My Deduction, Tax Dodge, Tax Gimmick, Write-Off, My Write-Off, Another Shelter, and Justa Shelter.

If you own a horse, you can deduct the costs of food, housing, vet bills, stud fees, transportation, insurance, interest charges, depreciation, attendance at horse shows, visits to horse farms, and state and local taxes.

Wilhelmina du Pont Ross, a member of one of the wealthiest families in the world, hired her husband to run their stables and wrote off his salary on their joint tax return. Her relative, William du Pont Jr., whose vast estate in Maryland contained a grandstand that could seat 12,500 people, deducted the cost of keeping professional foxhunters on staff.

You can trade an older horse for one that's younger and more valuable without paying any taxes on the exchange. And when you sell a horse, the profit is taxed at the lower capital gains rate rather than as ordinary income. If you don't want the bother of actually owning horses, you can even lease them and still cash in on the tax advantages, without any unpleasant odors on the estate.

All of this is kept in place by the vigorous lobbying of the American Horse Council, whose representatives virtually write the laws in this area. There isn't much opposition to these loopholes, both because most people don't know about them and because everybody loves horses. (Of course, it isn't the horses that get the tax breaks.) But like most tax shelters, they divert investment into unproductive uses simply for the purpose of tax evasion.[22] In the nonprofit sector, this would be like securing grant money to provide English-as-a-second-language classes even though your constituency is already completely fluent. Or more ominously, it is like getting debt reduction for your country through an IMF plan in exchange for switching supports for social services to underwriting private enterprise even though your private sector is not starving and your people are. Unfortunately, most business leaders don't see any of these situations as a paradox. "Free" money obscures clear thinking.

In creating a fiscal response to the 9/11 attacks, Congress allowed horses to be eligible for "bonus depreciation" (see p. 40) if purchased between September 11, 2001, and September 11, 2004. New tax rules in 2003 also quadrupled the limit on the horse deduction from $25,000 to $100,000. Now if that doesn't stop the terrorists, nothing will.[23]

Miscellaneous corporate tax breaks

Some economists make the following argument: Since corporations always pass their costs along to their customers, consumers ultimately pay all corporate taxes. Thus, there's really no such thing as corporate taxation. If this were true, then the lower the corporate tax rate, the higher consumer spending power would be. In the real world, however, the opposite is often the case.

In the 1950s, when the corporate tax rate was 52% and corporations paid almost a third of all income taxes, a single wage earner could support a family of four and could afford a new house, a car, and major appliances.[24] In the 2000s, when the corporate tax rate ranges between 15% and 35% and corporations pay less than 10% of all income taxes, more than half of all families have two or more wage earners, and businesses are laying off people left and right.[25] (According to the US Bureau of Labor

Statistics, average earnings of nonsupervisory workers peaked in 1973, and they've been going down ever since. By 1992, they were 12% lower than they were in 1965.)[26]

So it seems that corporations retain some of the savings they get from lower tax rates—which isn't surprising, since they lobby so ferociously for them. Their investment in certain key legislators can be repaid many times over.

For example, section 543(b) of the US tax code contains a provision that applies only to corporations formed in Nevada on January 27, 1972. It allows Cantor, Fitzgerald, and Co.—the only company incorporated in Nevada on that date—to exempt certain interest income involving securities and money-market funds from taxation.

Handcrafted tax breaks like this are nothing new. Movie mogul Louis B. Mayer had a provision inserted into the Revenue Act of 1951 that classified his retirement package as capital gains rather than ordinary income. As a result, it was taxed at 20% instead of 90%, and he saved nearly $2 million in federal taxes.[27]

Fly the friendly skies

As I discuss in Chapter 16, "Aviation Subsidies," if there's any rationale for governmental subsidies, it would be to help useful fledgling technologies that might not otherwise be developed. The airline industry isn't exactly a newcomer anymore, and yet we taxpayers still fork out for the air traffic control system, hand out grants for airport construction, and provide reports from the National Weather Service. The industry receives $1 billion annually in federal military research funds, the taxpayer-funded Commerce Department lobbies aggressively for foreign purchases of US-built aircraft, and the airlines are exempted from the 4.3 cents per gallon fuel tax that the rest of us consumers pay.

But even with all these handouts (and there are plenty more cited in that chapter), commercial aviation has never been all that profitable. Even before the 9/11 attacks (which left the country's entire fleet grounded for a week or so), the industry was in a world of hurt. It was simply a case of over-capacity; compared to the demand, there were too many planes flying. Demand slacked off even more after 9/11, but the airlines ended up with a $15 billion bailout from Uncle Sugar that was triple what they had lost in the shutdown. And as with so many other wealthfare programs described in this book, the lion's share of the bailout went to the biggest companies; many small firms received quite a bit less than they had lost in the 9/11 crisis.

So how did the big airlines show their gratitude? As you may recall, by laying off thousands of workers (who got absolutely no compensation from Congress) and shelling out huge bonuses for the executives. And did this elicit any outrage on Capitol Hill? Not particularly, though plenty of workers across the country were seething. In fact, Congress saw nothing wrong with setting up another $3 billion bailout for the airlines to get them through any economic turbulence arising from the war on Iraq. Welcome to the wonderful world of corporate welfare.

It's a system where the timber industry can spend $8 million lobbying to retain a threatened road-building subsidy and come up with $458 million in goodies. It's a world where Archer Daniels Midland can spread around $3 million in campaign contributions and be rewarded with a $7 billion subsidy. It's a country where the tobacco companies can buy themselves a $50 billion tax break with a mere $30 million investment in "good government."[28] And yes, it's your country; as the saying goes, these are your tax dollars at work.

HERE WE GO...

Even in election years, few politicians pay more than lip service to ending corporate welfare (this isn't surprising, considering who finances their campaigns). Of the budget cuts passed by the 104th Congress, more than 90% came out of programs for the poor.[29] Though some politicians appear to be working sincerely to limit welfare for the rich, it would be foolish to depend on them. Fortunately, there are plenty of ways ordinary citizens can force changes. For some ideas on how to start, see the "Activist's Toolkits" following each chapter.

If you run across terms you're not sure of—*constant dollars*, say, or *median*—consult the glossary that begins on p. 147. (It can also help you appreciate the full significance of terms you do know the meaning of, like billion and trillion.)

If you think something I'm saying just can't be true—a reaction I've had several times myself—you'll find backup for it in the endnotes. If a note is in error or you want to check out something that's not referenced, drop me a line at comicnews@earthlink.net. I can't promise how quickly I'll get back to you, but I do value the feedback.

And now—into the mire.

ACTIVIST'S TOOLKIT — GENERAL

Following each chapter, you'll find an "Activist's Toolkit" geared to that particular topic. But several organizations attack corporate welfare—and other injustices—on more than one front. This section lists some of the best of them. (For groups working mainly on tax policy, see the Toolkit at the end of Chapter 4.) All of the Activist's Toolkit sections will be archived and occasionally updated at this book's official website, http://www.markzepezauer.com/wealthfare.

The Cato Institute
A libertarian think tank • 1000 Massachusetts Avenue NW, Washington, DC 20001-5403 • phone: (202) 842-0200 • fax: (202) 842-3490 • website on corporate welfare: http://www.catoinstitute.com/fiscal/corporate-welfare.html

The Center for Public Integrity
910 17th Street NW, Seventh Floor, Washington, DC 20006 • phone: (202) 466-1300 • fax: (202) 466-1101 • website: http://www.publicintegrity.org/dtaweb/home.asp

The Center for Responsive Politics
1101 14th Street NW, Suite 1030, Washington, DC 20005-5635 • phone: (202) 857-0044 • fax: (202) 857-7809 • email: info@crp.org • "Your Guide to the Money in U.S. Elections," website: http://www.opensecrets.org/

Common Cause
2030 M Street NW, Washington, DC 20036 • phone: (202) 833-1200 • fax: (202) 659-3716 • website: http://www.commoncause.org/ • corporate welfare page: http://www.commoncause.org/issue_agenda/corporate_welfare.htm

Corporate Welfare and Foreign Policy
A report by Janice Shields for Foreign Policy in Focus • website: http://www.foreignpolicy-infocus.org/papers/cw/

Corporate Welfare: Communism in America
website: http://socialconscience.com/articles/welfare/

Corporate Welfare Information Center
A project of the ACTION Center • email: catalyst@actionpa.org • website: http://www.corporations.org/welfare/

Corporate Welfare Shame Page
A project of the Benjamin Banneker Center • 647 Plymouth Road, Baltimore, MD 21229 • email: banneker@progress.org • website: http://www.progress.org/banneker/cw.html

The Freedom Network Directory for Corporate Welfare
website: http://www.free-market.net/directorybytopic/corporatewelfare/

HR 2902, Corporate Subsidy Reform Commission
Sponsored by Rep. Adam Smith, (D-WA) • website: http://thomas.loc.gov/cgi-bin/bdquery/z?d108:h.r.02902:

Infact Campaign Headquarters
46 Plympton Street, Boston, MA 02118 • phone: (617) 695-2525 • fax: (617) 695-2626 • email: info@infact.org • website: http://www.infact.org/

OMB Watch
1742 Connecticut Avenue NW, Washington, DC 20009 • phone: (202) 234-8494 • fax: (202) 234-8584 • email: ombwatch@ombwatch.org • website: http://www.ombwatch.org/ • corporate welfare page: http://www.ombwatch.org/article/articleview/428/1/87/

Program on Corporations, Law and Democracy (POCLAD)
PO Box 246, South Yarmouth, MA 02664-0246 • phone: (508) 398-1145 • fax: (508) 398-1552 • email: people@poclad.org • website: http://www.poclad.org/

Public Citizen

1600 20th Street NW, Washington, DC 20009 • phone: (202) 588-1000 • fax: (202) 588-7799 • email: pnye@citizen.org • website: http://www.citizen.org/ • corporate welfare page: http://www.citizen.org/congress/welfare/index.cfm

United for a Fair Economy

37 Temple Place, Second Floor, Boston, MA 02111 • phone: (617) 423-2148 • fax: (617) 423-0191 • email: info@faireconomy.org • website: http://www.ufenet.org/

Welfare for the Well-Off: How Business Subsidies Fleece Taxpayers

A report by Stephen Moore for the Hoover Institution • website: http://www-hoover.stanford.edu/publications/epp/88/88d.html

What Corporate Welfare Costs You

A report for *Time* magazine by Donald L. Barlett and James B. Steele • November 9, 16, 23, and 30, 1998 • website: http://www.time.com/time/magazine/corpwelfare/

The White Rose Corporate Welfare Page

website: http://www.spiritone.com/~gdy52150/cw.htm

Yahoo! Corporate Welfare directory

website: http://dir.yahoo.com/Government/u_s__government/budget/corporate_welfare/

Part One: Individual Inequities

Chapter 1

Social Security Tax Inequities
($85 billion a year)

You remember Ronald Reagan, don't you? He was elected president in 1980 on a promise to cut taxes. ("When they insist we can't reduce taxes... and balance the budget too, one six-word answer will do: Yes we can, and yes we will." Of course that's seven words, but that's closer than he usually came.)[1]

Reagan did reduce taxes—for the rich. For everybody else, he signed the largest tax increase in US history (adjusted for inflation), which far exceeded his tax cuts. How did he manage that? By raising Social Security tax rates while he lowered income tax rates.[2]

Raising the Social Security tax is a major technique for transferring the tax burden away from the rich. One reason is that it only applies to "earned" income; income from investments is exempt. Another reason is that there's a ceiling—currently $87,000—on how much earned income is taxed. Everyone who earns $87,000 or more pays the same amount of Social Security tax dollars Bill Gates does—needless to say, it amounts to a slightly higher percentage of their income.[3] This makes Social Security one of our most regressive taxes. A teenager flipping burgers for minimum wage pays the Social Security tax at the same rate (6.2%) as a manager making $87,000. The kid shells out about $835 a year in Social Security taxes, and the manager pays about $5,400. But someone who makes $870,000 pays the same $5,400—just 0.62% of their income. A CEO taking in $8.7 million would also pay $5,400 in Social Security taxes, or 0.062%, and so on up to Mr. Gates. (Since Gates makes about $1 billion a year, he's got his Social Security taxes paid off in just under three minutes.)

As a result of tax changes over the past quarter century, some 80% of taxpayers now pay more in payroll taxes than income taxes.[4] The payroll tax consists of the OASDI (Old Age, Survivors, and Disability Insurance) tax, which funds all Social Security programs, and the HI (Hospital Insurance) tax, which funds Medicare. The OASDI tax is currently 12.4% on all wages below $87,000. The HI tax is an additional 2.9% and has no ceiling. The two taxes combined make up the 15.3% payroll tax. People who are self-employed pay the entire tax, whereas wage earners share the burden with their employers, so that each pays 7.65%.

There are no deductions, and everybody pays the same rate—except that the OASDI tax rate for all income over $87,000 is 0.0%. In contrast, the income tax is paid at four different rates ranging from 10% to 35%, and is subject to a bewildering array of deductions and exemptions, as detailed elsewhere in this book.

How much you get back from your payroll taxes depends on how long you live. But the benefits, unlike the taxes, are mildly progressive. That is, poor people (assuming they live long enough) tend to get more out than they put in. This has made Social Security one of the most successful antipoverty programs in our history. Poverty among seniors is far below what it once was. But the fact that wealthier individuals tend to live longer helps to balance that progressivity out a bit.

In any case, whatever the ultimate payoff people might see (if they live long enough), tax changes between 1977 and 1999 reduced after-tax income for the bottom 60% of the population by an average of 6%. During the same period, the top 40% enjoyed an average 19% increase in after-tax income (93% for the top 1% of the population).[5]

BUT THE TRUST FUND WAS JUST SITTING THERE

The Social Security tax has been raised nine times since 1977. Because these massive tax hikes were sold to the public as a way of saving Social Security, one of the government's most popular programs, both parties supported them, without much controversy or publicity. People have been told that the Social Security trust fund has to begin racking up huge surpluses or it will go bankrupt when the baby-boom generation begins to retire. (Since the baby boom lasted from 1946 to 1964, the first boomers will start collecting Social Security in 2008, at age 62.)

The extra money doesn't just sit in the trust fund; the government borrows it to pay for other things, like military waste and corporate welfare—making the Social Security tax, in effect, just another form of income tax. Or to put it another way, the Social Security surplus that you've paid for has become a cash cow for politicians seeking to cut other taxes for their wealthy patrons. Over $1 trillion, plus interest, will have to be repaid in order for Social Security and other trust funds like Medicare to meet their obligations in the coming century.[6] Can you guess who's going to repay it?

Borrowing from the Social Security trust fund makes it easier to cut taxes for the wealthy and masks the true size of the budget deficit. But when those IOUs come due, somebody has to pay for the Social Security outlays, either with higher taxes or fewer services. Taxes paid into the fund become "just another income tax" because they're transferred into the general fund, which is normally fed by income taxes. The Social Security taxes are thus used for a purpose other than that for which they're intended.

The government borrows money from itself to disguise the fact that it's spending more than it takes in. This shell game has been around for over 30 years. Back when the government was more honest, Social Security's income and expenditures were treated as separate from the discretionary part of the federal budget (the part the government could spend as it wished). The trust fund took in money and paid out benefits, and it wasn't included in the budgets passed by Congress and signed by the president.

But in 1969, the so-called unified budget was instituted.[7] By combining Social Security with other taxes, then-President Lyndon Johnson could claim that the United States was running a surplus, even though it was actually being bled dry by the Vietnam War. This is like counting money held in escrow for your tenant's security deposit as if it were income that could be spent, so it looks like spending is in the black—even though you can't actually touch the escrow account.

To this day, the unified budget makes military spending look like a smaller percentage of discretionary federal spending than it really is. The government likes to put out pie charts and other graphs (such as the one below) showing that it spends more on "social programs" than on "defense." But if you don't count entitlement programs like Social Security and Medicare in your "unified" budget, then it's obvious that the mili-

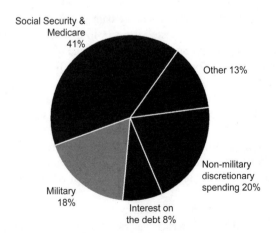

Source: War Resisters League, "Where Your Income Tax Money Really Goes: United States Federal Budget for Fiscal Year 2005," http://www.warresisters.org/piechart.htm.

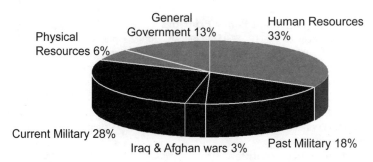

Source: War Resisters League, "Where Your Income Tax Money Really Goes: United States Federal Budget for Fiscal Year 2005," http://www.warresisters.org/piechart.htm.

tary is taking up the lion's share of the discretionary budget. (See graph above.)

It's important that we make the distinction between trust funds and discretionary spending. We need that clarity in order to be better consumers of the information the government gives us. And we need that money to actually be set aside—because the largest demographic bulge in our history is about to begin retiring.

Social Security tax receipts for fiscal year 2003 are estimated at $749 billion, and outlays at $472 billion. According to the Heritage Foundation, if the wealthy had to pay Social Security tax on all their earned income, the government would take in an additional $425 billion over five years—an average of $85 billion a year.[8]

Of course, the Heritage Foundation thinks that would be a terrible idea. They say it would be the largest tax increase in history. That's one way to look at it. Or you could consider that $85 billion a year to be the biggest tax dodge in history, since the people who would be paying it are now enjoying lower payroll tax rates than the rest of us.

In other words, if there were no ceiling, Social Security taxes could be reduced by $85 billion (assuming Social Security benefits stayed the same). Or we could set it aside to cover the trillion dollars' worth of IOUs to the Social Security fund, and we'd have it saved up in about a dozen years. That figure doesn't even include what could be raised with a Social Security tax on investment income, all of which is exempt, but let's be conservative and use $85 billion as the total for this category.

ACTIVIST'S TOOLKIT

Campaign for America's Future

1025 Connecticut Avenue NW, Suite 205, Washington, DC 20036 • phone: (202) 955-5665 • fax: (202) 955-5606 • email: info@ourfuture.org • website: http://www.ourfuture.org/ • Social Security page: http://www.ourfuture.org/issues_and_campaigns/socialsecurity/

Center for Budget and Policy Priorities

820 1st Street NE, #510, Washington, DC 20002 • phone: (202) 408-1080 • fax: (202) 408-1056 • email: bazie@cbpp.org • website: http://www.cbpp.org/ • Social Security page: http://www.cbpp.org/pubs/socsec.htm

Center for Economic and Policy Research

1621 Connecticut Avenue NW, Suite 500, Washington, DC 20009 • phone: (202) 293-5380 • fax: (202) 588-1356 • email: cepr@cepr.net • website: http://www.cepr.net • Social Security page: http://www.cepr.net/pages/Social_Security.htm

Economic Policy Institute

1660 L Street NW, Suite 1200, Washington, DC 20036 • phone: (202) 775-8810 • fax: (202) 775-0819 • email: epi@epinet.org • website: http://www.epinet.org/ • Social Security page: http://www.epinet.org/content.cfm/issueguides_so-cialsecurity_socialsec

Employee Benefit Research Institute

2121 K Street NW, Suite 600, Washington, DC 20037-1896 • phone: (202) 659-0670 • fax: (202) 775-6312 • email: info@ebri.org • website: http://www.ebri.org • Social Security page: http://www.ebri.org/SSproject/index.htm

National Committee to Preserve Social Security and Medicare

10 G Street NE, Suite 600, Washington, DC 20002 • phone: (202) 216-0420 • email: webmaster@ncpssm.org • website: http://www.ncpssm.org/

Social Security and Its Enemies: The Case for America's Most Efficient Insurance Program

by Max J. Skidmore (Boulder, CO: Westview Press, 1999).

Social Security Network

c/o The Century Foundation • 41 East 70th Street, New York, NY 10021 • phone: (212) 452-7743 • fax: (212) 535-7534 • email: info@tcf.org • website: http://www.tcf.org/

Social Security: The Phony Crisis

by Dean Baker and Mark Weisbrot (Chicago, IL: University of Chicago Press, 2001).

Chapter 2

Tax Breaks for Homeowners

($32.1 billion a year)

Homeowners get several different federal tax breaks—which add up to more than $100 billion annually—that the one-third of American families who rent their homes (or are homeless) don't get.[1] The best known of these breaks allows interest paid on mortgages for principal residences and/or vacation homes to be deducted on the federal income tax return.

IS THE MORTGAGE INTEREST DEDUCTION FAIR?

Supporters of this deduction say that it's in the public interest to encourage homeownership, yet more than three-quarters of the benefits go to families with incomes of $75,000 or higher—who hardly need encouragement to own property. (Canada, which doesn't have such a deduction, has about the same rate of homeownership as in the United States.)[2] Twenty percent of the benefit goes to families making over $200,000 a year, and these families also enjoyed an average tax break of more than $6,000. Those making $20,000 or less received less than 2% of the benefit—an average of about $411 per family.[3]

The mortgage interest deduction has been known as the "mansion subsidy" because it's available for the purchase of homes up to $1 million in value. Wealthy taxpayers have also used the write-off to help them purchase vacation homes and condos—even yachts can qualify as a second residence.

Studies have shown that the deduction has contributed to white flight from urban areas and the resulting suburban sprawl. It has made buying a house in the suburbs (rather than staying in the city as a renter) more attractive, and historically, because of redlining and other factors, that option was not widely available to non-white families until the late '60s and the early '70s. Nowadays, while there is still housing discrimination, it's more of a "middle-class pass."

It has also been argued that whatever benefit taxpayers get from the deduction, it is canceled by the higher interest rates resulting from an artificial stimulus to the mortgage market (which generates more demand). People are more likely to buy a home if they can deduct the cost of the mortgage insurance, since that reduces the cost of their investment. Thus, government policy is steering people toward this particular market.

Although about 68 million US families owned their homes in 1998, only 29 million—fewer than half—claimed the mortgage interest deduction. That's probably because it isn't worth it for most nonwealthy taxpayers to itemize their deductions. What's more, the lower your tax bracket, the less the deduction is worth to you. If a family in the 15% bracket pays $5,000 in mortgage interest a year, they save $750 ($5,000 x 15%) on their taxes. But if a family in the top tax bracket (35%) takes out the same mortgage, the deduction is worth $1,750 to them ($5,000 x 35%)—more than 2.5 times as much.

So, even though almost 43% of homeowners don't even claim the mortgage deduction, the congressional Joint Committee on Taxation calculates that this deduction will cost the Treasury slightly more than $68 billion in fiscal year 2004.[4] As of 2001, nearly 60% of the total deduction—$28 billion—went to people with incomes over $100,000. One study found that in 1997, the total amount of tax subsidies to homeowners was more than *seven times* what the Department of Housing and Urban Development (HUD) spent on its housing programs for poor people. (This is a reversal from the situation in 1978, when HUD subsidies to the poor were three times higher than tax breaks for homeowners.)

According to the Congressional Budget Office, only about 7% of home mortgages are over $300,000. By capping the deduction there, we'd save an estimated $4.7 billion a year. (We could also save another $800 million a year by eliminating the use of the deduction for second homes.) On the other hand, if we limited the availability of the deduction to families with incomes under $100,000, we'd save 60% of the total, or about $40 billion. (Some of you who make $100,000 a year may not think of yourselves as rich, but it'd be a stretch to call you poor.)

OTHER TAX ADVANTAGES OF OWNING A HOME

The mortgage interest deduction isn't the only way the law shifts the tax burden to renters. There used to be a couple of capital gains exceptions for homeowners. One allowed a one-time deferral of taxes for those over 55 on the first $125,000 of profit from a home sale. The other waived capital gains taxes every time you bought another home of equal or greater value. Those two tax breaks were costing us around $19.8 billion a year.

Fortunately, Congress "reformed" those rules and replaced them with an unlimited repeatable exclusion on up to $250,000 in profits on any home sale. The White House estimates that this now costs us $20.8 billion a year—so we're behind a billion bucks a year on the deal (and this was before the recent cut in the capital gains tax; data on the effects of that is not yet available).

Homeowners can also deduct state and local property taxes on their federal income tax returns. According to the White House, this deprives the Treasury of $23.6 billion a year. Beyond the money lost, however, there are issues of fairness. One, the deduction isn't available to home-owners who don't itemize (about half of them). Two, it's not available to those who rent (about a third of all families). Some who recognize this inequity have proposed replacing these homeowner deductions with a progressive system of housing credits (similar to the Earned Income Tax Credit), which would be of more benefit to lower-income households.

Finally, homeowners can deduct the interest paid on home equity loans (which sit on top of the basic mortgage). Let's say you have a mountain of credit-card debt. You take out a home equity loan and use the money to pay off the credit cards. Suddenly your interest payments, which weren't deductible, are. Phasing out this deduction alone would save $2.3 billion a year, according to the Progressive Policy Institute.[5] But that amount is included in the overall mortgage interest deduction.

THOSE ARE THE BREAKS

So, to add everything up: the capital gains deferral costs us at least $20.8 billion, and the property tax deduction another $23.6 billion. That comes to $44.4 billion, but not all of it is welfare for the rich. Since about 60% of the mortgage interest deduction goes to people with incomes above $100,000, we can use that as a benchmark and prorate the total amount. This gives us $26.6 billion.

But that doesn't include the $68 billion mortgage interest deduction itself, which brings the total in homeowner subsidies to $112.4 billion. One could make an argument for adding the portion of the deduction that goes to people with incomes above $100,000, but let's be conservative once again and just count the $5.5 billion a year we lose by not capping it at $300,000 homes. That brings us to a total of $32.1 billion a year for the wealthfare portion of homeowners' tax breaks.

Now, if you introduced legislation to openly provide $32 billion in housing subsidies to wealthy families, it wouldn't stand a chance (al-though you probably shouldn't put anything past Congress). But because these provisions are called "deductions" and "exemptions" rather than "subsidies," they're enshrined in our current tax code, and middle-class homeowners think they're the ones getting the deal.

If you believe that, you're being had. It's a classic case of being tossed a few scraps from the table. If we simply eliminate all the handouts and boondoggles this book documents, our tax rates would drop so far, so fast, that special little deals like these homeowners' loopholes would seem archaic and silly.

A HUMMER OF A TAX BREAK

Some of this stuff, you couldn't possibly make up. In the face of global warming and increased dependence on terrorist-friendly oil monarchies in the Middle East, the US government decided to increase the tax deduction for SUVs. But not just any SUVs. Only those over 6,000 pounds, the least fuel efficient of all gas-guzzling behemoths, would qualify. And with the quadrupling of the deduction, well-heeled consumers could write off the entire purchase price of these vehicles.

Does that sound like satire to you? Unfortunately, it's all too true. The deduction was originally created in the 1980s to help farmers and contractors purchase heavy equipment for their businesses. In those days, the deduction was for a maximum of $17,500, which gradually rose to $25,000. But in the meantime, gigantic trucks had become such a prestigious status symbol that they ended up accounting for more than half of all car sales by the end of the 1990s. Over the years, more and more doctors, lawyers, and other business owners took advantage of the loophole to acquire shiny new SUVs—over 100,000 a year by 2002.

In the face of this egregious abuse of the original intent, the Bush administration found a way to make it even worse. The economic stimulus package of 2002 changed the rules to allow "farmers" and other small business owners to deduct up to $100,000 of the purchase price of their "new equipment"— as a "bonus depreciation" in the same year it was bought.

The opportunity was not lost on car salespeople. They made sure that customers knew that cars and small SUVs wouldn't qualify. Only for those three-ton monsters, like the Humvee or the enormous Ford Excursion, would your Uncle Sam help pick up the tab. According to the Joint Committee on Taxation, that tab could run to some $1.3 billion over the next decade.

The largest SUVs get somewhere between 8 and 13 miles per gallon. Meanwhile, new high-tech hybrid vehicles, which get more than 50 miles per gallon, are also in line for a tax subsidy. But at a maximum of $2,000 per vehicle, that's 50 times less than the write-off for the guzzlers.

In October 2003, the Senate Finance Committee voted to scale the deduction back to $25,000 per vehicle—a limited victory for common sense. But given the arroused opposition of the Alliance of Automobile Manufacturers and their small army of lobbyists, the House flatly refused to go along. In fact, it is calling for the deduction to be extended further—to apply to all types of vehicles. If you think it can't possibly get any stranger, stay tuned.

SOURCES

Durbin, Dee-Ann. "Automakers Oppose Plan to Cut SUV Tax Deduction." *Salt Lake Tribune*, October 11, 2003, http://www.sltrib.com/2003/Oct/10112003/business/100817.asp.

Kamen, Al. "A Hummerdinger of a Tax Loophole?" *Washington Post*, September 26, 2003.

Onion, Amanda. "Driven to Buy: Tax Breaks May Help Small Businesses Buy Big SUVs, But Help for Hybrids May Vanish." *ABCnews.com*, October 1, 2003, http://abcnews.go.com/sections/scitech/Business/hybrid_suv_tax0301001.html.

Taxpayers for Common Sense, "Senate Committee Shrinks SUV Tax Break," press release, October 3, 2003, http://www.taxpayer.net/TCS/PressReleases/2003/10-03SUV.htm.

ACTIVIST'S TOOLKIT

Center for Community Change
1000 Wisconsin Avenue NW, Washington, DC 20007 • phone: (202) 342-0519 • email: info@communitychange.org • website: http://www.communitychange.org/

National Coalition for the Homeless
1012 14th Street NW, #600, Washington, DC 20005-3471 • phone: (202) 737-6444 • fax: (202) 737-6445 • email: info@nationalhomeless.org • website: http://www.nationalhomeless.org/

National Housing Institute
460 Bloomfield Avenue, Suite 211, Montclair, NJ 07042-3552 • phone: (973) 509-2888 • fax: (973) 509-8005 • website: http://www.nhi.org/index.html

National Housing Law Project
614 Grand Avenue, Suite 320, Oakland, CA 94610 • phone: (510) 251-9400 • fax: (510) 451-2300 • email: nhlp@nhlp.org • website: http://www.nhlp.org/

National Low Income Housing Coalition
1012 14th Street NW, Suite 610, Washington, DC 20005 • phone: (202) 662-1530 • fax: (202) 393-1973 • email: info@nlihc.org • website: http://www.nlihc.org/

The National Urban League, Inc.
120 Wall Street, New York, NY 10005 • phone: (212) 558-5300 • fax: (212) 344-5332 • email: info@nul.org • website: http://www.nul.org/

Chapter 3

Runaway Pensions

($7.6 billion a year)

Most federal employees enjoy a number of benefits not found in the private sector. The main perk is the ability to retire with full benefits after 30 years of service—or just 20 in the military. As a result, the average age of federal retirement is 58, compared to 63 in the private sector. (The average military retiree spends 22 years earning a pension and 35 years collecting it!)[1]

All federal pensions have automatic cost of living adjustments (COLAs) set at 100% of the consumer price index (CPI). Thanks to these, many civil service retirees get bigger checks than the people who are now doing their jobs. Only 5% of private pension plans have automatic COLAs, and very few of those increase by 100% of the CPI. (About half of state and local pensions have automatic COLAs.)

Of course, private-sector employees should get COLAs too. Part of the reason government employees do is that they're more heavily unionized. The problem here is not the inflation adjustments per se, but the overly generous pensions at the top end of the scale. $50,000 a year pensions don't need the same protections that $10,000 a year pensions do. At the top end of the scale, even small percentage increases can translate into huge outlays. One former Congressman has collected $1.2 million since his retirement because of these regular adjustments, and is actually asking to be cut off.[2]

In 1992, when the average private pension was around $600 a month, the average government pension was $1,420 a month—more than twice as much. It used to be that government workers received bigger pensions because they were paid less, but during the last 40 years, federal salaries have risen 25% faster than those in the private sector.

In 1991, $9.2 billion in pension payments went to households whose annual incomes (including salaries from jobs they took after retirement, investment income, retirement benefits, etc.) were over $100,000.[3] Former Speaker of the House Tom Foley's pension started at $123,804 a year—COLAs will increase that every year—and Dan Rostenkowski's at $96,468 (once chair of the powerful House Ways and Means Committee, he could even collect that money during his subsequent term in prison).

In 1994, government pensions cost us $65 billion. About 58% of that—$38 billion—was beyond what private companies would pay, on average, to people with the same salary histories. If public employees' pensions were equivalent to those in the private sector, the average person's income tax would drop by 8%. One proposal is to stop applying COLAs to federal pensions once they are equal to the maximum Social Security benefit. This would save taxpayers $900 billion in the long term, or around half the government's total pension liability of $1.8 trillion.[4]

Although most—if not all—of that $38 billion is excessive, a lot of it benefits people who aren't rich. To come up with a figure for the wealth-fare portion of it, we can use the fact that we'd save $7.6 billion a year just by shaving 25% off government pensions paid to households with annual incomes of $70,000 or more.[5] That's a pretty conservative estimate of how much welfare for the rich there is in excessive government pensions.

WHERE IS THE FEDERAL PENSION FUND?

Now we get into something that rightfully belongs in Part Two. But then, figuring out where the wealthy individual ends and the filthy-rich corporation begins is never easy, because they work hand in hand. Like the Social Security trust fund, the government pension fund hasn't been managed very carefully and is already committed to $870 billion more than its holdings; if you include state and military pensions, the figure is $1.7 trillion. All that money will either have to be borrowed, raised through taxes, or cut out of some other part of the budget.

Meanwhile, private-sector pensions are insured by a government agency, the Pension Benefit Guaranty Corporation (PBGC). After starting out 2002 with a $7.7 billion surplus, the PBGC paid out that entire amount in claims (and then some), ending the year with a $3.6 billion shortfall. By July 2003, that shortfall had grown to $5.7 billion.[6] A month later, the PBGC's deficit had soared to $8.8 billion.[7]

Underfunded pension liabilities at US companies added up to $23 billion in 1999. By 2002, the hole was more than $400 billion.[8] The PBGC funds its insurance program by charging premiums to the companies under its coverage. But under lax oversight, companies have been allowed to take "contribution holidays" in recent years. PBGC executive director Steven Kandarian admitted that it would take 12 years of premiums to cover just the claims from 2002.[9] In response, the Bush administration is, of course, calling for loosening the rules even further.[10]

Corporate America is lobbying strongly for legislation that would reduce its own liability for its pension funds.[11] And companies like Enron and Halliburton have used elaborate shell games to get out of their obligations, leaving millions of employees bereft of the coverage they had been depending on.[12] Interestingly, one study shows that "of the 30 companies with the greatest shortfalls in employee pension funds, CEOs collected 59 percent more compensation than the median CEO."[13]

As economist Robert Samuelson puts it, this sounds "eerily like the first reaction to the savings and loan problems of 20 years ago."[14] Actually, it could end up being much worse. The original bailout of the S&Ls cost $157 billion; go back two paragraphs and look at the number for underfunded pension liabilities. You and I are ultimately on the hook for that if the PBGC can't cover it. And that could make the S&L scandal look like a liquor store heist.

THE FREE MARKET OF IDEAS

ACTIVIST'S TOOLKIT

Employee Benefit Research Institute
   2121 K Street NW, Suite 600, Washington, DC 20037-1896 • phone: (202) 659-0670 • fax: (202) 775-6312 • email: info@ebri.org • website: http://www.ebri.org

National Committee on Public Employee Pensions
   22 Richardson, Centerville, MA 02632 • phone: (508) 790-3844

Part Two: Big Business Breaks

FOOD STAMPS

Chapter 4

Tax Avoidance by Transnationals
($137.2 billion a year)

"Why, man, he doth bestride the narrow world like a colossus, and we petty men walk under his huge legs, and peep about to find ourselves dishonorable graves."[1] Cassius's description of Caesar is hard to beat for giving the flavor of how transnational corporations have come to dominate the earth. (A transnational—or multinational—corporation is simply one that has operations in more than one country.)

Richer than many nations, more powerful than most, transnationals lumber about, settling where taxes are the lowest, and labor is the cheapest and most intimidated. But many are still headquartered in the United States, and virtually all of them have significant operations here. That brings up the sticky question of US taxes.

Not to worry. Both US- and foreign-based transnationals have lots of tricks for avoiding our taxes. And lately, they're getting a lot better at it.

THE TRANSFER PRICING SHELL GAME

Conducting an audit on a transnational would require the IRS to look at every transaction between the domestic and foreign branches of that corporation and then assess whether a fair price was charged for that transaction. Because that's an impossible task, for the most part, the IRS simply takes a transnational's word for how much taxable income it earns in this country. Thus corporations feel free to shift profits out of, and expenses into, the United States—thereby minimizing, on paper, the profitability of their US-based operations. One company bought a jar of salad dressing from Brazil for $720, essentially from itself. Another sold a missile launcher to an Israeli subsidiary for just $22.[2] This is called transfer pricing. Senator Byron Dorgan (D-ND) estimates that this scam costs US taxpayers more than $50 billion a year.[3]

There's an easy way to cut through the trickery of transfer pricing. Called the unitary method, it calculates taxes based simply on how much of the company's sales, assets, and payroll are in the United States (or any other country).[4] The unitary method is more accurate and easier to enforce, and makes it far more difficult for companies to hide their profits in offshore tax shelters. That's why it's so fiercely opposed by transnational corporations and their congressional hirelings.

Multinational corporations report profits and losses to their share-holders as one large enterprise—regardless of how many subsidiaries they control. But when it comes time to report to the IRS, or to the tax collec-tors overseas, then the corporation is a sprawling mass of interlocking subsidiaries, all of which do business with each other.

This is where the problem of transfer pricing comes in. The corpora-tion can essentially sell goods to itself (a foreign subsidiary) at dirt-cheap prices in order to report a loss in a high-tax jurisdiction. Or it can sell to itself at exorbitant prices and collect the profits in a low-tax country. Smart corporate lawyers can make the tangle of such transactions so complicated that they are virtually audit-proof.

Under the unitary method, that whole can of worms becomes moot. The corporation, no matter how many subsidiaries it has, is treated as a unitary entity. It reports all of its worldwide sales, assets, and payroll, just as it does in its annual report to its shareholders. Then the state or nation taxes the company on the basis of what percentage of its business is done in that jurisdiction. Thus there's no point in juggling assets or playing transfer pricing games. If all governments used this method, the corpora-tion would pay its taxes where it actually does business.

As Senator Dorgan has pointed out, it's estimated that the US Trea-sury is defrauded of $53 billion annually because we fail to use the unitary method. This gives an indication of why US-based multinationals are so adamantly opposed to the unitary method—and why they're willing to pay smart lawyers so much to take advantage of its absence.

Of the US-based transnationals with assets over $100 million, 37% paid no US federal taxes at all in 1991 (that's right, zero taxes), and the average tax rate for those that did pay was just 1% of gross receipts. (I'd tell you what it was as a percentage of profits, but nobody knows. That's just the point—transnationals avoid paying tax by concealing how much profit they make.)

Foreign-based transnationals did even better. 71% of them paid no US income tax on their operations in this country, and the average rate for those that did pay was just 0.6%—six-tenths of one percent—of gross re-ceipts. (You can see why they'd be eager to avoid a tax burden like *that*.)

How successful foreign-based transnationals are at avoiding taxes has a lot to do with where they're based, since it depends on what their tax laws are like back at home; many countries allow corporations to use transfer pricing schemes to avoid US taxation. In 1989, only 22% of Swedish-based transnationals managed the trick, compared to 64% of the British-based, 73% of the Japanese, 78% of the Dutch, 92% of the

Panamanian, and 95% of the Irish. The Saudis took the cake—99% of the transnational corporations based in Saudi Arabia paid no US income tax on the profits they earned in the United States.[5]

THE PUERTO RICAN EXEMPTION

In 1976, Congress decided to boost employment in Puerto Rico by completely exempting companies from taxes on the profits they made there. Between then and 1994, companies from the US mainland earned $35 billion in profits in Puerto Rico and paid not a penny of federal tax on that.[6]

The pharmaceutical industry made particular use of this tax break by writing off the cost of developing drugs—much of which is already taxpayer subsidized—on their US tax returns. They then produced the drugs in Puerto Rico, so they could assign the profits to their subsidiaries there and pay no taxes on them. (Puerto Rico also offers exemptions from income, property, municipal, and excise taxes.)

Then-President Reagan tried to eliminate the Puerto Rican tax exemption in 1986. It was part of the grand bargain of the 1986 tax reform bill, which allowed for still-lower marginal tax rates for the wealthy (after they'd already enjoyed a huge tax cut in 1981) in exchange for closing a number of egregious tax shelters and loopholes. Of course, to no one's surprise, many of the shelters and loopholes were later restored or extended. In any case, closing the Puerto Rican loophole failed in the face of fierce industry lobbying.

In 1996, Congress agreed to gradually phase out the loophole by 2004, so that US companies in Puerto Rico would only escape some $21 billion in taxes, rather than the $30 billion they would have avoided if the law hadn't been revised.[7] Current law calls for the credit to expire by 2007, but stay tuned because that could change. For instance, Congressmember Eni Faleomavaega of American Samoa has introduced legislation to extend the "possessions tax credit" permanently in his territory to help the tuna-canning industry there.[8]

CREDIT FOR FOREIGN TAXES

US-based transnationals are also allowed to credit any taxes paid to foreign governments against taxes they owe here. Supposedly, this is to prevent companies from being taxed twice on the same income. The problem is, there's no reliable method of making sure that a company is telling a foreign country the same thing it tells us.

There are rules to prevent this sort of abuse, of course, but companies can still find plenty of ways around them. In the late 1940s, when the king of Saudi Arabia began demanding higher royalty rates from US oil companies operating there, the oil execs suggested that he simply impose a corporate income tax on them instead. They'd pay no more in total taxes, but the king would get higher payments. Soon the other countries in the Persian Gulf all had corporate income taxes as well.[9]

Sometimes lying isn't necessary. After making millions of dollars from selling computer chips in Japan, Intel was able to exempt the profits from US tax by convincing the US Tax Court that they were Japanese income. But a tax treaty between the two countries requires Japan to treat the profits as US income, therefore exempting them from Japanese tax! Thus the profits became "nowhere income"—not taxable anywhere.[10] This happens more often than you might think. Tax treaties are, supposedly, agreements to exchange information to assist in the prevention of tax evasion and tax avoidance. Unfortunately, like a lot of other international treaties, the language is mostly drafted by corporate lawyers—the very people who assist in said evasion and avoidance.

There's one further problem with this setup. By treating US state and local taxes as deductions against federal income tax while treating foreign taxes as credits (which are much more valuable), our tax code creates an incentive for companies to ship US jobs abroad.[11]

THE BERMUDA SHUFFLE

The foreign tax credit has certainly made it more desirable for US-based multinationals to shift more of their operations overseas. But many companies have found that it's not strictly necessary to actually leave the United States, with its extensive highway system, well-equipped military, and affordable legislators. All that's necessary is to set up a corporation in a friendly tax haven like the Cayman Islands, Antigua, or Bermuda. Once you've paid your incorporation fees, presto, you're a foreign company. You can keep your physical plant in the United States, because it's a shorter commute, but your official address is a post office box in Vanuatu.

This shuffle has grown more popular in recent years. One study found that reported profits in these tax havens by the 10,000 largest companies in the United States jumped by 735% between 1983 and 1999.[12] (Again, using the unitary method of corporate taxation could easily eliminate this problem. If some company owned a post office box in Bermuda, but still had 90% of its assets and business in its US "subsidiary," it would still pay 90% of its tax in the United States.)

There is an estimated *$3 trillion* in US assets parked in offshore bank accounts.[13] Some $800 billion of that is in the Cayman Islands alone.[14] The Caymans are now host to 590 banks and more than 30,000 companies, making the islands a financial center to rival New York, London, and Frankfurt.[15] Bermuda has helped formerly American companies avoid significant chunks of taxes. Tyco International cut its US tax bill by $400 million. Ingersoll-Rand ducked out on $40 million.[16] Other "borderless" companies include Seagate Technology, Pricewaterhouse Coopers, and the infamous Arthur Andersen accounting firm (which changed its name to Accenture when it made the move).[17]

The IRS estimates that these tax dodges are costing the US Treasury some $70 billion a year.[18] That's a staggering number, but it doesn't even include the amount lost to the firms that create a flood of shell companies as Caribbean subsidiaries.

These havens are also attractive because of their notoriously weak protections for the shareholders of these companies—making it easier for management to rip them off. Perhaps that's one reason why companies like Enron and Halliburton set up so many subsidiaries in the Caribbean. Of course, another is that Enron was able to get away with paying zero taxes in the United States for four years. No, wait—less than zero. Enron picked up $382 million in refund checks from Uncle Sam during that time.[19] (Now, if Enron had paid taxes on the fabulous profits it had reported to its shareholders—instead of on what it reported to the IRS—it would have paid out more than a billion dollars in taxes.)

Corporations are not alone in finding tax havens attractive. Drug dealers, mobsters, and terrorists also hide money that way. Efforts to crack down on this money laundering have met some resistance, though. The Clinton administration instituted a rule that would have required US banks to report the interest they paid foreigners back to their home governments. The rationale was that, hopefully, we'd get a little more cooperation from foreign banks in tracking payments to Americans overseas. But the Bush administration, at the urging of First Brother Jeb and others, soon put a stop to that.[20] Likewise, the Bush White House worked to weaken an international treaty on money laundering.[21] It wasn't that they wanted to protect drug dealers and terrorists, but that too much of that sort of scrutiny might unduly discomfort US corporations.

After 9/11, this sort of overseas corporate tax dodge began to seem downright unpatriotic. It looked especially bad that some of the companies fleeing the United States to avoid taxes were doing big business with the US government. "Accenture," for example, got a contract to redesign the IRS website.[22] It didn't look good for these corporate traitors to be collecting nearly a billion dollars in contracts with Uncle Sam.

Republican leaders made indignant speeches about closing the Bermuda loophole, but behind closed doors they worked to make sure that reforms were either weakened or killed. In fact, the official line from GOP leaders like House Majority Leader Tom DeLay—and as the saying goes, I'm not making this up—is that no corporate tax loopholes should be closed unless equally large new ones are opened up to replace them.[23] (DeLay explains that this amount of tax evasion is simply proof that US corporate taxes are too tough, so we have to cut them yet again. His ostensible motivation is to stimulate the economy—though there are certainly more equitable ways of doing so.) There are a number of bills pending that would address these abuses, but at this writing none have passed. Most are bottled up in committee. (See the "Activist Toolkit" for more on this legislation.)

COUNT UP YOUR LOSSES

While most experts consider tax avoidance by transnational corporations to be a major problem, they disagree on the extent of it. According to Citizens for Tax Justice (and updated figures from the federal budget), there are an additional $15 billion in miscellaneous tax breaks for transnational corporations.[24] The Puerto Rican credit still costs $2.2 billion a year. Add in $50 billion for transfer pricing scams and the $70 billion in offshore shenanigans and, as the late-Senator Everett Dirksen put it, pretty soon you're talking about real money. That's $137 billion in unpaid taxes that the rest of us have to make up for.

ACTIVIST'S TOOLKIT

Center on Budget and Policy Priorities
820 1st Street NE, #510, Washington, DC 20002 • phone: (202) 408-1080 • fax: (202) 408-1056 • email: center@cbpp.org • website: http://www.cbpp.org/

Citizens for Tax Justice
1311 L Street NW, Washington, DC 20005 • phone: (202) 626-3780 • fax: (202) 638-3486 • email: mattg@ctj.org • website: http://www.ctj.org • *The Hidden Entitlements* report: http://www.ctj.org/html/hemenu.htm

Economic Policy Institute
1660 L Street NW, Suite 1200, Washington, DC 20036 • phone: (202) 775-8810 • fax: (202) 775-0819 • email: epi@epinet.org • website: http://www.epinet.org/

Taxpayers for Common $ense
651 Pennsylvania Avenue SE, Second Floor, Washington, DC 20003 • phone: (202) 546-8500 • fax: (202) 546-8511 • email: staff@taxpayer.net • website: http://www.taxpayer.net/index.html

Tax Policy Center
A project of the Urban Institute and the Brookings Institution • website: http://www.taxpolicycenter.org/ • Their "Tax Facts" page is absolutely invaluable: http://www.taxpolicycenter.org/taxfacts/

United for a Fair Economy
37 Temple Place, Second Floor, Boston, MA 02111 • phone: (617) 423-2148 • fax: (617) 423-0191 • email: info@faireconomy.org • website: http://www.ufenet.org/

Chapter 5

Lower Taxes on Capital Gains

($89.8 billion a year)
(not counting home sales)

The larger someone's income is, the larger the portion of it (in general) that comes from investments rather than a salary. Some investment income takes the form of dividends and interest, but a major part of it is capital gains—profits made from the sale of assets like stocks, bonds, and real estate whose value went up while the investor owned them. Any kind of profit is new income, money you didn't have before. When you get money—whether it's a paycheck, a lottery winning, or a gift—it counts as income. So do your stock profits. Conservatives argue such profits should be taxed at a lower rate to encourage investment—as if nobody would ever invest money for profit unless they got a tax break to go with it.

One of the slick things about capital gains (for those who have them) is that they aren't taxed until the asset is sold. But you can still cash in on them in the meantime—all you have to do is borrow money, using the appreciated value of the asset as collateral. (You do have to pay interest on the loan, of course, but interest on business loans is tax-deductible.)[1]

As of 1998, the richest 1% of Americans held nearly 48% of all stock, while the bottom 80% owned 4.1%.[2] And the IRS reports that in any given year, 93% of all Americans filing tax returns receive zero income from capital gains.[3] Sometimes people who aren't rich have capital gains too—when they sell houses that have appreciated in value, for example—but people who make $50,000 a year or less (two-thirds of all taxpayers) paid only 1.2% of their total tax burden on capital gains taxes. People making $50,000–$100,000 a year paid 2.3% of their taxes on capital gains. Over three-quarters of all capital gains taxes are paid by taxpayers making over $200,000—just 2% of the population.[4]

As Citizens for Tax Justice puts it, "More than any other kind of income, capital gains are concentrated at the very top of the income scale." Of the benefit from the 1993 capital gains tax cut, 97% went to the richest 1% of the population. But that's not enough for them—they want to pay nothing. Thus, proposed "flat tax" plans advanced by GOP politicians like

Dick Armey and Steve Forbes would exempt capital gains from taxation completely.[5]

TWO KINDS OF CORPORATE TAXES—LOW OR NO

When capital gains are taxed, they get special treatment. For the 65 years from 1921 to 1986, the capital gains rate was lower—often enormously lower—than the rate for salaries and other "ordinary income." The 1986 tax reform bill made the rates the same—and lasted for four years. That radical idea was eliminated in the tax "reform" bill of 1990, and the 1993 tax "reform" bill widened the gap even further.[6] The budget agreement of 1997 cut capital gains taxes once again (from 29% to 21%),[7] and the rate was cut down to a maximum of 15% (and a minimum of 5%) in the 2003 tax bill.[8] At this point, only the poorest Americans pay a lower tax rate for their labor than millionaires do for their investment profits. Meanwhile, the top rate for ordinary income is 35% (38% for corporations).

In addition to the basic unfairness of penalizing people for working (by taxing earned income at a higher rate), the tax code is riddled with exceptions and special treatment for various groups. For example, coal, timber, iron ore, and certain agricultural enterprises are allowed to cut their tax bill by treating part of their normal business profits as capital gains rather than as ordinary income.[9] (Those loopholes are quantified in subsequent chapters.)

Owners of certain "small business corporate stocks" get another special break: they can deduct investment losses up to $100,000 from ordinary income (for everyone else, capital losses beyond the first $3,000 can only be offset against capital gains).[10] In 1993, another special exclusion was added: half the capital gains from certain risky ventures (deemed "likely to fail") aren't taxed at all.[11] (Though why we would want to encourage businesses that are likely to fail is a mystery to me.)

Real estate speculators get an especially sweet deal. They can avoid capital gains taxes on appreciated properties indefinitely, simply by trading them in what are called Starker or 1031 exchanges. Not until they finally sell a property without buying another do they have to pay capital gains tax on the increased value of all the properties in the chain.[12]

But there's even a way around that. If they keep trading properties until they die, their heirs can sell the property without paying any capital gains tax on the accumulated appreciation. And when property is bestowed as a gift, no capital gains tax is due on it until the person receiving the gift sells it.[13]

LOW RATES ARE BAD FOR BUSINESS

As with accelerated depreciation (see next chapter), defenders of a lower capital gains tax rate argue that it encourages greater savings and more investment. This, they say, results in more jobs, a higher rate of economic growth, and even higher tax revenues (since the wealthy have less incentive to hide their income in tax shelters).

But by cutting the capital gains rate, the government is simply creating a new and better tax shelter—one that's more attractive to the rich than the ones they've been using. And using tax rates to encourage investments that otherwise make little business sense ultimately sabotages economic growth.

When investment decisions are made mainly to take advantage of a tax break, rather than on the soundness of the businesses being considered for investment, it tends to cause speculative bubbles, as we've just seen in the late '90s. The value of the stock market was inflated by trillions of dollars. Much of the resulting wealth simply disappeared when the bubble burst in 2001. Before that happened, corporate swindlers had siphoned off immense sums, and similarly vast sums had been overinvested in questionable sectors like fiber optics. The world now has four times as much fiber optic cable as it can use, and other manufacturing sectors are suffering from similar over-capacity, which contributes to the global recession. Nobody's going to hire more workers when they have far more inventory than they can sell.

The jobs-and-growth argument in defense of this loophole is even less convincing. When the capital gains tax was *raised* in 1976, employment grew by nearly 2% over the next two years, and the GDP grew by 1.3%. The same thing happened after the 1987 hike in the capital gains tax; both employment and the GDP grew by 1.6% over two years. On the other hand, the 1978 cut was followed by several years of falling employment and slower growth rates. Since that didn't work, Congress cut the capital gains rate again in 1981. After two years, employment was down by 2%, and growth rates declined by 2.5%.[14]

Now, obviously, factors other than the capital gains rate affect employment and the growth of the economy. After all, the 1997 capital gains tax cut came in the middle of an economic boom that didn't need much goosing.[15] That boom continued for three more years before sliding back down. But the tax cut arguably contributed to the speculative bubble whose burst has rendered the US economy stagnant since late 2000. Either way, it's amazing that people can blithely make the argument that lower capital gains taxes mean more jobs and a healthier economy, when so much of the evidence goes in the other direction.

The lower tax rate for capital gains isn't a trivial matter. Between 2003 and 2007, it will cost us an average of $87 billion a year—and that doesn't include capital gains on home sales.[16] But wait—it doesn't include the cost of the capital gains cuts in the 2003 tax bill either. That will cost us an extra $22.4 billion through 2009, or an average of $3.2 billion a year.[17]

So if capital gains were taxed at the same rate as ordinary income, $90 billion more per year would be available to Uncle Sam. If those who profit from our economy get an exemption, the rest of us have to make up for that revenue shortfall, either in higher taxes or fewer services. The bottom line: wage earners like coal miners and kindergarten teachers are kicking in an extra $90 billion a year so that people living off of trust funds can pay $90 billion less.

ACTIVIST'S TOOLKIT

(See taxpayer resources for Chapter 4, p. 33.)

Chapter 6

Accelerated Depreciation
($85 billion a year)

In 1971, the Nixon administration issued an executive order allowing, for the first time, accelerated depreciation—that is, writing off the costs of equipment and buildings faster than they actually wear out. This led to a massive decline in corporate tax payments. When a company is allowed to write off an investment more quickly than usual, it is in effect getting an interest-free loan from US taxpayers.[1]

Say your business buys a widget, which normally wears out over 15 years. Every year, you'd get a little tax deduction for the depreciation of the widget. But then President Richguy comes along and lets you take all 15 years of deductions right away. You just got an advance on all your deductions from now until 2019. So now you have more money to play with, and Uncle Sam has less. The rest of us taxpayers, who didn't get to use this scam, either have our taxes raised to fill in the gap, make do with fewer services due to budget cuts, or pay the interest on the deficit spending Uncle Sam does to cover the shortfall. Either way, we pay, you don't.

When the accelerated depreciation write-off was expanded in Reagan's 1981 tax plan, an even more massive decline in tax receipts occurred; by 1983, the percentage of total federal tax revenues paid by corporations was half of what it had been just three years earlier.[2] Of the 250 largest and most profitable companies in the United States, a quarter—whose pretax profits totaled $50 billion—paid no federal income tax at all from 1981 to 1983, and half of them didn't pay in one or more of those three years.[3]

The 1986 tax reform disallowed the accelerated depreciation of real estate, but left the loophole for machinery and other equipment. So the accelerated depreciation scam is still with us and costs us, on average, nearly $50 billion a year.

A company can even generate a negative tax rate by buying equipment and leasing it to another company in return for tax deductions the other company can't use. (Being able to trade deductions and credits is a leftover from the huge 1981–86 Reagan corporate tax pig-out.) Company A never sees the equipment but still accelerates depreciation on it; company B gets to write off the leasing costs. General Electric, one company that used this strategy, saved a billion dollars in taxes between 1986 and 1992. And it wasn't the only one.

Business leaders like to argue that tax breaks such as accelerated depreciation stimulate the overall economy. But the evidence runs the other way. In the heyday of accelerated depreciation (1981–86), the economy grew an average of 1.9% a year. After accelerated depreciation was limited (1986–89), the economy grew an average of 2.7% a year. As a former Reagan Treasury official told *Business Week* magazine, "In 1981, manufacturing had its largest tax cut ever and immediately went down the tubes. In 1986, they had their largest tax increase and went gangbusters [on investment]."[4] Robert McIntyre of Citizens for Tax Justice explains that the 1986 tax bill sharply limited depreciation loopholes opened wide in the 1981 tax bill. "As money flowed out of wasteful tax shelters, industrial investment jumped by 5.1% a year from 1986 to 1989, after actually *falling* at a 2% annual rate from 1981 to 1986."[5] Of course, correlation is not causation, but this makes it pretty hard to claim that these tax breaks boost the economy.

That's not surprising, since corporate tax savings are seldom used to boost the economy. For example, Westinghouse got a $215 million tax break from accelerated depreciation in 1993; over the next two years, it cut 24,700 jobs. Accelerated depreciation reduced American Brands's 1994 tax bill by $115 million; in gratitude, the company laid off 10,780 workers.[6]

There's one final problem with accelerated depreciation: because it's such a gigantic tax break, it distorts business decisions. The tax benefit it confers often outweighs the actual risks and rewards of an investment, and in the long run, that sort of distortion is bad for the economy. The accelerated depreciation loophole provides an incentive for companies to divert funds into tax-sheltering activities, regardless of whether such investments are otherwise sound.

During the extended wrangling over the federal budget for fiscal year 1996, a group of business leaders fired off a stern letter to President Bill Clinton and Congress, urging them to get their act together. Among the signers of the letter were the CEOs of Ford, Exxon, General Motors, Chrysler, IBM, Amoco, and Chevron—companies that had each used accelerated depreciation to defer a billion dollars in tax payments. When consumer advocate Ralph Nader asked them if they'd consider forgoing tax loopholes of this kind to help balance the budget, their reply was a stony silence.[7]

In addition to benefiting corporations, accelerated depreciation also helps wealthy individuals (who own most of the stocks and bonds that the corporations issue). On average, tax breaks from accelerated depreciation are worth more than $13,000 a year to households making over $200,000, but less than $70 a year to households earning under $50,000.[8]

In early 2002, Congressmembers decided that one of the best ways to respond to the 9/11 attacks would be to create some new tax breaks for businesses. So they came up with something called "bonus depreciation," which allowed businesses to immediately deduct 30% of the cost of any new equipment or facilities.[9] The break was set to expire in September 2004, to encourage corporations to make new investments sooner rather than later. By mid-2003, it was apparent that this was not helping the economy, so the 2003 tax bill extended the deadline and kicked the deduction up to 50%[10] (*that* ought to scare the terrorists).

The bonus depreciation loophole was originally estimated to cost some $97 billion over its three-year life. The Joint Committee on Taxation projected that the 2003 extension would add another $9 billion to the cost. But as the Center on Budget and Policy Priorities (CBPP) has pointed out, Congress is unlikely to allow this provision to expire. The legislation "sunsets" the bonus in the same month (December 2004) as more popular provisions such as the increase in the child tax credit. The coincidence makes it more likely that both will be renewed shortly before the end of 2004—say, just before the election.[11]

The CBPP projects that a permanent bonus depreciation (if that's not an oxymoron) would cost as much as $400 billion over the next ten years. But we won't count that golden goose before it's hatched. Let's just average the current bonus breaks at $35.3 billion a year, and add the ongoing accelerated depreciation provisions at $49.7 billion. Right now the various depreciation tax breaks are costing you some $85 billion a year. So far.

ACTIVIST'S TOOLKIT

(See also resources for Chapter 4, p. 33.)

The Bermuda Project

> 1158 26th Street, #428, Santa Monica, CA 90403 • phone for press only: (415) 901-0111 • email: bermuda@ariannaonline.com • website: http://www.thebermudaproject.com/

CorpWatch

> 2288 Fulton Street, #103, Berkeley, CA 94704 • phone: (510) 849-2423 • email: corpwatch@corpwatch.org • website: http://www.corpwatch.org

Essential Information, Inc.

> PO Box 19405, Washington, DC 20036 • phone: (202) 387-8030 • *Multinational Monitor* • email: monitor@essential.org • website: http://www.multinationalmonitor.org/ • Multinationals Resource Center • email: mrc@essential.org • website: http://www.resourcesfirst.org/research.html

When Corporations Rule the Earth

> by David Korten (Bloomfield, CT: Kumarian Press, 1995).

Chapter 7

Insurance Loopholes
($23.5 billion a year)

If you heard that Wal-Mart, America's biggest retailer, spent around a billion dollars a year on life insurance it gave free of charge to about 325,000 of its employees, your initial reaction would probably be, "Isn't that nice? Some big companies really do care about their workers." Unfortunately, there's a twist to the story.

EEEK!—COLI

To encourage workers to sign up for the insurance, Wal-Mart offered them other free benefits. The company would even continue to pay for the policy after workers left their employ.

Now you're probably feeling a little confused. Why should Wal-Mart offer additional inducements to get employees to sign up for free insurance? And why in the world would it continue coverage for people who no longer work for Wal-Mart?

The answer is very simple. When an employee died, Wal-Mart—not the employee's heirs—would collect $60,000. Out of that, Wal-Mart gave the heirs $5,000—about 8%. (If the insured was a former employee, the heirs got just $1,000; if the death was accidental, they got $10,000.)[1]

This boondoggle is called corporate-owned life insurance, or COLI. More notoriously, it was known in one insurance company memo as "dead peasants insurance."[2] It's designed to avoid taxes by taking advantage of the fact that life insurance proceeds are tax free. In 1994, Wal-Mart used COLI to save $36 million in taxes; in 1995, it saved an estimated $80 million.

"But wait," you say, "the insurance cost Wal-Mart a billion dollars a year, right?" Wrong. It cost them nothing. To pay the premiums, the retailer borrowed money from the same company that sold it the insurance (in effect, the insurance company bills the premiums, pays them itself, and charges Wal-Mart interest). When an employee (or former employee) died, Wal-Mart used the insurance proceeds—minus the pittance it sent to the heirs—to pay off the loans it got from the insurance company.

But what about the interest Wal-Mart had to pay on those loans from the insurance company? Well, first of all, like all business interest, it's tax deductible. Second, Wal-Mart didn't actually pay the interest—the retail giant borrowed more money to cover it, and the interest on those loans is also tax deductible. So in a nutshell, COLI allowed companies to deduct from their taxes all the interest on these loans, and then let them pay back the loans themselves with tax-free insurance proceeds.

Once upon a time, businesses could only insure essential personnel considered vital to the business. But when state rules were revamped in the 1980s, there was a rapid expansion of a new kind of COLI, covering rank-and-file employees. Originally promoted as a tax break for small businesses, COLI ended up benefiting giant corporations like Disney, Coca-Cola, and AT&T, at a cost to the US Treasury of about $1.5 billion a year (in 1994).[3]

Starting in 1996, the IRS began to take a dim view of the deductions for the loans and began investigating more than 85 companies for tax-shelter violations. Courts agreed with the IRS that the deal was "a sham in substance."[4] By late 2002, the government was offering a final 45-day amnesty allowing other companies that turned themselves in to keep 20% of the deduction.[5] Wal-Mart and other COLI carriers settled with the tax man, but the nation's largest retailer faced a number of lawsuits from irate employees and employee heirs.[6] Wal-Mart in turn sued its insurance companies, claiming it had been misinformed about the viability of the deduction.[7]

COLI isn't dead yet. Even without the deduction, companies can still profit from the tax-free investment gains on the policies—and, of course, from the death benefits. Congressmember Rahm Emanuel (D-IL) estimates that COLI scams still deprive the Treasury of $1.9 billion a year. He's introduced legislation to offset the tax shelter and use the revenue to fund college grants.[8] And Representative Gene Green (D-TX) has repeatedly sponsored bills to prevent companies from taking out policies on their employees without their consent.[9] Such legislation has yet to pass, but taxpayers have had a partial victory over COLI.

OTHER LOOPHOLES

COLI is far from the only loophole available in the creative world of insurance. Insurance companies whose net income from premiums is less than $350,000 a year are tax exempt. Those whose net premium income falls between $350,000 and $2.1 million get to pay tax on either their investment income or their premium income, whichever is less; the other income is tax free.

Life insurance companies get to deduct the entire amount they set aside as a reserve each year, whether or not it exceeds the actual amount they have to pay out in claims. (Needless to say, this gives them a powerful incentive to increase the size of the reserve.) Property and casualty companies get a similar deduction. Between them, these reserve loopholes cost us more than $4 billion a year. Presumably, the government encourages large reserves to prevent insurance companies from going bankrupt due to huge losses. (One might assume that being in the business of insurance, insurance execs might be prudent enough to avoid unnecessary risks. Then too, insurance companies buy their own insurance to cover them in such situations.)

If you run a certain type of nonprofit organization—a fraternal society, say, or a voluntary employee benefit association—you might want to consider setting up your own in-house insurance operation. It won't be taxed either, and you can pay huge salaries to your top executives, just like any other self-respecting insurance company.

The insurance industry has carved out several other loopholes for itself. Put them all together and they cost us about $21.6 billion a year.[10] Add in the COLI costs and that's $23.5 billion for insurance loopholes. That is, unless we have another terrorist attack. After getting a whiff of the post-9/11 bailouts for the airline industry (see pp. 113–114), the insurance sector decided it needed some help, too.

CRISIS IN THE INDUSTRY?

This section rightly belongs in Part Three, since the breaks here are specific to the insurance industry, but I kept it here because this chapter discusses insurance scams, and the federal bailout is the biggest of them all. (Besides which, even the initial costs of this scam are not yet known.)

Within ten days of the attacks, insurance executives met with President Bush and Commerce Secretary Don Evans to discuss the details. Evans was friendly with several of the execs from his days as candidate Bush's fundraiser; the insurance industry gave $1.6 million to the Bush-Cheney ticket and kicked in another $1.1 million for the inaugural. Plus, the insurance industry gave $39 million to congressional candidates and their parties.[11]

The insurance industry claimed that a crisis was about to take place—because most of their terrorism insurance policies were set to expire by the end of 2001. (I bet you didn't know you could buy terrorism insurance, did you?) So unless the government stepped in with some assistance, the reinsurance companies—who insure the insurers—would refuse to renew this protection. And then banks would refuse to finance major new construction projects, and the whole economy would collapse.

Maybe this sounded plausible at the time, but six months after the deadline, Congress still hadn't finished the legislation. In the meantime, the companies had dipped into their 12-figure reserve funds to pay their 9/11 claims, and happily went back to work devising new forms of terror and construction insurance, for which they charged premium prices.[12] And banks continued to finance large buildings, with or without terrorism coverage.

But that didn't stop President Bush from continuing to proclaim the urgent need for the federal government to step in and back up the industry. The legislation, he said, would create 300,000 new jobs that had been held back by its absence.[13] It turned out that the lack of terrorism insurance was the only thing keeping the economy from roaring back to life. On the campaign trail, he accused Democrats of indifference to the plight of workers, saying the terrorism insurance bill was vital to economic recovery. A spokesperson for the Construction Trades Council of California said that he didn't know of "a single job being delayed" because of post-9/11 jitters, but few took notice.[14]

After the 2002 election, a lame-duck session of Congress passed the bill—and still the economy continued to shed tens of thousands of jobs every month. But you can take comfort, taxpayer, knowing that now you too are in the insurance business. If we should be unlucky enough to be attacked by terrorists again, you'll be covering 90% of the costs, after the old insurance industry pays off a $10 billion deductible.[15] The new law simply puts taxpayers on the hook for future losses, so no money is appropriated up front. In a sense, it's an "entitlement" for the insurance industry. But if these provisions had been in place on 9/11, taxpayers would have paid more than $30 billion in claims.[16] That's more than the entire cost of the various loopholes described above.

ACTIVIST'S TOOLKIT

Congressmember Gene Green
  2335 Rayburn House Office Building, Washington, DC 20515 • phone: (202) 225-1688 • fax: (202) 225-9903 • website: http://www.house.gov/green/

Congressmember Rahm Emanuel
  1319 Longworth House Office Building, Washington, DC 20515 • phone: (202) 225-4061 • fax: (202) 225-5603 • website: http://www.house.gov/emanuel/

Consumer Federation of America
  1424 16th Street NW, Suite 600, Washington, DC 20036 • phone: (202) 387-6121 • website: http://www.consumerfed.org/

National Association of Insurance Commissioners
  2301 McGee Street, Suite 800, Kansas City, MO 64108-2662 • phone: (816) 842-3600 • fax: (816) 783-8175 • website: http://www.naic.org/

Chapter 8

Business Meals and Entertainment
($8.8 billion a year)

When the 1986 tax reform lowered the deductibility of business meals and entertainment from 100% to 80%, the restaurant industry worried that businesspeople would stop eating out—or that, at the very least, they'd shift from expensive restaurants to fast-food outlets. Neither of those things happened, nor were there any appreciable job losses when the deduction was lowered further, to 50%, in 1993.[1]

But even if there had been, that still wouldn't justify continuing this loophole. Money not spent on entertainment is likely to be spent on other business expenses and will create other jobs to compensate for those lost. Or if it isn't spent, corporate overhead will go down, and ultimately, so will the price of products and services.

The meals and entertainment deduction amounts to an annual subsidy of $8.8 billion for fancy restaurants, golf courses, skyboxes at sports arenas and the like. And it's applied unequally. Factory workers can't deduct meals or sporting events at which they discuss their jobs with colleagues—nor can any taxpayer who doesn't itemize deductions. Also, like any deduction, this one is worth more to higher-bracket taxpayers, and it's particularly subject to fraud and abuse. Since the chance of an audit is low, the odds favor taxpayers who take an aggressive stance on the deductibility of their entertainment expenses.[2]

After the 9/11 attacks, the "three-martini lunch deduction" was deemed a matter of urgent national security; Congress voted to gradually raise the deduction to 65% in 2002, then 70% by 2004, 75% by 2006, and back to good old 80% in 2008.[3] The mind-set seems to be, as always, that what's good for business is good for the country. So whatever new tax breaks you can come up with, that's all to the public good. Since the economy was slumping after 9/11, the only thing they could come up with was more tax cuts and handouts. But the economy was slumping before 9/11, and it didn't work then either.

ACTIVIST'S TOOLKIT
(See taxpayer resources for Chapter 4, p. 33.)

Chapter 9

Tax-Free Muni Bonds

($6.4 billion a year)

Bonds are basically IOUs—a promise to pay back funds with interest. Unlike stocks, they don't give you a piece of the company, but they're much less risky. If the bond issuer defaults, you are guaranteed a place in line at the bankruptcy court before any stockholders. To help attract investors to bonds issued by state and local governments—generally called municipal bonds, muni bonds, or simply munis—the federal government has made the interest most of them garner exempt from federal income tax.

Leaving aside the question of how worthy the projects are that munis finance—they can be anything from water treatment plants to prisons—these tax exemptions cost the US Treasury a lot more than they save state and local governments. According to Citizens for Tax Justice (CTJ), interest rates on long-term munis averaged around 5.8% in the mid-'90s, while rates on comparable taxable Treasury and corporate bonds averaged 7.6% (after subtracting any state taxes that were due). This means state and local governments were able to pay 24% less interest to investors than they would have had to pay if the interest on their bonds were taxable.[1]

But most of that interest went to wealthy investors in tax brackets substantially higher than 24%. So while state and local governments are saving 24% on the bonds, corporations are saving between 34% and 39%, and wealthy individuals between 28% and 35%. The difference between those rates and 24% represents the net loss to government on all levels. (What's more, if the muni bond is from the same state as the taxpayer, the interest on it is exempt from state income tax as well.)

CTJ estimates that, overall, only 46% of this muni-bond subsidy actually benefits state and local governments, while 27% goes to individual investors, 18% to corporations, and 9% to nonprofit hospitals and schools. In the end, "about a quarter of the federal subsidy ends up as a windfall to well-off investors." Since the total tax subsidy is expected to cost the federal government $24.3 billion a year between 2003 and 2007,[2] the wealthfare portion of it runs $6.08 billion a year (a quarter of $24.3 billion).

For instance, if a city wants to fund, say, a new sports stadium for the local football franchise and issues $7 billion in tax-free bonds to pay for

it, federal taxpayers will pick up $2.4 billion of the tab. The city will then pay back the bondholders through other taxes, including property taxes and various fees. If the feds had simply transferred the $2.4 billion to the city, they could have specified that it pay for schools and hospitals, instead of handouts to team owners. And besides, then the entire amount would have gone to the designated project, instead of also lining the pockets of investors.

But that's not the worst of it. To quote CTJ again: "In many circumstances, private companies and individuals can 'borrow' the ability to issue tax-free bonds from state and local governments." If your city or state makes this cookie jar available to private industry, it can be used to build things like stadiums and shopping malls as well as schools and hospitals. As such, at least some of this counts as state and local wealthfare (see "State and Local Corporate Welfare," pp. 133–134).

Before the mid-'80s, "there was almost no limit on what states could authorize tax-exempt financing for—and since the federal government was picking up the bill, there was no [reason for] the states [not to go] hogwild. Reforms now generally limit the total amount… but it still remains a major drain on the federal Treasury." In fact, CTJ estimates that about 36% of all muni-bond revenues finance private projects.

ACTIVIST'S TOOLKIT

(See taxpayer resources for Chapter 4, p. 33.)

Chapter 10

Export Subsidies

($1.8 billion a year)

Export subsidies take many forms. Under various programs—I won't bore you with all their names—the US Department of Agriculture (USDA) currently spends nearly $637 million a year helping US-based transnational corporations market their products abroad.[1] Back in 1996, that figure was over $1 billion a year.[2]

These programs provide information on foreign markets, loans at below-market rates, funding for trade shows, and advertising subsidies. This is over and above the tax deduction for advertising (see Chapter 14). It's a straight handout to help defray the cost of advertising overseas. (As Friends of the Earth points out, there's been little effort to ensure that these funds actually increase overseas promotions rather than simply pay for marketing the transnationals would be doing anyway.)

The USDA also provides "bonuses" to transnationals—many of them foreign firms—so that they can "sell US agricultural products in targeted countries at prices below the exporter's cost of acquiring them."[3] (When other countries do this to us, we call it "dumping" and protest vociferously, since it has the effect of destroying any unsubsidized competition.) Corporations that have benefited from the USDA's largesse include (all figures are totals for 1985–94):[4]

- Cargill (annual sales of $7 billion)—$1.3 billion
- Continental Grain (the fourth-largest privately held corporation in the United States, with sales of $15 billion)—$1.1 billion
- the US subsidiary of the French firm Louis Dreyfus (US sales of $1.7 billion)—$938 million
- Bunge Corp.—$282 million
- the US subsidiary of the Italian firm Ferruzzi—$246 million
- Pillsbury—$163 million
- Mitsubishi USA—$114 million

Other struggling companies you were generous enough to subsidize include: McDonald's, Dole, Sunkist, General Mills, Ernest & Julio Gallo, Campbell's Soup, Miller Beer, M&M Mars, and American Legend (to help them peddle those mink coats overseas, where there's less chance paint will get thrown on them).

BEYOND THE USDA

There's almost another billion in export subsidies outside the USDA. The Export-Import Bank (Ex-Im), an independent federal agency with a $770 million budget (in fiscal year 2004), provides low-interest loans and loan guarantees to foreign users of US products.[5]

In 1994, for example, the murderous government of Indonesia got over $125 million in Ex-Im loans to buy equipment from Hughes Aircraft. Ex-Im insured a $3 million loan to General Electric to build a factory in Mexico that cost 1,500 jobs in Indiana. The Chinese government used an $18 million loan to modernize a steel plant—even though that company was accused of illegally dumping steel onto US markets below cost.[6]

Other Ex-Im beneficiaries include needy corporations like Boeing, AT&T, IBM, General Motors, and good old Enron and Halliburton. According to Congressmember Bernie Sanders (I-VT), Enron has taken in more than $673 million in loans and loan guarantees over the past decade. Ex-Im covered a $300 million loan for an Enron project in India—even after the World Bank had turned down the project as "not economically viable."[7]

The Bush administration, eager to exploit overseas oil supplies, has doubled the amount of debt Ex-Im is authorized to assume on your behalf—to $100 billion. Since Bush took the White House, the two largest oil companies receiving Ex-Im funding have cut their US workforces by more than 20,000 jobs.[8]

The federally funded Overseas Private Investment Corporation (OPIC) works the other side of the street. Instead of lending money to foreign governments and companies so they can buy US products, it will commit over $800 million in loans and guarantees (in FY2004) financing US companies' investments in "developing" countries.[9]

OPIC used to hand out a lot more money. Under the Clinton administration, the OPIC budget went from less than $100 million to more than $3 billion. In FY1994, US West alone got $170 million in OPIC financing for projects in Russia and Hungary. (Just coincidentally, the company made $320,000 in campaign contributions that year.) Other OPIC welfare kings included Citibank ($388 million), Kimberly-Clark ($9.3 million), and Levi Strauss ($1.1 million). The last two companies were so happy with the overseas operations we financed that Kimberly-Clark transferred 600 jobs out of the United States, and Levi Strauss transferred 100.[10]

OPIC has always been subject to political influence. During the Reagan years, it directed a loan toward a prominent supporter of the contra war against Nicaragua. During the Clinton years, 14% of its loans went to Citibank, which was affiliated with Treasury Secretary Robert Rubin. OPIC also funded a mining project in the Philippines run by the notorious Freeport-McMoRan company, but canceled it due to environmental disasters associated with the company. That is, until former Secretary of State Henry Kissinger, a Freeport director, launched a huge lobbying campaign—at which point OPIC canceled its cancellation.[11] (Of course, Enron got in on some OPIC goodies as well.)

The State Department gives $125 million a year to foreign importers of US goods. The Commerce Department runs the International Trade Administration, which gets over $300 million a year.[12] And then there's the Pentagon. It runs several overseas loan programs, but since I'm discussing them in the following chapter on military waste and fraud, I won't detail them here. Even without the Pentagon's programs, export subsidies total over $1.8 billion a year.

ACTIVIST'S TOOLKIT

Congressmember Bernie Sanders

2233 Rayburn House Office Building, Washington, DC 20515 • phone: (202) 225-4115 • fax: (202) 225-6790 • email: bernie@mail.house.gov • website: http://www.bernie.house.gov

ECA Watch

c/o Pacific Environment • 1440 Broadway Street, Suite 306, Oakland, CA 94612 • phone: (510) 251-8800, ext. 314 • fax: (510) 251-8838 • email: info@eca-watch.org • website: http://www.eca-watch.org

Global Exchange

2017 Mission Street, #303, San Francisco, CA 94110 • phone: (415) 255-7296 • fax: (415) 255-7498 • website: http://www.globalexchange.org

MAJOR US GOVERNMENT
EXPORT SUBSIDY PROGRAMS
(ALL FIGURES ARE FOR FY2004)

Commodity Credit Corporation
USDA program administering credit guarantee programs for agricultural exports—$4.2 billion a year in taxpayer guarantees.

Dairy Export Incentive Program
Cash payments to dairy producers to subsidize exports—$57 million.

Economic Support Fund (ESF)
Grants to foreign governments with "special security interests" generally solved by US arms merchants—$2.53 billion.

Export Enhancement Program (EEP)
Direct subsidy of farm exports, ostensibly to counter "unfair" trading practices by other countries—$28 million, with "some flexibility" to go above that level.

Export-Import Bank (Ex-Im)
Provides low-interest loans and loan guarantees to foreign customers of US corporations—$76 million in administrative costs; over a half billion in guarantees.

Foreign Agricultural Service (FAS)
Supports trade-related initiatives in developing countries so that they might buy from us—$145 million.

Foreign Market Development (FMD)
Promotes exports of bulk farm products, in contrast to the Market Access Program, which does the same thing for brand-name products—$34.5 million.

Foreign Military Financing (FMF)
Direct grants to foreign governments, administered jointly by the Pentagon and the State Department to help finance export sales of US-made weaponry—$4.4 billion.

Foreign Military Sales (FMS)
Manages government-to-government sales of military equipment, as opposed to FMF, which gives other governments money to buy from US arms merchants—$11.1 billion in contracts; $361 million in administrative costs.

International Military Education and Training (IMET)
Military training for dozens of foreign countries, including some of the planet's worst human rights abusers—$91.7 million (combined with up to $625 million in "drawdowns," or outright gifts of US military equipment, which will of course need spare parts).

Market Access Program (MAP)
Notorious marketing subsidy for the likes of McDonald's and Pillsbury, which need help in foreign countries—$125 million, rising to $200 million by 2007.

Overseas Private Investment Corporation (OPIC)
Finances US corporate investments overseas—$800 million.

SOURCES

Federation of American Scientists, "Fast Facts." http://www.fas.org/asmp/fast_facts.htm.

Hamnes, Bruce, "Trade Policy Statement: The Future of U.S. Agricultural Export Programs," testimony of the US Wheat Associates before the Senate Subcommittee on Production and Price Competitiveness of the Committee on Agriculture, Nutrition, and Forestry, July 18, 2000, http://www.uswheat.org/marketnews.nsf/0/45ba2548a2b3b0118525691f00707de9?OpenDocument.

Office of Management and Budget, *Fiscal Year 2004 Budget of the United States* (Washington, DC: GPO, 2003).

Part Three: Industry Chicanery

Chapter 11

Military Waste and Fraud
($224 billion a year)

More than a quarter of the $815 billion we spend each year on wealthfare comes from waste, fraud, and abuse in military expenditures. When it comes to throwing away money, the Pentagon has no peer.

For one thing, there's the simple question of scale. The Pentagon budget for fiscal year 2003 (October 1, 2002, to September 30, 2003) was $393 billion—a $70 billion increase in just the past two years.[1] That increase alone is more than the annual military budget of any other nation (Russia is the next-largest military spender at $65 billion a year).[2] The Pentagon shells out more than six times as much as Russia, more than eight times as much as China, more than nine times as much as Japan, more than ten times as much as Britain, and more than thirteen times as much as France.

The proposed 2004 budget ($399.1 billion) is the size of the next 22 largest military budgets combined, and it's 37 times larger than the combined military budgets of all our "regional adversaries"—Cuba, Syria, Iran, Iraq, North Korea, Sudan, and Libya.[3] In 2000 (the last year for which data was available globally), the United States accounted for 36% of all military spending on the planet.[4] Since then, US military spending has shot up by an additional 28%, reaching close to half of the total global estimate.

As enormous as the Pentagon's budget is, there's more military spending buried elsewhere—in the Department of Energy's production of fuel for nuclear weapons, in the military portion of the NASA budget, in the Veterans Administration, the Homeland Security Department, and so on. These hidden military expenses come to nearly $123 billion.[5]

Adding them in, the War Resisters League has estimated FY2004 military spending at $522 billion.[6] But that doesn't include what we have to pay for past Pentagon budgets. The Center for Defense Information (CDI), a Washington-based think tank run by retired admirals and generals, went back to 1941 and multiplied the military's percentage of each year's budget by the deficit for that year. Using that method, CDI figured that interest on past military spending costs us $93 billion per year.[7] (The

War Resisters League went all the way back to 1789 and came up with $282 billion per year, or 80% of our annual interest payments.)

Since the Center for Defense Information's estimate is lower, let's be conservative and use it. Adding it to the $522 billion estimated for FY2004 gives us a figure for total military spending—past and present—of $615 billion a year ($11.8 billion a week, $1.7 billion a day, or $70 million an hour).

WASTE BEYOND YOUR WILDEST DREAMS

But just the scale of the Pentagon's budget alone can't explain its prodigious ability to waste money. Another quality is required—either world-class incompetence or unparalleled deceitfulness (or both). There are so many examples of this that they tend to blur together, numbing the mind. Here are just a few:

According to a US Senate hearing, $13 billion that the Pentagon handed out to weapons contractors between 1985 and 1995 was "lost."[8] Another $15 billion remains unaccounted for because of "financial management troubles." That's $28 billion—right off the top—that simply disappeared. (This is one of those places where I can hardly believe what I'm writing. But it's true.) It doesn't faze the Pentagon, though; in 1999 alone, it lost an additional $2.7 billion in equipment.[9]

In the *New York Times,* Anthony Lewis described the amount of Pentagon waste as "literally incalculable. That is because financial managers in the Defense Department cannot produce auditable books. The director of its accounting service so testified to a congressional committee."[10] As Colman McCarthy commented in the *National Catholic Reporter,* "The money might as well have been thrown out of airplanes for all anyone knew where it went."[11]

Since no one raised much of an uproar over the lost billions, the Pentagon seems to have decided that it can keep its books however it pleases. Auditors for the Office of Management and Budget found that in FY2000, the Pentagon entered "unsubstantiated balance adjustments" totaling $1.1 *trillion.*[12] As reporter Joel Brinkley explained, that doesn't mean the whole trillion was gone. What it does mean is that the Pentagon's books are cooked as thoroughly as a Thanksgiving turkey. The elaborate charade of congressional hearings and budgetary oversight has virtually nothing to do with how the Pentagon actually spends its money.

For instance, when one Defense Department agency "discovered" that its accounts were out of balance with the Treasury Department by $3.9 billion, instead of trying to explain how that happened, it just made a "balance adjustment" so its account would come out even. As Brinkley noted, hundreds of similar adjustments—some debits, some deposits—

added up to the $1.1 trillion figure. But hey, that's an improvement. The previous year's cheat sheet totaled $2.3 trillion.

According to the General Accounting Office (GAO), 80% of the Navy's purchase orders are inaccurate. An Air Force purchase of $888,000 in ammunition was listed as $333 million—an increase of 37,500%. In 1992 alone, the Army Corps of Engineers "lost" $1.3 billion worth of equipment.[13]

But let's not sweat a few billion dollars here and there—the way the Pentagon really wastes money is by overpaying contractors. The reference on that subject is a wonderful book called *The Pentagon Catalog*, published in 1986 by Christopher Cerf and Henry Beard.[14] This book was the greatest bargain in history. To quote its cover copy: "Buy this catalog for only $4.95 and get this $2,043 nut for free." Attached to each book was a small metal nut, the kind that costs a few cents at the hardware store—and that McDonnell Douglas sold to the Navy for $2,043 each.

Here are some other examples of your tax dollars at work:

- a plain metal bolt from Grumman Aerospace for $898 (a bargain compared with the nut)
- a pair of duckbill pliers Boeing originally proposed charging $2,548 for, but whose price the Air Force slashed to $748
- a $469 box wrench, a $437 tape measure, a $435 hammer, a $265 set of screwdrivers, and a $243 pair of Vise-Grip pliers (all from Gould Simulation Systems)
- a half-inch socket for $504, and a $660 ashtray (both from Grumman)
- a coffeemaker Weber Aircraft priced at $7,622, but in fairness, it was designed to handle a 100-degree drop in room temperature or 40 G's of acceleration (I don't know about you, but the first thing I want after being frozen solid or turned into a blob of jelly is a nice, hot cup of coffee)
- a $670 armrest pad from Burns Aerostat
- a toilet seat for which Lockheed charged $640
- a $214 flashlight from Grimes Manufacturing
- my personal favorite: a plastic cap that goes over the end of a stool leg—at the special price from Boeing of just $1,118.

The Project on Government Oversight (POGO) has continued to track procurement outrages. In 2000, it found dozens more examples, including what may be the record breaker: microcircuits worth 11 cents each, which the Pentagon picked up for $5,788.76 apiece. The markup? A staggering 5,262,500%.[15]

There is some speculation that the outrageous pricing is just a bookkeeping maneuver for the lazy accountants employed by defense contractors. (This is not a slap at the accountants—they can afford to be lazy since, after all, nobody is really paying that much attention.) In other words, when defense contractors go over budget on a new jet fighter, for instance, they take the billions of dollars extra they're charging and split them up among all the components. Thus, they add hundreds of dollars to the bolt as well as to the alternator or the engine, or whatever, and it just seems that much more outrageous in the case of the bolt. That doesn't make the extra billions any less outrageous, but it does make it easier to explain.

I should also point out that for a few of these items, the government eventually did negotiate a refund—of about 10%. To make sure contractors are never again inconvenienced by refunds like these, Vice-President Al Gore's Reinventing Government program cut the staff of the Defense Contract Audit Agency (which saves taxpayers $10 for every $1 it spends) by 19%. Other auditing agencies were also decimated: the Inspector General's office by 21%, and the GAO by 33%.[16]

More recently, Defense Secretary Donald Rumsfeld has decided that even this minimal amount of oversight is too onerous. In April 2003, he proposed the Defense Transformation for the 21st Century Act. This bill would end protection for whistle-blowers, waive ethics rules, exempt the Department of Defense from environmental laws, allow no-bid service contracts, and repeal scores of reporting requirements for congressional oversight.[17] Hopefully this will allow the Pentagon to struggle along without anybody else poking a nose into its business.

CAREER CRIMINALS

Take one bloated budget. Add the most incompetent and/or duplicitous bureaucrats on earth. Only two more ingredients are needed: greed and (more) guile. For every $640 toilet seat the Pentagon buys, there's some unctuous predator selling it for $640.

Actually, "unctuous predator" is far too kind. Many military suppliers are—quite literally—criminals. According to the *Bulletin of the Atomic Scientists*, every single one of the top ten weapons contractors was convicted of or admitted to defrauding the government between 1980 and 1992.[18] For example:

- Grumman (now Northrop Grumman) paid the government $20 million to escape criminal liability for coercing subcontractors into making political contributions.
- Lockheed (now Lockheed Martin) was convicted of paying millions in bribes to obtain classified planning documents.

- Northrop (now Northrop Grumman) was fined $17 million for 34 counts of falsifying test data on its cruise missiles and fighter jets.
- Rockwell (still unmerged) was fined $5.5 million for committing criminal fraud against the Air Force.

More recently, POGO has searched public records from 1990 through 2002 on civil, administrative, criminal, and alleged violations by the top 43 Pentagon contractors. It found over 400 instances, which resulted in $3.4 billion in fines.[19] (Of course, $3.4 billion divided by 13 years makes $260 million a year, which in the context of the Pentagon budget is a rounding error.) Sixteen of the contractors had 28 criminal violations between them; four of the companies in the top ten had at least two criminal convictions.

It's not as if this kind of behavior is universal; thirteen companies had zero violations and consequently paid out a total of zero dollars in fines. But too many of the Pentagon's vendors are, to put it mildly, repeat offenders. For example:

- Fluor had 19 cases on the list, and paid $70 million in fines and settlements.
- Raytheon had 24 cases, and paid $128.7 million in fines and settlements.
- Boeing had 36 cases, and paid $358 million in fines and settlements.
- Lockheed Martin had 63 cases, and paid $231.9 million in fines and settlements.

But General Electric (GE) was the champ. POGO lists 63 cases, including a conviction for mail and procurement fraud that resulted in a criminal fine of $10 million and restitution of $2.2 million. From 1990 to 2002, GE ended up paying out a total of $982.9 million in fines, penalties, restitution, and settlements. And during that time, out of all 43 companies, GE was the only one that was suspended from doing business with the government. That mighty tap on the wrist lasted a total of—tada!—five days. In my own research, I found a few other examples of GE crimes and civil violations over the years:

- In 1961, GE pleaded guilty to price fixing and paid a $372,500 fine.
- In 1977, it was convicted of price fixing again.
- In 1979, it settled out of court when the State of Alabama sued it for dumping PCBs in a river.
- In 1981, it was convicted of setting up a $1.25 million slush fund to bribe Puerto Rican officials.

- In 1985, GE pleaded guilty to 108 counts of fraud on a Minuteman missile contract. In addition, the chief engineer of GE's space systems division was convicted of perjury, and GE paid a fine of a million dollars.
- In 1985, it pleaded guilty to falsifying time cards.
- In 1989, it paid the government $3.5 million to settle five civil lawsuits alleging contractor fraud at a jet-engine plant (which involved the alteration of 9,000 daily labor vouchers to inflate its Pentagon billings).
- In 1990, GE was convicted of criminal fraud for cheating the US Army on a contract for battlefield computers; it declined to appeal, and paid $16 million in criminal and civil fines. (Of this amount, $11.7 million was used to settle government complaints that GE had padded its bids on 200 other military and space contracts—which comes to just $58,000 or so per contract.)
- In 1992, GE pleaded guilty to defrauding the Pentagon in an embezzlement scheme that ended up funding the Israeli military (by diverting Pentagon funds into the bank account of an Israeli general, who then used the money for Israeli military programs not authorized by the US foreign aid budget). GE paid out over $69 million in fines—one of the largest Pentagon fraud settlements ever.
- In 1995, GE was fined $1.5 million for contaminating the Hudson River. This came on top of $7 million in compensation to fishermen and over $2.5 million in cleanup costs. The case is still far from settled.
- In 1998, GE was ordered to pay £2 billion in the United Kingdom for asbestos contamination, and $4.2 million in Puerto Rico for contamination of drinking water.
- In 1999, a Chicago court ordered GE to reimburse consumers $147 million for unfair debt collection practices.
- In 2001, a New York court ordered GE to refund over $4 million in overcharges for mortgage insurance.

This is, believe it or not, only a partial list.[20] GE sold its weapons division to Martin Marietta (now part of Lockheed Martin) in 1993 for $3 billion (retaining 23.5% of the stock and two seats on the board of directors).[21] But despite its lengthy criminal rap sheet, GE is still the twenty-third largest Pentagon contractor, raking in over $1.5 billion a year.[22]

After watching this parade of criminality for eight years, the Clinton administration decided to do something about it—on its way out the door. In January 2001, Bill Clinton issued an antiscofflaw rule that would have given federal contracting officials the authority to deny contracts to corporations that violate environmental, labor, and other laws. The incoming Bush administration suspended the implementation of that rule "for further study." The rule was quietly revoked just after Christmas the next year. This was a great gift to contractors, who had given $2 million in 2000 campaign contributions, 96% of it to the GOP.[23]

IT'S AN ILL WIND

The largest investigation of Pentagon fraud, Operation Ill Wind, took place between 1986 and 1990. Initiated by the Justice Department and pursued by the FBI, the investigation began when Pentagon official John Marlowe was caught molesting little girls. He cut a deal to stay out of jail; for the next few years, he secretly recorded hundreds of conversations with weapons contractors.

There's no way of knowing how much the crimes that Ill Wind looked into cost the taxpayers, but the investigation, which cost $20 million, brought in ten times that much in fines. According to *Wall Street Journal* reporter Andy Pasztor, "More than 90 companies and individuals were convicted of felonies… including eight of the military's fifteen largest suppliers…. Boeing, GE and United Technologies pleaded guilty… Hughes, Unisys, Raytheon, Loral, Litton, Teledyne, Cubic, Hazeltine, Whittaker and LTV… admitted they violated the law."[24]

Unisys signed the largest Pentagon fraud settlement in history: $190 million in fines, penalties, and forgone profits (which means they weren't allowed to overcharge the way military contractors usually do).

Assistant Navy Secretary Melvyn Paisley was the central figure in the Ill Wind scandal and the highest-ranking person convicted (he was sentenced to four years in prison). He ran his office like a supermarket for weapons manufacturers, soaking up bribes, divvying up multibillion-dollar contracts, and diverting work to BDM, a firm he secretly controlled with a partner (and a firm owned by the Carlyle Group, a name well-known by watchers of the military-industrial complex).

Paisley may have been a bit more flamboyant than most, but there was nothing terribly unusual about his approach. As of 1994, nearly 70 of the Pentagon's 100 largest suppliers were under investigation. Fines for that year totaled a record $1.2 billion.[25] That may sound like a lot, but it was less than 2% of the weapons industry's net income (which averaged $64 billion a year in 1994 and 1995).[26] A billion or two in fines is hardly an incentive to end the corruption and waste in Pentagon contracting.

THE BLACK BUDGET

Not all Pentagon waste is visible. Hidden within the military budget is a secret "black budget" that's not subject to any congressional oversight—toothless as that usually is. It includes money for the CIA (tucked away in the Air Force budget, where it gets about 10% of the total), and for less-well-known but better-funded "intelligence" organizations like the National Security Agency and the National Reconnaissance Office.

In 1997, a lawsuit from the Federation of American Scientists argued that with the Cold War over, there was no harm in publishing the total amount of the intelligence black budget, without giving details of how it was spent. A court agreed, and a figure of $26.6 billion for 1997 was released, followed by $26.7 billion for 1998. But in 1999, Pentagon officials raised the issue again, and this time the court sided with them.[27] So the 2003 figure—estimated, without too much difficulty, at $41.5 billion—is still an official secret.

That number has jumped nearly $10 billion over the previous year's due to increased intelligence spending for the so-called war on terrorism. John Pike of GlobalSecurity.org estimates that the black budget ran about $36 billion a year during the Reagan years. The number dropped gradually in the 1990s to a low of $24.4 billion in 1995. That's not because the operations stopped or someone cut off the funding, though. Pike attributed the lower levels to a couple of projects that grew too huge to be hidden and "surfaced" in the public budget.[28]

One of these is the B-2 bomber. Originally projected to cost $550 million, B-2s ended up costing $2.2 billion each—literally more than their weight in gold. The Air Force had planned to purchase a fleet of 133 planes, but given the sticker shock, it ended up buying only 21—for a total cost of some $45 billion. The B-2 has been plagued by technical problems from the beginning. Its "stealth" capability is extremely fragile, and requires costly and time-consuming maintenance. It has to be kept in expensive climate-controlled hangars. This prevents it from being based overseas and keeps it unavailable for any mission about two-thirds of the time.[29]

How did the project survive such massive cost overruns? As humorist Dave Barry described it, "The B-2 has demonstrated a breathtaking capacity, unmatched in aviation history, to deliver, with pinpoint accuracy, extremely large payloads of taxpayer dollars into the districts of strategic members of Congress."[30] In fact, the B-2's manufacturer, Northrop Grumman, subcontracted work on the plane to 383 of the 435 congressional districts.

Another once-black project is Milstar, a satellite system designed to "fight and win a six-month nuclear war... long after the White House and the Pentagon are reduced to rubble."[31] The Air Force tried to kill this idiotic program four times since it emerged from the black budget, but Congress wouldn't listen. So far, Milstar has cost us between $10 billion and $20 billion and has been plagued with technical glitches. According to the GAO, it has a 65% chance of degrading "below a minimally acceptable level" by 2006.[32] At that point, the Department of Defense plans to implement a new, improved version of the system. But if the United States is destroyed in a nuclear holocaust between now and then, we might miss out on our chance for revenge.

Since the black budget is completely off the books, it encourages waste on a titanic scale. As one Pentagon employee put it: "In a black project, people don't worry about money. If you need money, you got it. If you screw up and need more, you got it. You're just pouring money into the thing until you get it right. The incentive isn't there to do it right the first time. Who's going to question it?"[33]

Well, the founding fathers would have, since the Constitution states that "no money shall be drawn from the Treasury, but in consequence of appropriations made by law" and it requires that the government publish a "regular statement… of the receipts and expenditures of all public money."[34] Unfortunately, in 1974, the Supreme Court ruled that if we don't like the black budget, our only recourse is to elect politicians who won't allow it. (Or we could get better people on the Supreme Court.)

DON'T CALL IT BRIBERY

Why do our legislators put up with military waste and fraud? For the same reason they do anything. Defense PACs (political action committees) gave congressional candidates $8.4 million in 2001 and 2002. And PAC money is just part of the story. Pentagon contractors also came up with $3.2 million in soft-money donations and another $2 million in individual contributions from industry executives. That makes at least $13.6 million in the last election cycle, about two-thirds of which went to the GOP.[35] So it's no wonder that Congress usually finds a way to give the Pentagon even more than it asks for.

Of the $4.5 billion in unrequested weapons funding added to the Pentagon budget for FY1996, 74% was spent in or near the home districts of representatives who sit on the House National Security Committee.[36] For FY2000, the two top unrequested items were the $375 million LHD-8 helicopter carrier, to be built in Mississippi, the home state of then-Senate Majority Leader Trent Lott, and $275 million for five F-15 fighters, to be built in the home district of then-House Minority Leader Dick Gephardt.[37]

After shelling out for its fleet of B-2 bombers, the Pentagon insisted that it really didn't need any more of them. But Senator Ted Stevens (R-AK) didn't care. Stevens—who's second on the list of the largest recipients of military PAC money—tried to get Congress to pony up another $27 billion for nine more of the planes. Stevens got more than $207,000 between 1989 and 1994, making him one of the top ten recipients of PAC contributions from B-2 contractors.[38] (Isn't it amazing how little politicians cost?)

If PAC money isn't enough, military lobbyists can always argue jobs. Liberal Californian Representative Maxine Waters defended her vote to continue B-2 funding by candidly admitting that it was one of the few ways she knew to bring federal jobs to her district.[39] (Since her district is South Central Los Angeles, you can understand her desperation.)

In the election 2000 debates, Al Gore proposed raising defense spending by $10 billion a year over the next decade. George W. Bush painted Gore as a big spender, saying that an extra $5 billion a year was plenty.[40] One would have to have had the ability to look into Bush's heart to know if he was lying, but one could certainly make an educated guess. The annual Pentagon budget is now more than $100 billion higher than when that debate took place.

The second Bush administration came into office making noises about trimming costs and "skipping a generation of military technology." Some officials on the transition team hinted at "rethinking" bloated weapons systems like the V-22 Osprey and the F-22 Raptor.[41] But the Bush administration faced a different fiscal outlook before 9/11. Its own pre-election planning documents show that Bush and his inner circle knew they could not increase military spending dramatically without some sort of "new Pearl Harbor" to scare the hell out of the American public.[42] Once they got that event, they had a blank check to spend as much as they wanted.

Prior to that event, there were restraints on military spending. To advance their imperial plans for military adventures in oil-rich regions (also spelled out in planning documents), they had to find some savings in the budget; hence the rhetoric about possible cancellation of ridiculously useless weapons systems. It is even possible that they were sincere in their belief that some of the deadwood had to go. But 9/11 freed them of the necessity to fight any such politically dicey battles with Congress.

The only weapons system that has been phased out is the absurdly overweight Crusader artillery system, which had sucked up a mere $2 billion.[43] Even so, Defense Secretary Rumsfeld faced a major fight with his own generals and members of Congress to cancel the Crusader. United Defense, the Crusader's contractor, had wisely increased its campaign contributions from $49,500 in the 1998 election cycle to $180,000 in 2000 and $287,000 in 2002. This didn't help save the big gun, but United is currently contracting for over a dozen other weapons systems. It probably doesn't hurt that it's owned by the Carlyle Group, for which the president's father was a consultant (he resigned in late 2003).[44]

The Seawolf submarine, designed to counter the Soviet Union's submarine fleet, was a poster child for Pentagon pork.[45] Given a more-than-adequate existing submarine fleet and a defunct adversary, there was no conceivable need for the Seawolf (which cost $2.4 billion apiece)—except for the votes in Connecticut, where it was built, and in surrounding states. That's why liberal New England senators like Ted Kennedy and John Kerry supported it, as did Bill Clinton—who needed votes from those states in his 1992 campaign.[46] After years of opposition, the Seawolf program was discontinued with only three subs built—to be replaced by an equally redundant fleet of 30 "Virginia" submarines, projected to cost $73 billion.[47]

Neither the Air Force nor the Navy wanted to continue funding the V-22 Osprey assault plane, which has so far killed 22 soldiers in accidental crashes.[48] The first Bush administration tried in vain to kill it, though the second Bush administration is funding it at $1.7 billion for FY2004—for a total program cost of $46 billion.[49] The V-22 was rescued in its hour of need by legislators from Texas and Pennsylvania—the two states that do the most contracting for it—and by then-President Clinton,[50] who—oh, you get the idea.

WHAT ABOUT THE JOBS WE'D LOSE?

If new weapons systems are nothing more than make-work programs, they're really inefficient ones. A 1992 congressional study estimated that shifting money from the Pentagon to state and local governments would create two jobs for every one it eliminates.[51] Building weapons we don't need is so wasteful that the economy would probably be better off if we just paid people the same money to stay at home. The Congressional Budget Office concluded that a billion dollars spent on successfully promoting arms exports creates 25,000 jobs, but if that same billion is spent on mass transit, it creates 30,000 jobs; on housing, 36,000 jobs; on education, 41,000 jobs; or on health care, 47,000 jobs.[52]

Aside from the cost, using federal money to prop up military contractors creates a disincentive for them to convert to civilian products. Shifting Pentagon funds to urgently needed domestic uses would be good for both the United States and the rest of the world. As then-President Dwight Eisenhower put it, "Every gun that is made, every warship launched, every rocket fired signifies, in the final sense, a theft from those who hunger and are not fed, those who are cold and not clothed."[53]

THE REVOLVING DOOR

Another reason for Pentagon waste and fraud is the revolving door between military contractors and government personnel. Before taking a pay cut to become vice-president, Dick Cheney was the CEO of Halliburton, which is currently building and maintaining new bases for the US military.[54] And before that, he was the secretary of defense. Before Caspar Weinberger was the secretary of defense, he was a top executive at Bechtel, which does massive engineering projects for the Pentagon and foreign clients like Saudi Arabia. Before he was the secretary of state, George Shultz was the president of Bechtel.[55] Unsurprisingly, both Halliburton and Bechtel are profiting handsomely from the second Gulf War.[56]

Before his days as a famous Navy felon, Melvyn Paisley worked for Boeing—as did his boss at the Pentagon, Navy Secretary John Lehman.[57] Secretary of Defense William Perry and CIA Director John Deutch both did consulting work for Martin Marietta before they joined the Clinton administration.[58] As mentioned before, the first President Bush helped to run the Carlyle Group, along with former Defense Secretary Frank Carlucci, former Secretary of State James Baker, and other luminaries.[59] The list goes on and on.

Generals have an interest in keeping weapons contractors happy—at least if they want to sit on the boards of corporations after they retire. Contractors can use their connections at the Pentagon to find work there and, like Paisley, feed lucrative contracts to their friends in the private sector.

On both sides of the revolving door, militarists live in the lap of luxury. Nobody batted an eyelash when Paisley entertained contractors in staterooms on the *Queen Elizabeth,* nor is there ever much dismay when military aircraft are used, at a cost of tens of thousands of dollars an hour, to fly politicians, lobbyists, and weapons contractors on pleasure trips.[60]

DIRECT HANDOUTS

Still, personal perks don't cost us much compared with corporate perks. For example, when Lockheed and Martin Marietta merged to become Lockheed Martin, $92 million in bonuses—or "triggered compensation," as they prefer to call it—was handed out to top executives and members of the board. US taxpayers helpfully chipped in $31 million of that. While he was at the Pentagon, Deutch quietly reversed a 40-year ban on triggered compensation. (Both Deutch and Perry obtained waivers from an ethics regulation that prohibits Pentagon officials from dealing with people they formerly did business with until a year has passed.) The government reimbursed the company for "merger expenses," including the golden parachutes for the departing executives. The biggest bonus, $8.2 million, went to the new company's president, Norman Augustine, for whom Deutch and Perry had done work at Martin Marietta.

The handouts were justified on the theory that the resulting new company would be more efficient than the two parent companies and hence would save taxpayers money in the long run. It seems like it would be hard to prove this theory either way, but we do know that the merger put a lot of people out of work; up to 30,000 employees lost their jobs.[61]

MAKING A KILLING ON WAR

Once upon a time, the president of the United States said, "I don't want to see a single war millionaire created in the United States as a result of this world disaster." That was Franklin Roosevelt in 1940, and that was a long time ago. Today, the president is blithely appointing his friends and former business associates to oversee the reconstruction of Iraq. The Bush administration has worked hard to make sure that US firms get the bulk of this business—even if US troops have to bear the brunt of resistance attacks because excluded countries refuse to assist the occupation forces.

Perhaps most shockingly, on May 22, 2003, President Bush issued an executive order (EO 13303) that places US oil companies operating in Iraq above the law for any activities "related to" the extraction of Iraq's petroleum resources. The order is good until the end of 2007, and covers any lawbreaking either on US soil or in occupied Iraq. Specifically, Bush's text declares that "any attachment, judgment, decree, lien, execution, garnishment, or other judicial process is prohibited, and shall be deemed null and void."

According to Tom Devine of the Government Accountability Project, "The Executive Order cancels the concept of corporate accountability and abandons the rule of law. It is a blank check for corporate anarchy, potentially robbing Iraqis of both their rights and their resources."

Perhaps the most notorious of the oil companies operating in Iraq is the corporate criminal Halliburton. From 1995 through 2000, while Vice-President Cheney was running the company, Halliburton was fined for illegal exports to Libya and sued by the US government for fraudulent "contract inflation" in the maintenance of a California military base. Subsequent investigations also showed that Halliburton had overcharged the US military in Kosovo by millions of dollars and had done business with Saddam Hussein, using an offshore subsidiary to evade US sanctions. So you can see why they might need a "get out of jail free" card.

Cheney, who served as defense secretary in the first Bush administration, used his government contacts to turn Halliburton into a poster child for corporate welfare. Under his guidance, the company pulled in at least $3.8 billion in federal contracts, many through pork-dispensing agencies like the Ex-Im bank (see Chapter 10). Halliburton also ran a string of dozens of Enron-like subsidiaries in Caribbean tax havens (see Chapter 4).

But the company stands to do even better with its former chief working in Washington, DC. Today, Halliburton and its subsidiaries provide construction and maintenance services to dozens of US military bases around the world, including the new bases springing up in and around Afghanistan and Iraq. The ten-year contract covering this work is both open-ended and "cost-plus." This means not only that nobody knows how much it will ultimately cost (the company took in $2.5 billion for such services during the 1990s), but also that Halliburton is guaranteed a profit no matter what. That profit will be a fixed percentage of whatever the eventual costs turn out to be—which doesn't exactly encourage a frugal stewardship of the public trust (see above).

Halliburton was also handed a contract worth up to $7 billion, in a secret, no-bid process, to repair Iraq's oil infrastructure. This contract was awarded before the war began, but announced afterward. So it may well be that Cheney's old firm is in line for even more of your tax dollars; we just don't know about it yet.

SOURCES

Chaterjee, Pratap. "The War on Terrorism's Gravy Train: Cheney's Former Company Wins Afghanistan War Contracts." *CorpWatch,* May 2, 2002, http://www.corpwatch.org/issues/PID.jsp?articleid=2471.

Gongloff, Mark. "Halliburton Contract Could Reach $7B." *Money,* April 11, 2003. http://money.cnn.com/2003/04/11/news/companies/war_halliburton.

Leser, Eric. "Halliburton, Principal Beneficiary of Iraq's Reconstruction." *Le Monde,* June 20, 2003, http://www.globalpolicy.org/security/issues/iraq/after/2003/0620halliburton.htm.

Rosen, James. "Cheney, Halliburton Ties Facing More Questions." *Modesto Bee,* October 14, 2003, http://www.modbee.com/local/story/7589897p-8498586c.html.

Royce, Knut, and Nathaniel Heller. "Cheney Led Halliburton to Feast at Federal Trough." Center for Public Integrity, August 2, 2000, http://www.public-i.org/story_01_080200.htm.

Sustainable Energy and Economy Network. "Groups Demand Repeal of Bush Immunity for U.S. Oil Companies in Iraq." Press release, July 23, 2003, http://www.seen.org/BushEO.shtml.

Trilling, Roger. "Bush's Golden Vision: President Sees Election Cash in Rebuilding Iraq." *Village Voice,* October 15–21, 2003, 36–37.

Verloy, Andre, and Daniel Politi. "Windfalls of War: US Contractors in Iraq and Afghanistan." Special report for the Center for Public Integrity. http://www.publicintegrity.org/wow/.

Military contractors milk the government in other ways as well. It's common for the State Department to give foreign aid to brutal dictatorships like Uzbekistan and Eritrea, with the requirement that the money be used to buy US weapons. Each year, this program results in the transfer of $5 billion to $7 billion from US taxpayers to US arms merchants (not to mention the murder of lots of innocent people in the countries involved).[62] In fact, more than a third of the State Department's foreign aid budget is actually hidden military spending. What's more, many of these loans are ultimately defaulted on or forgiven. Egypt, for example, was let off the hook for $7 billion in loans as a reward for participating in the first Gulf War.[63]

Just since September 2001, Lockheed alone has received deals worth up to $8 billion from the Foreign Military Sales program.[64] That's quite a return on its $2.4 million in campaign contributions in the 2000 election cycle.[65] (As I've already remarked, politicians sure are a bargain.)

The Pentagon has similar programs that not only provide subsidies to foreign countries to buy from US weapons suppliers but also help them negotiate the sale. Thanks in large part to these Pentagon programs—on which we spend $7.9 billion a year, or almost half our total foreign aid expenditure—the United States is the largest arms supplier on earth, with 46% of the world trade (as of 2001).[66] The variety of programs we provide to help our contractors overseas have made them the second most subsidized of all US industries, after agribusiness. But the arms merchants don't really need any extra help from the US taxpayer. Given the economies of scale gained from selling to the biggest military on the planet, they have built-in advantages over smaller foreign arms makers.

SELLING THE STORY TO THE PUBLIC

It is clear why politicians, military contractors, and Pentagon bureaucrats support the Pentagon system. But how do they sell it to the rest of us, who are harmed by it?

After World War II, then-President Harry S. Truman faced the same problem: how to keep the war industries going without a war to justify them. Senator Arthur Vandenburg of Michigan supplied the answer: "Scare the hell out of the American people."[67] For the next 40 years, the Soviet Union was used for this purpose. There was just one hitch—the USSR's military capabilities were always significantly inferior to ours.[68] Ah, that's where the guile comes in.

First there was the "bomber gap." In 1955, Air Force intelligence warned that the USSR would have between 500 and 800 intercontinental bombers within five years. At the time, the United States had over 1,000 such bombers; the Soviets had fewer than 40 and never built more than 200.

Then there was the "missile gap." Introduced in 1957, it warned that the Soviets "could" have 3,000 ICBMs (intercontinental ballistic missiles) by 1960. Apparently the Soviets decided not to bother, since by 1960, they had a grand total of four ICBMs. Still, the missile gap served its real purpose, which was to generate billions of dollars in military spending.

Military expert Seymour Melman identified seven other fictitious "gaps" in our defenses that were used to scare the hell out of the American people: the antiballistic missile gap, the fighter gap, the megatonnage gap, the submarine gap, the survivability gap, the strategy gap, and the security gap.[69] And then there was the "window of vulnerability."[70] Reagan used that one to justify his $1.5 trillion increase in military spending, which helped turn us from the world's largest creditor nation to the world's largest debtor nation.[71]

The Strategic Defense Initiative—better known as SDI or Star Wars—is another example. It is extremely expensive, counters a "threat" that's virtually nonexistent, and almost certainly will never work.[72] (Missile experts are fond of saying that SDI is like trying to deflect a bullet that's coming at you by hitting it with another bullet.)[73]

The Pentagon admits to faking the results of Star Wars tests it ran in 1984.[74] They said they did it to deceive the Soviets, but of course they also deceived the media and Congress, which poured more money into this useless boondoggle. Between 1983 and 1993, more than $35 billion was spent on Star Wars, with basically nothing to show for it.

In one of the weasel fests Bill Clinton has become famous for, he announced he was killing Star Wars. Only later did the story come out in the alternative press that SDI wasn't actually dead—it had just been renamed the Ballistic Missile Defense Organization.[75] Removed from public debate, minimal attention was paid to SDI—er, BMDO—until Clinton and Congress decided they wanted to give it more money. They planned to spend another $10.5 billion of our money on Star Wars between 1999 and 2005—on top of some $95 billion spent up to then—whether we ever decided to deploy it or not.[76] But when the time came to make the decision on deployment, Clinton decided to pass the buck to his successor.

Since that successor turned out to be the hawkish Bush II administration, Star Wars funding quickly mushroomed into a variety of new boondoggles. The Pentagon staged new tests, which were faked to help sell taxpayers on the efficacy of the program[77] (the only justification, since the Soviets were long gone), and it was decided to begin deploying components of the system beginning in 2004—whether they work or not![78] Star Wars programs are budgeted at nearly $10 billion for 2004 alone; they

WHAT ABOUT THE WAR ON TERROR?

Whatever your response to the 9/11 attacks was, you probably didn't see it as an "enormous opportunity" that we must "move to take advantage of." But that's how National Security Advisor Condoleezza Rice described it, and it epitomizes how the White House and the defense industry have exploited the nation's legitimate fears. The military budget is projected to rise by a third or more from already bloated pre-9/11 levels.

But wait, you say. We have a war on terrorism to fight, so why shouldn't we spend, as the president says, whatever is necessary? There are two answers to that. The first is that most of the new spending is absolutely unnecessary, and the second is that most of the spending for the war on terrorism doesn't really count as part of the military budget.

War spending—for both Iraq and Afghanistan—comes in the form of "supplemental" bills, which are not included in the Pentagon's annual appropriations. Immediately after the 9/11 attacks, Congress passed an emergency $40 billion spending bill, about $28.5 billion of which was used to fight the war in Afghanistan. Or so we're told. The Pentagon has been more vague than usual in reporting how any of that money was actually spent. For instance, $4.8 billion was spent on "Increased Worldwide Posture." That's about the going rate for something like that, isn't it?

Let's set aside the question of whether or not Iraq had anything to do with the 9/11 attacks against us. Congress appropriated $79 billion when the war began, and the White House asked for another $87 billion to handle the postwar war. Add that $166 billion to the previous spending, and that's almost $200 billion for the war on terror—on top of the Pentagon's annual $400 billion budget. In effect, we not only have the world's most expensive military, but we have to pay extra to use it.

And what about the additional $100 billion plus a year we've tacked on to the Department of Defense's budget? The bulk of it is going to overpriced weapons systems that have almost nothing to do with catching terrorists. Most of the senior al-Qaida figures in custody have been apprehended as the result of international police operations.

And while we may need to spend more on, say, unstaffed reconnaissance planes or special operations forces, we aren't likely to stop many terrorists by throwing billions more into the Star Wars boondoggle. Nor do we need to order thousands of new fighter planes that were designed to penetrate the Soviet Union. Likewise, it seems of negligible value to add a tenth aircraft carrier group. The terrorists don't have even one—and neither does anyone else in the world.

According to retired Vice-Admiral Jack Shanahan, "About a third of the total Pentagon budget will actually go to the funding of weapons systems and programs designed to fight the former Soviet Union or the People's Republic of China." Eliminate Cold War weapons and duplication, says defense expert Lawrence Korb, and "America would save more than enough to fight the war on terrorism—and have tens of billions of dollars extra that could be returned to taxpayers or spent elsewhere."

Prior to September 11, 2001, the United States was burdened with a military establishment that couldn't pass an audit, routinely lost track of millions of dollars in equipment, and came up with trillions of dollars in accounting errors. Since then, nothing has changed—except that our military contractors now have enormous opportunities to take advantage of.

SOURCES

Business Leaders for Sensible Priorities. "Terrorism Doesn't Justify Pentagon Hike." Press release, January 24, 2002. http://www.usnewswire.com/topnews/temp/0124-135.html.

Editorial, "The Pentagon Spending Spree." *New York Times,* February 6, 2002.

Hartung, William D. "War Shouldn't Bar US Military Cuts." *Newsday,* January 7, 2002, http://www.commondreams.org/views02/0109-04.htm.

Peña, Charles V. "A Bigger Defense Budget Is Not Needed to Win the War on Terrorism." Cato Institute, February 5, 2002, http://www.cato.org/dailys/02-05-02.html.

could eventually end up costing us another $1.2 *trillion,* according to the Center for Arms Control and Non-Proliferation.[79]

All this nonsense succeeded in denying us the "peace dividend" we were promised at the end of the Cold War. Even though the Soviet system had completely collapsed, the Pentagon's budget during the '90s was only

7% lower (adjusted for inflation) than the Cold War average, and by 1999 it was 50% higher than it was in 1980, before the Reagan buildup began.[80] The second Bush administration now proposes to spend $2.7 trillion over the next six years, reaching levels close to the peak of the Reagan spending spree.[81] This of course doesn't count the cost of invading and rebuilding Iraq—or of any other "war on terror" we might get into before the end of the decade (see sidebar, pp. 70–71.)

HOW MUCH MILITARY SPENDING IS WASTE?

Even if you accept high levels of military spending, lots of savings are still possible:

- We have more Trident missiles than we could ever use, and nobody to aim them at. But the Navy isn't happy with its old Tridents (currently funded at $780 million a year). It wants to spend $37.5 billion to replace them with a newer version, even though both kinds of Tridents are likely to be eliminated under the next arms-control agreement, START III.[82]
- According to POGO, the Army's Comanche helicopter is one of the "poster children for bad weapons development." The Comanche was first projected in 1988 to cost $3.6 billion over eight years. Oops, make that 18 years and $48 billion. And yet, for all that, the Comanche is "too heavy to exit hostile battle environments." Apparently, having a helicopter that would get our troops to safety will cost extra.[83]
- The rationale for the F-22 fighter, designed to achieve air superiority in the 1990s over the now-defunct Soviet Union, is especially weak. We already have 900 F-15s—which the GAO calls the best tactical aircraft in the world—and none of our real or potential enemies have more than a handful of planes that even come close to matching its capabilities. For the cost of three F-22s, we can build eight F-15s, but that hasn't stopped the Pentagon from asking for 295 F-22s. Total cost: $69.7 billion.[84]
- But even if you believe we need to buy a fleet of F-22s, then we certainly don't need to develop 2,866 copies of the new Joint Strike Fighter (JSF) on top of that. At a total program cost of $226.5 billion, the JSF is the most expensive weapons system in Pentagon history—so far. To help pay for it, the Department of Defense is giving early retirement to hundreds of perfectly good planes (removing the expense of maintaining, stationing, or providing crew for the old planes—which then frees up funds to procure new ones).[85]

- Even a hawk like the late Barry Goldwater pointed out the waste involved in the Army, the Navy, the Air Force, and the Marines each having its own air force.[86] The JSF is meant to be shared among the services, which would be great—except that the Air Force and the Marines are both building Cold War–style aircraft on top of that. Likewise, both the Marines and the Army have light infantry divisions, and the Navy and the Air Force each insist they need to have their own kind of cruise missiles and satellites.
- The Pentagon keeps 100,000 troops in Europe and 70,000 in Korea and Japan. We spend $80 billion a year on NATO, $59 billion a year in South Korea, and $48 billion a year in the Persian Gulf. In all of these cases, the countries we're supposedly defending have militaries that are better equipped and much better funded than do their enemies.[87]
- Although our 121 C-5 and 265 C-144 transport planes are perfectly adequate, the Pentagon wants to replace a bunch of them with 180 new C-17s, at a total cost of $59 billion. It will purchase 60 of these planes under a special "commercial" provision that shields the project from any sort of financial oversight.[88]
- Meanwhile, the plane's manufacturer, Boeing, has gotten another unprecedented sweetheart deal. The US government will lease a fleet of 100 Boeing 767s for a decade, which will cost taxpayers far more than if we simply purchased the planes outright.[89] That is, first we have to retrofit them for military duty, and then we have to return them to the original condition when the ten years are up. The Pentagon didn't even ask for these planes. But try telling that to the politicians whose campaigns are funded by Boeing or who have subcontractors in their districts. (The Boeing tanker deal resulted in such a stink that in December of 2003 Boeing CEO Phil Condit had to resign following whistleblower allegations of misconduct involving "promises made" to an Air Force acquistions officer who joined the company. Red-faced Pentagon officials then announced that the deal would be put on hold pending an investigation.[90])

By now it should be obvious that the so-called defense budget isn't based on any rational calculation of what the defense of this country actually requires—it's based on what US arms manufacturers can get away with (almost anything, it turns out). Attaching the word "defense" to this spending isn't just misleading; it's the complete opposite of the truth, since military waste and fraud make our country weaker, not stronger. By overspending on the military, we short-change human needs in the overall budget, thus undermining the economic security of our country. The preposterously obese Pentagon budget is the single greatest threat to our national security.

It's not just wild-eyed radicals who think we're overfunding the Pentagon:

- Lawrence Korb, a military planner under Reagan who's now with the Council on Foreign Relations, says that $300 billion a year is enough to keep the US military overwhelmingly more powerful than any other in the world.[91]
- The conservative Cato Institute laid out a detailed military budget that includes funding for a lot of unnecessary programs like Star Wars. Even so, it called for scaling down the military budget to $154 billion.[92]
- Philip Morrison and Kosta Tsipis of MIT—who say that we would be safer if we reduced our gigantic Cold War forces than we are in keeping them so large—have called for a $140 billion Pentagon budget.[93]
- Military expert John Pike of GlobalSecurity.org has argued for a military budget of just 1% of the GDP, or about $105 billion in 2003.[94]

The average of those four estimates is $175 billion a year—quite a bit less than the $399 billion a year we actually spend. And remember: that $399 billion doesn't include $44 billion in veterans' benefits and the $92 billion or more we lay out each year to service debt that's the result of past military spending. (Unfortunately, all we can do about that past debt is to cut down on present military budgets, so the amount gets smaller rather than larger.)

Subtracting $175 billion from $399 billion gives us a figure for current military waste and fraud of $224 billion a year.[95] That's more than $600 million a day—virtually all of which goes to large corporations and super-rich individuals. (Sure, some of it pays for ordinary people's salaries, but they'd also be earning money if they were doing something useful.)

Half a billion dollars a day could buy a lot of medical care, or fill a lot of potholes, or—you name it. After all, it's your money—or it was, before you gave it to the government.

ACTIVIST'S TOOLKIT

Antiwar.com

520 South Murphy Avenue, #202, Sunnyvale, CA 94086 • email: egarris2@antiwar.com • website: http://www.antiwar.com/

Bulletin of the Atomic Scientists

6042 S. Kimbark Avenue, Chicago, IL 60637-2806 • phone: (773) 702-2555 • fax: (773) 702-0725 • website: http://www.thebulletin.org/

Center for Defense Information

1779 Massachusetts Avenue NW, Washington, DC 20036-2109 • phone: (202) 332-0600 • fax: (202) 462-4559 • email: info@cdi.org • website: http://www.cdi.org/index.cfm

Center for Strategic and Budgetary Assessment

1730 Rhode Island Avenue, Suite 912, Washington, DC 20036 • phone: (202) 331-7990 • fax: (202) 331-8019 • email: info@csbaonline.org • website: http://www.csbaonline.org/

Council for a Livable World

322 4th Street NE, Washington, DC 20002 • phone: (202) 543-4100 • email: clw@clw.org • website: http://64.177.207.201/pages/91_10.html

Federation of American Scientists

1717 K Street NW, Suite 209, Washington, DC 20036 • phone: (202) 546-3300 • fax: (202) 675-1010 • email: fas@fas.org • website: http://www.fas.org/

Fortress America: The American Military and the Consequence of Peace

by William Greider (Boulder, CO: Perseus Publishing, 1998).

Friends Committee for National Legislation

245 Second Street NE, Washington, DC 20002 • phone: (202) 547-6000 • fax: (202) 547-6019 • toll-free (in the US) phone: (800) 630-1330 • email: fcnl@fcnl.org • website: http://www.fcnl.org/

GlobalSecurity.org

300 N. Washington Street, B-100, Alexandria, VA 22314 • phone: (703) 548-2700 • fax: (703) 548-2424 • email: info@globalsecurity.org • website: http://www.globalsecurity.org/

Institute for Defense and Disarmament Studies

675 Massachusetts Avenue, Cambridge, MA 02139 • phone: (617) 354-4337 • fax: (617) 354-1450 • email: info@idds.org • website: http://www.idds.org

Project on Defense Alternatives

The Commonwealth Institute • PO Box 398105, Inman Square Post Office, Cambridge, MA 02139 • phone: (617) 547-4474 • fax: (617) 868-1267 • email: comw@comw.org • website: http://www.comw.org/pda/

Project On Government Oversight

666 11th Street NW, Washington, DC 20001-4542 • phone: (202) 347-1122 • fax: (202) 347-1116 • website: http://www.pogo.org/

Veterans for Peace

World Community Center • 438 N. Skinker, St. Louis, MO 63130 • phone: (314) 725-6005 • fax: (314) 725-7103 • website: http://www.veteransforpeace.org/

War Resisters League

339 Lafayette Street, New York, NY 10012 • phone: (212) 228-0450 • fax: (212) 228-6193 • email: wrl@warresisters.org • website: http://www.warresisters.org/

Chapter 12

The S&L Bailout

```
($32 billion a year)
(every year for 30 years)
```

The savings and loan (S&L) industry began over a century ago for the sole purpose of providing home mortgages. Until the 1930s, S&Ls (sometimes called thrifts, which is pretty ironic considering their recent history) got along quite nicely more or less on their own. But when nearly 2,000 failed during the Great Depression, the government began regulating them in earnest and providing deposit insurance to quell fears of further S&L failures.[1]

Compared to the greener pastures of the commercial banks, the S&Ls' opportunities for financial chicanery were slight, so there wasn't a great deal of corruption there. The trouble began when President Jimmy Carter appointed Paul Volcker as chair of the Federal Reserve Board (commonly called "the Fed") in late 1979.

The Fed is supposed to minimize unemployment as well as inflation, and before 1979, it tried to achieve some sort of balance between the two goals. But under Volcker and his successor, Alan Greenspan, it has simply aimed for low inflation, regardless of the effect that has on jobs. In fact, Greenspan has asked Congress to relieve the Fed of responsibility for keeping unemployment down.[2]

Inflation was high when Volcker took over—13% or so. To get it under control, he tightened the money supply. This brought on a monster recession, the biggest since World War II. Within a year, the prime rate shot up to the unheard-of level of 21.5% (compared to an average of 7.6% for the 14 previous years). Unemployment peaked at just under 11%.[3]

Ideally, the Fed functions like a thermostat. It keeps the economy from getting too overheated (inflation) or too cold (unemployment). But the Fed is a political institution, and as such, it tends to reflect the interests of bankers and investors at the expense of the rest of us. It is also not above manipulating the economy for the benefit or detriment of the party in power, depending on where the loyalties of the Board of Governors happen to lie. Then too, the Fed is populated by fallible human beings and has a history of overcompensating one way or the other.

That said, the Fed can influence the economy both by raising or lowering interest rates and by increasing or decreasing the money supply. In this case, the Fed under Volcker sharply contracted the money supply. This reduced the amount of reserve funds on hand in the nation's banks, which led the banks to raise interest rates on their loans, which led to decreased investment, which slowed down the economy, which led companies to lay off workers, which reduced their disposable income, which reduced demand for goods and services, which led to lower prices in order to attract customers, which led (eventually) to lower inflation.[4]

It could be argued (and it has been) that Volcker overdid it, leading to the nastiest recession since World War II, but he also had the nastiest postwar inflation to contend with. In effect, we traded the latter for the former.

According to author Robert Sherrill, Volcker stated, on taking office, that "the standard of living for the average American has to decline."[5] Sherrill says Volcker was recommended by David Rockefeller because

> Wall Street and the international banking fraternity loved [Volcker]. They hated inflation—bankers don't like to be repaid in money that is softer than the money they lend, even if the softer money makes the economy hum—and they knew that Volcker was mean enough to destroy the economy to save the hardness of their dollars.[6]

Volcker's policies caused a combination of inflation and recession called "stagflation." This put the squeeze on S&Ls. Most S&L mortgages were fixed rate, so the S&Ls couldn't raise the interest they charged on those. But because their depositors were withdrawing money by the billions and placing it in higher-yielding money market funds or government bonds, the S&Ls did have to raise the rates they paid on savings accounts and CDs, thus laying out more than they could take in. Finally, because of the recession, homeowners started defaulting on their mortgages in droves, and S&L bankruptcies skyrocketed.

IF IT IS BROKE, FIX IT

By the time Reagan took office in 1981, two-thirds of the nation's S&Ls were losing money, and many were broke. If all the problem thrifts had been shut down right then, the government's insurance fund would have been able to cover their debts.[7]

Instead, the government delayed an average of two years—and, in some cases, as many as seven years—allowing bankrupt S&Ls to go on losing billions of dollars. This delay also gave S&Ls a chance to gamble on questionable investments in an attempt to regain solvency. But first they had to convince Congress to deregulate them.

As with bank deposits, there was a government agency that insured deposits in your local S&L: the Federal Savings and Loan Insurance Corporation (FSLIC). If your S&L went belly up, this government insurance fund would make good on your deposit—up to a point. Before 1980, that point was $40,000.

One night in 1980, Representative Fernand St. Germain (D-RI), whose $10,000-to-$20,000-a-year restaurant and bar tab was being paid for by the S&L industry's chief lobbyist, proposed raising federal insurance on S&L savings accounts from $40,000 to $100,000—even though the average size of an S&L account was $6,000. He waited until after midnight, when only 11 representatives were still on the House floor; they approved his proposal unanimously.[8]

But St. Germain was just getting warmed up. In 1982, he cosponsored a bill that removed all controls on what S&Ls could charge for interest and released them from their century-old reliance on home mortgages.[9]

Around the same time, the Reagan administration ended the requirement that S&Ls lend money only in their own communities, allowed S&Ls to offer 100% financing (that is, no down payments), let real estate developers own their own S&Ls, and permitted S&L owners to lend money to themselves.

This meant that the white-collar criminals playing around with insolvent thrifts knew that ultimately any liability would be the government's problem. For one thing, as economist Bert Ely puts it,

> Had the deposit-insurance limit been kept at $40,000, a depositor intent on putting $200,000 of insured funds into insolvent S&Ls paying high interest rates would have had to deposit his money, in $40,000 chunks, into five different S&Ls. Because of the higher limit, two $100,000 deposits would keep the $200,000 fully insured.[10]

These changes were like taping a sign to the S&Ls' backs that read Defraud Me. In fact, it's widely rumored that Mafia lawyers and accountants carefully monitored the progress of this bill as it worked its way through Congress, ready to pounce the moment it became law.

SCOUNDREL TIME

Whatever truth there is to that rumor, the Defraud Me sign worked. The examples abound. J. William Oldenburg bought State Savings of Salt Lake City for $10.5 million, then had it pay him $55 million for a piece of land he'd bought for $874,000.

With the help of a shadowy figure named Herman K. Beebe, who had served a year for bank fraud, Don Dixon bought Vernon Savings and Loan—one of the nation's healthiest—and then set up a series of corporations for it to loan money to. Four years later, he left Vernon $1.3 billion in debt. Beebe also had money in Silverado Savings, an S&L partly owned by then-Vice -President Bush's son, Neil. Silverado told a prospective borrower he couldn't have $10 million; instead, he should borrow $15 million and buy $5 million in Silverado stock.[11]

Although federal examiners knew Silverado was leaking cash as early as 1985, it wasn't closed down until December 1988, a month after Bush Senior was elected president. Because Silverado kept leaking cash for those three years, it ended up costing taxpayers more than a billion dollars, funneled through the FSLIC, to cover the insured deposits.[12]

Robert Corson, who helped the CIA smuggle and launder money, bought Kleburg County Savings and Loan and bankrupted it in nine months. *Houston Post* reporter Pete Brewton found 24 failed S&Ls with ties to the CIA, including several run by James Bath (a former friend and business partner of George W. Bush). Another Corson purchase was Peoples Savings and Loan in Llano, Texas, which loaned $3 million to Ray Corona, a drug smuggler, and $2.3 million to his associate Harold White.

One of Corona's drug-smuggling associates was Frank Castro, a Cuban exile involved in Oliver North's contra resupply network. Herman Beebe's Palmer National Bank was also involved with North; it loaned money to customers who then channeled it to the Swiss bank accounts used to supply the contras. Basically, the people running the contra war saw defrauding S&Ls as an easier way to get taxpayers to pay for their war than going through Congress to have funds appropriated for it.[13] (While this is undoubtedly true, it's hardly democratic.)

The Reagan administration not only failed to police the industry while all this was going on, it dreamed up ways to keep insolvent S&Ls propped up even longer. By 1988, the government was spending a billion dollars a month keeping "zombie thrifts" afloat.[14]

Everyone in both the S&L industry and Congress knew that a bailout would be necessary, but a conspiracy of silence kept the issue out of public debate. There was an institutional reluctance to face the truth lest it become an issue in the 1988 presidential campaign. Democratic presidential candidate Michael Dukakis tried to raise the issue[15] but dropped it under pressure from his running mate, Lloyd Bentsen (who had been part-owner of a couple of Texas S&Ls).[16] For obvious reasons, the Bush campaign displayed a similar reticence.

THEY ROB, WE PAY

As previously mentioned, if the insolvent S&Ls had been shut down in 1981, the government's insurance fund would have covered the losses and only administrative costs would have been incurred. If the S&Ls had been liquidated in May 1985, it would have cost less than $16 billion. By the end of 1985, the costs were estimated at $30 billion.[17]

In 1989, Congress finally came up with $157 billion to bail out the S&Ls. But by that time, the costs were over $200 billion (and they continue to rise to this day). To make up the difference, the Resolution Trust Corporation was formed; it sold off the assets of failed S&Ls, mostly at bargain-basement prices in sweetheart deals.

For example, Robert Bass, one of the richest people in America, bought American Savings and Loan for $350 million, and then received $2 billion in government subsidies to help him resurrect it. (With that much money, you could probably raise the dead.) During one week in 1988, the government promised $8 billion in assistance to nine S&L purchasers; one of them put $20 million down, and the other eight paid nothing.

That same year, the First Gibraltar Bank was merged with four failing S&Ls and sold to Ronald Perelman (at the time, the fifth richest person in the United States). Perelman and his partners paid just $315 million for $7.1 billion in good assets; the government then gave them $5.1 billion to cover bad assets, plus $900 million in tax breaks. (A good asset would be an office building full of rent-paying tenants; a bad asset would be a large empty building in an oversaturated market.) In the first year Perelman and his cronies owned it, Gibraltar made a profit of $129 million and got an additional $121 million in tax breaks.[18]

CHECK, PLEASE

The $157 billion bailout was financed by floating 30-year bonds, the interest on which will make the ultimate cost much higher. The actual total will depend on the level of interest rates between 2004 and 2020, but estimates have ranged from $500 billion to $1.4 trillion (in other words, $1,400 billion!).[19]

If I could predict interest rates, I'd be vacationing on Jupiter right now, so let's just split the difference between these two estimates and predict that the ultimate cost for the S&L bailout will be $950 billion. That comes to about $32 billion a year—and we're locked into it for 30 years, no matter what we do or who we elect.

All this money will come from taxpayers and will go to the people who bought the bonds. So ultimately, the S&L bailout amounts to a massive transfer of wealth from ordinary people to investors (most of whom are wealthy)—as well as to the crooks who looted the S&Ls. (Few of them were convicted, by the way, and the average sentence of those who were was less than two years.)[20]

Probably the worst part of the S&L bailout is the message it sends to high-flying con artists. It says, "Plunder all you want. As long as your political connections are solid, you'll get to keep the money and probably won't suffer more than a slap on the wrist."

Charles Keating was the most notorious of the S&L swindlers. He used his political connections to evade regulation, sucked millions out of his thrift for himself and his family, and left his depositors defrauded of their life's savings. His name was later attached to the Keating Five scandal, for the five US Senators who helped him to throw his weight around Washington (though for some reason this opprobrium didn't stick to Alan Greenspan, who performed similar services). But Keating only went to jail because his abuses were so extreme; he was the exception, not the rule.

The authors of the best book on the S&L scandal, *Inside Job,* conclude that, rather than a lot of mindless blundering, there was

> some kind of network... a purposeful and coordinated system of fraud. At each step of our investigation our suspicions grew because, of the dozens of savings and loans we investigated, we never once examined a thrift—no matter how random the choice—without finding someone there we already knew from another failed S&L.[21]

But hey—don't worry too much about that $32 billion a year. We only have 17 more years to go on it.

ACTIVIST'S TOOLKIT

We can't undo the last bailout, but these two books tell us more about how it happened. Also, Citizen Works is fighting the battle for greater corporate accountability—to try to prevent the next bailout.

Citizen Works
PO Box 18478, Washington, DC 20036 • phone: (202) 265-6164 • fax: (202) 265-0182 • email: info@citizenworks.org • website: http://www.citizenworks.org

Inside Job: The Looting of America's Savings and Loans
by Stephen Pizzo, Mary Fricker and Paul Muolo (New York: Harper Perennial, 1991).

The Mafia, CIA & George Bush
by Pete Brewton (New York: SPI Books, 1992).

Chapter 13

Agribusiness Subsidies
($30.5 billion a year)

When agricultural subsidies began during the Great Depression, their main purpose was to keep farmers on the farm by enabling them to earn roughly what people in cities did. Of course, in those days, some 25% of the population lived and worked on farms. Today, only 2% of us do.[1] These days the average net worth of farm households is $564,000—nearly double the $283,000 for nonfarm households.[2] Farmers' household income from all sources (an average of $64,347 in 1999) has exceeded that of nonfarmers' income every year since 1986.[3]

Agricultural subsidies are particularly bizarre these days because they go mostly to relatively few states, for relatively few crops, to benefit relatively few farmers. The wealthiest 10% of subsidized farmers take 74% of the handouts, while the bottom four-fifths get 12% of the total. The bottom half? Just 2%. And 60% of US farmers get nothing at all.[4] Five crops—wheat, corn, rice, cotton, and soybeans—receive 90% of all federal subsidies.[5] Almost two-thirds of total US farm production—including most fruits and vegetables—remains unsubsidized.[6]

Concentrating the subsidies on certain crops also concentrates them geographically. Just 15 states receive 74% of the benefit from federal agriculture programs, while paying only 24% of the cost.[7] In California, the largest agricultural producer, only 9% of the farms received any subsidy at all. (These were mostly big cotton and rice farms, while the state's many orchards and vegetable farms didn't get a penny.)[8] The Northeast gets a particularly raw deal, paying for 30% of the cost of crop subsidies (that is, it contributes 30% of federal taxes), while receiving just 2.4% of the benefit.[9] In an effort to get in on the party, New York's congressional delegation helped create a new subsidy for its dairy farmers in the 2002 farm bill.[10]

Not surprisingly, many of the "luckiest" states are those that can help swing the results of national elections or that have powerful representatives in Congress who help to write farm legislation. The 2002 farm bill gave the most money to Iowa, and the largest increase to Texas. Iowa is the home of Senator Tom Harkin, then the chair of the Senate Agriculture Committee. And Texas sent Republican Larry Combest, chair of the

House Agricultural Committee, and Democrat Charles Stenholm, a member of the same committee, to Washington, where they helped double the amount of subsidies for their home state.[11]

And just coincidentally, Representative Stenholm himself is a subsidized farmer, receiving more than $39,000 under the 1996 farm bill (from 1996 through 2002). At least ten of his colleagues, including Senators Grassley (R-IA), Lugar (R-IN), and Lincoln (D-AR), are also on the dole. Representative Marion Berry of Arkansas (not to be confused with the former mayor of Washington, DC) took in more than $750,000 in subsidies between 1996 and 2002. Perhaps you will not be surprised to hear that Berry feels that federal farm subsidy programs are "woefully underfunded."[12]

Not only is the US Department of Agriculture (USDA) generous in its handouts to farmers, it's also quite generous in who it calls a farmer. Making a complete mockery of the supposed aims of the farm subsidies (to help keep 'em down on the farm), the USDA doled out almost $3.5 billion to recipients in urban zip codes between 1996 and 2001.[13] Many recipients aren't even located in the same state as their farms. Among celebrity farmers (outside of Congress) are billionaire David Rockefeller, basketball star Scottie Pippen, broadcaster Sam Donaldson, tycoon Ted Turner, and corporate crime poster boy Kenneth Lay of Enron.[14] In fact, any land that produces $1,000 or more in agricultural products can be officially regarded as a farm.[15] So if you see the word "farmers" in quotes below, you'll know why.

Of course, it's not even necessary to be a human being to qualify as a farmer. One study found farm subsidies going to 413 municipal governments, 44 universities, and 14 prison systems.[16] And such Fortune 500 companies as Chevron Oil, John Hancock Life Insurance, Caterpillar Manufacturing, and Eli Lilly Pharmaceuticals are also quote, farmers, unquote—subsidized with your tax dollars.[17] That's why this chapter is called "Agri*business* Subsidies."

One last thing before we dive into the details. Despite all the booty being siphoned off to the wealthy, these programs are routinely justified by the need to help combat rural poverty or save small family farms. But there's an alternative that would be a whole lot simpler and cheaper. We could bring the income of every full-time farmer in the United States up to at least 185% of the federal poverty level (about $33,000) for just $4 billion a year.[18] If the agribusiness subsidy's goal were to reduce rural poverty, we could simply write a check to every poor farmer. But of course that's not the goal anymore, is it?

Agribusiness subsidies take several forms:

- With price supports, quasi-governmental agencies or cooperatives buy up "excess" production of a crop to keep the price high. (It's like government-sanctioned price fixing.)
- Production quotas limit who can farm a particular crop (peanut and tobacco farmers, for example, must be licensed by the government).
- Market quotas control how much of a crop can be sold; the "excess" is warehoused (at taxpayer expense) or destroyed.
- Import restrictions limit how much of a crop can be imported into the United States.
- Crop insurance provides low-cost insurance against crop failures and disasters.
- Deficiency payments, which I discuss on pp. 89–91.

THE "CHEAPER FOOD" RUSE

One rationale for agribusiness subsidies—to the extent that they have any—is that you get cheaper food prices out of the deal. Dream on.

First of all, we pay for many of these handouts with our income taxes, so you'd have to add a portion of those taxes to your food bill to come up with an accurate total. According to one estimate, the average household can tack on $1,805 over the next decade.[19] Besides that, there are indirect subsidies you pay for at the checkout counter without even realizing it.

Price supports, import restrictions, and market and production quotas keep the prices of sugar, dairy products, and peanuts higher in the United States than on the world market. They cost consumers $2 billion a year in higher sugar prices, $1.7 billion in higher dairy prices, and $500 million in higher peanut prices. That's $4.2 billion at the cash register right there.[20]

But crop subsidies actually help drive up the price of many other foods, because they help inflate the cost of rural real estate—by some 25% in 2000 alone.[21] Land that produces subsidized crops is worth more, thus bidding up the price of neighboring land. But more important, because subsidies are paid according to the number of acres planted (instead of farmer need), land becomes overvalued. Land prices are the single biggest contributor to the cost of food.

As a further illustration of the law of unintended consequences, the higher land prices are pushing more small family farms out of business and contributing to the dominance of corporate factory farms. Subsidies push up the price of land beyond what many poor farmers can afford. If they're tenant farmers, their rent goes up, and if they're owner-operators, their property taxes go up. Since neither group can afford to expand their operations, big corporations are able to gobble up more of the available land—which then makes the remaining land that much more valuable.

On top of that, the larger agribusiness concerns bid up the price of land in competition with each other, leaving small family farms in the dust.[22]

Even when agribusiness subsidies actually do bring down the cost of food, you typically end up paying for them in other ways. For example, diverting productive salmon streams to grow potatoes in the desert may be great for fast-food outlets and the corporate farmers who supply them, but it's hell on fishermen and recreational workers. Their unemployment insurance is part of the cost of your cheaper meal.

The bottom line is that as agribusiness consolidation has increased, farm employment has declined. There have been jobs created in peripheral sectors, but not as many; employment in these sectors grew by 36,000 from 1975 to 1996, while farm employment dropped 667,000 jobs. More tellingly, the job "growth" in these sectors comes largely at the expense of the environment. Larger farms require more pesticides and machinery, leading to more pollution in our skies and streams as well as our food. So once again, we're subsidizing the deterioration of our environment, and we pay for it in health care costs as well as in taxes.

LIVESTOCK SUBSIDIES

Many Americans are cutting back on meat and dairy products for health reasons. But whatever your diet, you help pay for these products with your taxes (not to mention the Medicare costs for those who over-consume meat and dairy products).

While most farmers have to treat their profits as ordinary income, livestock profits are classified as capital gains and are taxed at a lower rate (now just 15%). But the costs of buying, breeding, and raising livestock are ordinary expenses that can be deducted immediately.[23] This best-of-both-worlds tax treatment encourages people to get into the livestock business, and there are nontax inducements as well.

Cattle ranchers graze their herds on public lands leased to them at about one-eighth of their market value—which works out to pennies per acre. In 2001, the Bureau of Land Management (BLM) took in $4.5 million from grazing leases and spent more than 17 times as much—$77 million—managing the lands. Note that even if the BLM had charged market value, we still would have lost more than $40 million on the deal.[24]

As far as I can tell, the main justification for this seems to be that ranchers are "cultural icons" who maintain a "way of life" that is worth preserving. (There may be a more sophisticated rationale, but I haven't come across it yet.) It's an emotional argument that ignores the facts about how little of the nation's livestock ranching is actually done on public lands—less than 0.1%, according to one study.[25] Besides, maintaining this lifestyle contributes to plenty of destruction.

Cattle trample native plants and grasses, foul local streams, and contribute to erosion. The BLM and the Forest Service have to deal with the effects on wildlife and watersheds in the lands they manage. Add in those environmental factors and the true cost of grazing leases comes to about *$500 million* a year, according to a study by the Center for Biological Diversity in Tucson, Arizona.[26]

Like most agribusiness handouts, cattle subsidies go disproportionately to the very rich—75% of the grazing land leased by the BLM is controlled by fewer than 10% of the lessees. Among these "welfare cowboys" are computer moguls Bill Hewlett and (the late) David Packard of Hewlett-Packard, as well as Jack Simplot, one of the 500 richest people in America. Other handouts go to Texaco, the Mormon Church, and Anheuser-Busch (which presumably grazes its famous Clydesdale horses at your expense). One study of Arizona's Prescott National Forest found that 64% of all leases were held by doctors, lawyers, art dealers, and other business owners—who are hardly dependent on ranching for their livelihoods and certainly aren't clinging to a bygone way of life.[27]

Amazingly, we are paying all this money—and subsidizing the destruction of our public lands—to benefit just 3% of all livestock producers in the United States.[28] This welfare ranching takes up 300 million acres of federally held land. That includes 90% of the BLM's land, 69% of the Forest Service's land, as well as various national parks, wildlife refuges, and nature preserves.[29] But other uses of federal lands contribute far more to local and regional economies. One study of the Kaibab Plateau in Arizona found that recreational activities and hunting licenses generated $1.5 million for the local economy, compared to $46,000 from federal grazing.[30]

Another handout to ranchers is the Western Livestock Protection Program, which spent $9.8 million in 1996 to protect livestock by exterminating predators—in the same year that livestock losses from predators totaled $5.8 million.

In 1998, Congress appropriated $28.8 million for this program, even though the House voted 229 to 193 for the Bass-DeFazio amendment, which would have killed the funding. Supporters of cowboy welfare forced a second vote the next day. As Taxpayers for Common Sense noted,

> After it passed, an inadvertent technical drafting error in the amendment was discovered. On June 24, the technical error was fixed by a unanimous consent request by the amendment's sponsor. Later that same day opponents of the original amendment sought a revote and inaccurately claimed that the error had not been fixed, even though House members were clearly told it had been fixed by Representative Bass. On June 24, the House rejected the amendment, 192–232.[31]

In fiscal year 2003, the program is budgeted at $68 million.

However, the Livestock Protection Program (LPP) is not to be confused with the Livestock Compensation Program (LCP), an emergency program with $750 million to cover drought losses, or the Livestock Assistance Program (LAP), which compensates ranchers for losses not covered by the LCP or the LPP. The LAP kicks in with another quarter billion for FY2003.[32] You'll be relieved to know, though, that nobody is allowed to collect from both the LCP and the LAP at the same time.

Of course, ordinary people have to buy their own insurance to cover losses from natural disasters. The ranchers seem unwilling to shoulder the risks inherent in their chosen business. And once again, it would actually be cheaper to simply write a check to each welfare cowboy for predator losses than to fund these programs.

SUBSIDIES FOR DRUG PEDDLERS

But at least beef and milk are edible. Tobacco, a drug that kills 48 Americans every hour, is also subsidized with a combination of price supports, import restrictions, and production and market quotas.[33]

By keeping foreign tobacco out and limiting domestic production, the government creates a lower supply for the same amount of demand, allowing domestic producers to charge more. There is no rational justification for this; tobacco does far more harm to the economy than any conceivable benefit that could be gained from government support. When the program started in 1933, the health effects of tobacco were not widely known, and there were far more farmers in need of assistance. The program survives

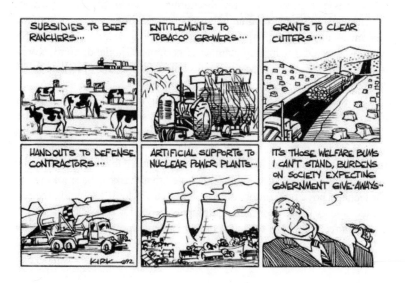

today because of sheer political clout. While some tobacco farmers are definitely hurting because of industry outsourcing, the bulk of the subsidy goes to absentee landlords, not farmers. Then again, the mythical promise of a subsidy might keep these smaller farmers producing tobacco, rather than switching to a more useful, though unsubsidized, crop.

In 1996, then-Representative Richard Durbin (now a Democratic senator from Illinois) introduced a proposal to end tobacco subsidies, estimating their direct cost at about $41 million.[34] The price supports also generate higher costs to consumers, at an estimated $857 million. (This doesn't count the additional cost to taxpayers of dealing with smoking-related illnesses through Medicare, Medicaid, veterans hospitals, and government employees' health plans. That costs you an extra $38 billion a year.[35] And that doesn't count the money the Social Security Administration pays out in survivors' benefits to kids whose parents have died from smoking. That puts another $1.8 billion on the tally.[36])

In June 1996, the House of Representatives voted down Durbin's measure by a smoke-thin margin of 212 to 210. There hasn't been a serious effort to end the subsidies since. Usually the tobacco lobby does better than a two-vote margin. Its 13 PACs, among the most generous on Capitol Hill, handed out almost $9.5 million in the 2001–2002 election cycle alone.[37] This is quite a boost from the $10 million distributed between 1986 and 1995.[38] (When you kill off 400,000 of your customers every year, you need all the friends you can get.)

Although the tobacco lobby has made sure that some portion of the federal government supports tobacco farmers, public pressure has forced other parts of the government to discourage smoking. Seeing the writing on the wall, US tobacco manufacturers are making a big push for new customers overseas. US tobacco exports have risen 275% since 1985, when we started threatening countries like Japan, Thailand, South Korea, and Taiwan with trade sanctions unless they opened their markets to US cigarettes.[39]

Taiwan has been trying to restrict smoking in public areas, and to ban cigarette ads and vending machine sales. That should sound familiar, because the same efforts are being made here. But when they do it, we call it an unfair trade practice. If this hypocritical coercion of ours succeeds, the results will be as disastrous for Taiwan as they were for South Korea. One year after the US tobacco giants penetrated that market, the smoking rate for teenage boys had almost doubled (from 18% to 30%), while the rate for teenage girls had more than quintupled (from 1.6% to 8.7%).[40]

Meanwhile, as US tobacco companies have moved more production offshore to service foreign markets, they've also been importing more foreign tobacco to use in domestic cigarettes. This has put the squeeze on

US tobacco farmers, the very people these subsidies are supposed to help. At the same time, the USDA has cut tobacco quotas in half in the past few years. To compensate for market losses, the USDA paid out $350 million in direct payments to tobacco farmers in FY2001. This amounts to eight times the previous annual subsidy.[41] (Of course, many of the beneficiaries are absentee landlords who don't farm tobacco but get rich selling their quotas to tenant farmers.) The big payout was not repeated in 2002, but a 2003 farm bill added a new $53 billion program to pay off the farmers again.[42] That brings the current total in tobacco subsidies to $96 million.

DEFICIENCY PAYMENTS

Like price supports, quotas, and import restrictions, deficiency payments keep the cost of certain crops artificially high. Before the 1996 "reforms," they made up the difference between a target price set by the USDA and the actual market price for that year (so if the target price was $15 a bushel and the market price $12, the USDA gave farmers $3 a bushel). This smoothed out the highs and lows of commodity prices, which fluctuate with the weather and other factors.

Between 1985 and 1994, deficiency payments cost us an average of $8.3 billion a year (the range was $4.1 to $14.3 billion).[43] Here's the breakdown:

Corn	45%
Wheat	24%
Cotton	12%
Rice	7%
Sorghum	4%
Dairy	3%
Barley	2%
Wool and mohair	2%
Oats	0.2%

In 1994 the "Republican Revolution" swept Newt Gingrich and the GOP into control of Congress. Eager to cut the size of government, they set their sights on agricultural subsidies and by 1996 came up with something called the Freedom to Farm Act. Although supporters of the 1996 farm "reform" bill claimed it would eliminate deficiency payments by 2002, the legislation actually planned to phase them down to a level of $4 billion, which is almost exactly what they were in 1994.

Only "farmers" who got deficiency payments before 1996 were eligible for them under the 1996 bill, and how much they got was determined by what they got before. There was no work requirement and no means test; recipients needn't be active farmers or managers. If the price of corn hit $1,000 a bushel, they got the payments. If they sat on a beach and let the crops rot in the field, they got the payments. Maybe the Act should have been called "Freedom from Farming!"[44]

The 1996 bill also allowed recipients to keep $1.7 billion in deficiency payments from previous years that, under the previous law, they would have had to apply against future payments. Even more freedom.

Freedom to Farm also supposedly replaced the old market-based system with a new flat rate. Thus, in bad years, farmers would get only the predetermined payments and no more, but in good years, they'd get the same amount, even if they raked in far more than the market price of their crop. This is what happened in 1996 and 1997, when there were exceptionally high market prices for many of the subsidized crops; farmers ended up getting $11 billion more than they would have under the old system.[45]

But when prices fell in 1998 and 1999, the promised flat rate turned out not to be so flat after all. Congress voted an additional $5.5 billion in "emergency assistance" to agribusiness in 1998 (even though disaster-related crop losses were only $1.2 billion), and added another $8.7 billion in 1999.[46] And $7.1 billion in 2000.[47] And another $5.5 billion in 2001.[48]

(The explanation for this largesse would seem to be, once again, "because we can." There were, in fact, natural disasters in those years that made emergency assistance justifiable. But Congress ended up throwing far more money than necessary at the problem. This leads one to believe that the "political disaster" of declining subsidies was what Congress was really responding to.)

But those are just the supplemental appropriations. Under the 1996 "reform" (which, you'll recall, was supposed to phase farm subsidies down to a level of $4 billion a year), total farm subsidies shot up from $7.5 billion in 1997 to $12.4 billion in 1998 and then topped $20 billion for each of the next three years.[49] Freedom to Farm was advertised as a bill to "phase out" subsidies by 2002 (or, well, almost) and was projected to cost $47 billion over six years. The final tab? More than $123 billion.[50] Clearly, further reform was needed.

So in 2002, it came time to pass a new farm bill (Congress passes a new farm bill every six years). The legislation that was passed will cost $190 billion over the next decade, a $73 billion hike from the last farm bill.[51] The reason it ended up costing so much? Lobbyists were lining up ten deep, and both sides wanted to placate them one way or another. The upcoming congressional elections featured a number of volatile swing seats in crucial farm states.[52]

Most of the actual reforms left over from Freedom to Farm were canceled. The 2002 bill added new subsidies for lentils, dried peas, and garbanzo beans. Wool, mohair, and honey subsidies, which had been phased out, are being phased back in. Peanuts and dairy are being shifted from price supports to direct payments. Cotton farmers and sugar producers received new goodies as well.[53]

Limits on the amounts available to high-income farmers and corporations have been eliminated or raised, while loopholes make even these limits laughably easy to circumvent.[54] Funding for a program to protect water supplies was boosted to include manure cleanup for giant factory farm operations, which crowd thousands of animals into feedlots. (The late Senator Paul Wellstone successfully introduced an amendment to make these corporate manure producers clean up their own pollution. However, the provision was stripped from the final bill, along with many other reforms, by the conference committee that marked it up.)[55]

We can look forward to further "reforms" in 2007, when this bill expires, along with a few more "emergency" appropriations along the way. On top of that, the Heritage Foundation estimates that price supports will cost US consumers an extra $270 billion over the next decade.[56]

THE WATERS OF BABYLON

Subsidized irrigation water is another good example of how agribusiness handouts distort our economic life. Because the official purpose of the subsidy is to help small farmers, no farm larger than 960 acres is supposed to receive subsidized water. It hasn't quite worked out that way.

The giant agribusiness companies waltz around the 960-acre limit by setting up networks of corporations and trusts to disguise their massive landholdings. (They're not fooling anybody, of course, but their political clout prevents the law from being enforced.) A more enforceable limit would require the full price from any operation with a gross income of more than $500,000 annually. Breaking your landholdings into various subsidiaries wouldn't work if you still owned all of them. Friends of the Earth estimates such a change would save taxpayers $440 million a year.[57]

Water users are also supposed to help pay for constructing irrigation projects, but the government fronts the money, waits ten years before starting to collect, charges no interest, and then only asks for 2.5% of the principal each year.[58] Between 1902 (when the program began) and 1986, these policies cost us an estimated $70 billion in lost interest payments.[59]

Once the canals are built, the water is provided free of charge—or at very low cost—though it isn't free to produce. It's estimated that irrigation projects, public dams, and the sale of water at below-market prices cost us more than $3 billion a year nationwide. Small farmers get very little of the benefit from this. In California, corporate "farmers" like Southern Pacific, Chevron, Getty Oil, Shell Oil, and Prudential Insurance use more than two-thirds of the state's agricultural water.[60]

FARMS WITHOUT SUBSIDIES

So what would happen if we stopped subsidizing agriculture? Would small farmers disappear altogether? Well, ask the farmers of New Zealand, the least subsidized in the industrialized world. What happened when their subsidies were ended in 1984? They thrived!

The 104th Congress, under GOP control, promised—and failed—to phase out US farm subsidies between 1986 and 2002. In contrast, the government of New Zealand simply ended its farm support programs overnight. Any farmers who thought they couldn't cut it anymore without government assistance were offered a one-time "exit grant."

At the time, New Zealand's economy was about five times as dependent on the farm sector as ours is today. And its farm subsidies covered 30 % of the nation's agricultural output (ours cover about 22 %). So this was not exactly risk free. Farmers protested bitterly, and even the government predicted that one in ten would go out of business.

Instead, only one in a hundred farms went bankrupt over the next ten years. The value of New Zealand's agricultural output has risen 40%. Farming grew from 14% to 17% of the overall economy. The country's farmers have cut costs and diversified their land use, and annual productivity growth is six times what it was before 1984. Environmental protection has improved as well. The overuse of fertilizers has ended along with farm subsidies. Marginal farmland, used only to collect government payments, has since been returned to nature.

Is there any reason that couldn't work here in the United States? Only one: the stranglehold that agribusiness has on our legislative process.

SOURCE

Edwards, Chris and Tad DeHaven, "Save the Farms: End the Subsidies," *Washington Post*, March 3, 2002.

The main effect of irrigation subsidies is to encourage agribusiness to waste water, depleting the nation's watersheds as well as its treasury. Many subsidized irrigators actually turn around and sell their excess water at a profit—sometimes to local governments.[61] (Isn't free enterprise great? We spend a fortune on dams and canals so some bloated welfare parasite can sell water back to us at a profit. We pay for it once with our federal taxes and then again—at a higher price—with our local taxes.)

MISCELLANEOUS PORK

The Conservation Reserve Program will pay farmers $2 billion in FY2004 (including administrative costs) not to grow crops. Supposedly this is to help control soil erosion, but much of the erosion is caused by unsustainable farming practices. One study suggested we could achieve better conservation simply by cutting farm subsidies in half.[62]

The USDA funds various research programs that help farmers take advantage of new technologies, improve the quality of agricultural products, and find new uses for them. One program even funds marketing research for farmers. Agribusiness derives the benefits from all this, but it doesn't pay the $987 million a year it costs. We do.

The National Agricultural Statistics Service collects and publishes data on agricultural crops and farm program payments, at a cost of $104 million a year.[63]

If the government's crop insurance program were eliminated, private insurers would bear the risk, rather than taxpayers. Subsidizing insurance leads to abuses like the farmers in Texas who planted a type of cotton that couldn't grow in their area and insured it through Uncle Sam with $4.4 million in premiums. Then they collected $15 million when the crops failed. This program is budgeted at $3.4 billion for 2004 (up from $1.5 billion in 1999).[64]

Another form of deficiency payment is found in the USDA's Marketing Assistance Loan Program. The government sets loan prices for various commodities like corn, wheat, and soybeans, and farmers can thus subsidize their crop production. Previously, if the price of the crop (as posted daily by the USDA) fell below the loan price, farmers could either forfeit their grain to the government or repay the loan. That has the effect of setting a floor price for these crops.

But under the 1996 farm bill, if the market price falls below the loan price, producers also have the option of repaying the loan at the lower price, and then keeping the crop and either selling it or storing it, presumably to wait for a better price. For instance, a farmer wants to grow 10,000 bushels of corn. The government bankrolls a loan, setting the loan price at $1 per bushel and giving the farmer $10,000. When the crop is harvested, and the market price comes in at 75 cents, the farmer can give the corn to the government as payment for the loan. So the farmer is guaranteed a certain minimum price. In this case, the government would be out $2,500. Under the old system, this is all the farmer could do. Under the new bill, however, beyond this minimum price, the farmer can now also keep the crop and sell it—say, at the market price of 75 cents. Now the farmer's gotten the $2,500 from the government loan plus $7,500 from the market.

Or the farmer could simply skip the loan program altogether and take a Loan Deficiency Payment (LDP). This removes the incentive for the farmer to forfeit the crop to the government. The LDP is a direct payment for a harvested crop that pays the difference between the loan rate, as above, and the market price, again guaranteeing a minimum price. As the USDA notes, the cost of this program doubled between 1997 and 2000, peaking at $8 billion in 2002. Because the agency predicts "improved market conditions," it projects the program will cost $1.6 billion in 2004.[65]

THE WELFARE KING

No discussion of agribusiness would be complete without the story of Dwayne Andreas, the undisputed king of American welfare. The Cato Institute estimates that his company, Archer Daniels Midland (ADM), derives at least 43% of its profits from products that are heavily subsidized or protected by the US government.[66]

But Andreas knows how to share. Back in 1972, he stopped by the Nixon White House to personally hand over an envelope that contained $100,000 in hundred-dollar bills. Later on, he sent a check for $25,000 that was cashed by Watergate burglar Bernard Barker.[67]

Andreas later became known as an equal-opportunity influence buyer, lavishing donations on both parties. He was one of Bill Clinton's top contributors. He also made a lifetime project of cultivating Viagra spokesmodel Bob Dole, Clinton's 1996 opponent. That investment continues in the form of Senator Elizabeth Dole's political career.[68]

In 1992 alone, Andreas gave a combined total of $1.4 million to the Republican and Democratic parties.[69] According to Common Cause, his political contributions between 1987 and 1997 came to more than $4.5 million.[70] Andreas calls this "tithing."[71] What does he get in return? ADM has profited from deficiency payments on corn, sugar quotas, and subsidized grain exports. Then there's the tax credit for ethanol production.

THE ETHANOL HANDOUT

There are lots of kinds of alcohol. Ethanol is the scientific name for the kind that's in alcoholic beverages. When one part ethanol is added to nine parts gasoline, the result is gasohol. Like the ethanol in bourbon, the ethanol that's added to gasoline is made from corn (something ADM grows a lot of). Or as columnist Paul Gigot puts it, ethanol is a mixture of corn and your tax dollars.[72]

Gasohol is a cleaner-burning fuel, but since ethanol contains about two-thirds as much energy as gasoline, gasohol doesn't work as well as gasoline. The Department of Energy calculates that gasohol-powered vehicles average 4.7 fewer miles per gallon than gasoline-powered ones.[73]

Not only that, but ethanol costs nearly twice as much to produce as gas. And the process is much less efficient. According to ADM's own figures, so much natural gas and electricity is required that the net energy gain is only about 12%.[74] But even that measly 12% gain is vastly overstated. It doesn't take into account the fact that many ethanol producers burn coal, which is less efficient than natural gas, nor does it include the energy spent growing the corn, powering the tractors that harvest it, or fueling the trucks that haul it to the production facility. (Ethanol also contributes more pollution, including carbon monoxide and formaldehyde emissions, when it is manufactured.)

Factor all that in, and you get an amazing picture. According to the Department of Energy, producing a gallon of ethanol results in a net energy loss of between 11% and 16%. So we've spent more than $7 billion since 1979 to make ourselves more fossil-fuel dependent, and not less.[75]

And how can anyone make money on that? Welcome to the ethanol tax credit. Companies receive a tax break of 5.3 cents for each gallon of gasohol sold; since one gallon of ethanol makes ten gallons of gasohol (there's no tax break for the gasoline portion), this translates to 53 cents for each gallon of ethanol used. In 1994, when a barrel of oil cost $18, this tax break was equivalent to a subsidy of $23 for each barrel of ethanol produced. In other words, for $5 less than we're paying merely to subsidize gasohol production, we could buy a barrel of oil flat out![76]

You can see why there'd be no market for ethanol without the subsidy, which cost us $850 million in 1999. ADM made 60% of all the ethanol produced in the United States that year, which means that taxpaying schnooks like us contributed about $505 million to subsidize Andreas's bottom line. (No other federal subsidy went so disproportionately to one company that year.)[77]

The ethanol handout currently costs us over $1 billion a year, and pending legislation has a provision that would triple that amount by 2012.[78]

HOW SWEET IT IS!

ADM does a triple dip into our pockets. First it profits from the price supports on corn to the tune of some $200 million a year. Then it turns a bunch of the corn into sweetener, the price of which is kept artificially high by import restrictions and market quotas on sugar. (If sugar were cheaper, corn sweetener would have to be cheaper too, in order to compete.) Finally, some of the corn is turned into subsidized ethanol.[79]

Call me crazy, but I think all this may have something to do with Andreas's "tithing." Maybe it's just a coincidence, but just days after Andreas contributed $100,000 to a presidential dinner, President Clinton issued an order that 30% of the gasoline in nine US cities must contain ethanol (it was later overturned in court).[80]

As for Bob Dole, he was as devoted to Andreas as an old hunting dog. He kept the 53 cents a gallon credit from being applied to competing gasoline additives like methanol (wood alcohol)—which is too bad, since methanol is cheaper, easier to get to market, and cleaner burning. Dole also helped impose tariffs on imported alcohol fuels.[81]

Andreas stepped down as head of ADM in 1999, at the age of 80. At the time, the company was rocked by scandals and ended up paying a $100 million fine for price fixing. Andreas's heir apparent, his son Michael, was unavailable to take over the family business because he had a three-year appointment at a federal penitentiary. But ADM continues to thrive at the public trough under the guidance of Dwayne's nephew, Allen Andreas.[82]

WALK IN, PIG OUT

There used to be a ribs place in Berkeley, California that had this motto painted on its window (maybe it still does). It would serve as a wonderful slogan for the USDA as well.

Let's review what's in the agribusiness trough. Price supports, import restrictions, and production and marketing quotas on sugar, peanuts, and dairy products cost us $4.2 billion a year; on tobacco, they cost about $857 million. That's more than $5 billion right there, but it's not part of the federal budget. Since it comes directly from the wallets of consumers (except the bureaucratic costs), I'll be conservative and not count that amount.

Under the 2002 farm bill, crop subsidies for 2004 are projected at $16.4 billion. Subsidized irrigation water costs more than $3 billion. We lose about $500 million a year on grazing leases, and another billion to the ethanol subsidy. We spend about $8.1 billion to the programs listed under "Miscellaneous Pork." Finally, agribusiness gets an additional $1.5 billion in tax breaks every year. The total agribusiness pig-out amounts to almost $30.5 billion per year. And that doesn't include one-time "emergencies," export subsidies (see that chapter for details), or the damage to our health and the environment—here and abroad—that's caused by current USDA policies.

ACTIVIST'S TOOLKIT

Corporate Agribusiness Research Project
PO Box 2201, Everett, WA 98203-0201• phone: (425) 258-5345 • email: avkrebs@earthlink.net • website: http://www.electricarrow.com/CARP/

Environmental Working Group
1436 U Street NW, Suite 100, Washington, DC 20009 • email: info@ewg.org • website: http://www.ewg.org/ • farm subsidy database: http://www.ewg.org/farm/

Food First/Institute for Food and Development Policy
398 60th Street, Oakland, CA 94618 • phone: (510) 654-4400 • fax: (510) 654-4551 • email: foodfirst@foodfirst.org • website: http://www.foodfirst.org/
Forest Guardians
312 Montezuma, Suite A, Santa Fe, NM 87501 • phone: (505) 988-9126 ext. 153 • email: swwild@fguardians.org • website: http://www.fguardians.org
National Public Lands Grazing Campaign
c/o The Larch Company • 1213 Iowa Street, Ashland, OR 97520 • email: andykerr@andykerr.net • website: http://www.publiclandsranching.org

Chapter 14

Media Handouts
($14.2 billion a year)

The Communications Act of 1934 declared that "the airwaves belong to the people." Part of the rationale was that, like land, the broadcast spectrum is finite, so regulation is required to govern the common good. The right to the airwaves was originally retained by the government in order to provide public service—leasing the airwaves out to nongovernmental entities is also supposed to ensure that we get nongovernmental, and varied, views. Theoretically, there should be a balance of interests, rather than allowing only rich corporations to have access—just as cable companies are supposed to provide public access in exchange for monopoly of a local market, normal people should be able to broadcast on TV and radio.

What happened instead was that the government handed out big chunks of the people's airwaves free of charge to businesses, which then made as much money off them as they could, without having to pay the government anything for the privilege.

Thanks—at least in part—to this generosity, the combined profits of the four largest TV networks were $2.26 billion in 2000 (on revenues of almost $14 billion).[1] The entire TV industry sold $44 billion worth of advertising that year.[2] And just one of the TV channels the government gave away was recently purchased (in New York) by Dow Jones and ITT for $207 million.[3]

Under the Communications Act of 1934, the government licensed the airwaves to private interests with the requirement that they would be used (at least in part) to provide services to the public. The definition of public interest has become so loose today that the chair of the FCC (Federal Communications Commission) says that he has no idea what it is (I'm not making this up). So broadcasters have been paying less and less lip service to the toothless public service requirements of their licenses. That's understandable, since not one of them has ever had a serious challenge from the FCC—not even General Electric, which owns NBC and has been convicted of many felonies (for details on some of them, see the section on career criminals in the chapter on military waste and fraud).

GIVE THEM A FINGER, THEY WANT A HAND

The government and the electronics industry want to encourage the development of high-definition TV (HDTV). While we're shifting to that new standard, TV stations will need to broadcast two signals—one for the TV sets we all have now, and one for new sets that receive HDTV.[4] At the time this policy was implemented, it was argued that the Japanese were way ahead of us on this technology and that US companies would somehow be unable to compete without some sort of government intervention. Again, I'm not making this up.

To make the transition as painless as possible, the Telecommunications Act of 1996 gave TV broadcasters an extra, free channel for each one they currently controlled—both for VHF (channels 2 through 13) and UHF (channels 14 through 69). Eventually, the FCC wants to narrow TV's spectrum (portion of the airwaves) so that it only runs from channel 7 to 51. (More spectrum is needed for cell phones and other wireless devices, and much of the remainder is reserved for police and military uses. With the widespread availability of cable TV, there is less demand for the UHF spectrum.)

Needless to say, the broadcasters applaud the first part of the proposal and oppose the second. And having spent some $9.5 million in political contributions in the decade before the extra spectrum handout, they're now using their influence to agitate for relaxed restrictions on when they have to give some part of the spectrum back.[5]

As of this writing, they have to give it back when 85% of TV sets in their market can receive HDTV. That's liable to be quite some time after 2006. Also, they may be allowed to *sell off* their excess UHF frequency to cell phone companies—and keep the proceeds for themselves. (One other bonus for the broadcasters is that if you switch to digital cable, they'll be able to track which programs and commercials you watch as easily as your internet browsing habits can be tracked today.)[6]

Ironically, new digital technology makes it possible to broadcast up to six channels on the same amount of spectrum currently used for one—which means the broadcasters don't actually need the new, free spectrum to make the transition to digital TV. That didn't stop them from running zillions of commercials warning us that free TV would disappear if they couldn't get this handout.[7] Now they're sitting on twice as much spectrum as they need to broadcast analog TV signals—and 12 times what they need to broadcast digital TV.

Broadcasters are used to getting spectrum for free, but since 1992, new spectra (that's the plural) have been auctioned off. Between 1994 and 2002, the wireless phone industry paid some $36 billion to Uncle Sam for the use of radio spectrum.[8] (That's not bad, but the Commerce Department has estimated that cell phone spectrum is worth as much as $86 billion in metropolitan markets alone.[9] And the so-called Baby Bells—giant local phone companies spun off from the breakup of AT&T—have been allowed to keep $4.68 billion worth of free spectrum, giving them a huge advantage over their competitors.[10])

The FCC claims the TV channels that were given away in 1996 would have fetched $37 billion if auctioned off. Common Cause (and virtually every other analyst) says they're worth more like $70 billion.[11] But let's split the difference and say $53 billion. Since there are the same number of these new channels as the ones the broadcasters had previously controlled, let's assume the latter are also worth $53 billion.

So if we forced TV broadcasters to pay for what they've been using for free for more than six decades, we'd have an extra $106 billion in the Treasury. Then the national debt would be that much lower, and interest payments (the single-largest item in the federal budget after military spending) would be that much lower, too. That means the government could issue $106 billion less in Treasury bonds. Assuming it would pay about 7% on the bonds, having the $106 billion in hand would add $7.4 billion each year to the Treasury (7% of $106 billion).[12]

But all those TV licenses are likely to be bid up considerably higher. In June 2003, the FCC all but threw out the limits on how many TV stations any one company could own.[13] The new rules will allow one company to own both a newspaper and a radio station in the same city, or to own two or three "competing" stations. Plus, they would allow any one TV network to own enough local TV stations to reach 45% of the national market. One of the biggest beneficiaries of this deregulation is Rupert Murdoch's Fox Network. Fox had been prevented from buying TV stations because it owned so many newspapers. Also, Fox already owned more broadcast TV stations than allowed by the previous 35% limit (without penalty).[14] So the FCC obligingly made legal what had previously been illegal. A federal court ordered a stay on the implementation of these rules, and both the House and the Senate voted to overturn them—in the face of a veto threat from the White House. Then in November 2003, in a last-minute backroom deal with the White House, the Senate Appropriations Committee voted to change the ownership cap from 35% to 39%.[15] Even though this is less than the FCC's preferred 45%, it still lets Murdoch off the hook—if it holds up in court.

The FCC made these changes despite considerable public opposition. It received more than 500,000 emails and postcards, running at least ten to one against the changes. More than 120 members of Congress expressed their opposition. When FCC Chair Michael Powell refused to hold public hearings, dissenting FCC commissioners held their own meetings across the country. As one commissioner put it, "Of all the hundreds of citizens I heard from, not one person stood up to say, 'I want to see even more concentration in our media ownership.' Not one."[16]

On the other hand, FCC commissioners had over 2,500 trips and junkets paid for by telecommunications firms and lobbyists—at a cost of some $2.8 million. More than 300 of those junkets were to Las Vegas—which suggests that the commissioners were being showered with benefits over and above those that they might have received by meeting in less entertaining cities. The FCC and its staff held more than 71 off-the-record meetings to discuss the proposed changes with industry executives. They did manage to meet with five public interest groups as well, before giving away the store.[17]

The new FCC rules will most likely result in an orgy of mergers and consolidation, reducing the diversity of programming and stifling the quality of news operations. How do we know this? Because that's exactly what happened when radio was deregulated.

THE RADIO SPECTRA

Ask the people of Minot, North Dakota, where Clear Channel Communications owns six of the seven radio stations. When a train derailment spilled chemicals that formed a huge toxic cloud, authorities tried calling the radio stations to get an announcement on the air. But there was nobody there to answer the phones—or to go on the air.[18] At many of these chain stations, all the programming is prepackaged thousands of miles away and piped in by satellite. Even the "local" news is often read by an actor trained to mimic the local accent.

Until the Telecommunications Act of 1996, there were strict limits on how many radio stations one company could own. Nobody could own more two stations in any one market or more than 40 stations nationwide. A little-noticed provision in the bill threw those limits out the window. Little noticed, that is, by everyone but radio station owners. "We were high-fiving each other," remembers one executive.[19] Small wonder—Congress just put $17 billion worth of spectrum up for grabs.[20] Like TV spectra, AM and FM radio slots were also given to broadcasters free of charge. When they sell them to each other, however, they don't continue that tradition.

Since then, roughly 10,000 radio stations have been sold, and resold, for a total of some $100 billion. Now there are 1,100 fewer station owners,[21] and just two companies—Clear Channel and Infinity—control 45% of the market. Clear Channel, the largest, went from owning 40 radio stations to more than 1,200.[22] And of course, now Clear Channel is ready to buy up a lot of TV stations as well.[23]

A radio station in a major market can run at least $100 million (one in Chicago brought $165 million in 2000).[24] And, even in the smallest town, it's rare for a station to be sold for less than $100,000. Here are some recent valuations.

According to *US News and World Report,* the 21 radio stations Disney acquired when it bought ABC were worth $2 billion—more than $95 million each. After Westinghouse bought CBS, the 39 radio stations it controlled were worth $1 billion—almost $26 million each.[25]

In just the first half of 2003, two stations in the Napa Valley went for $3 million, and two in Ohio brought $4.3 million. Six in Kansas fetched $9.2 million, with four Florida stations going for the same price. Two in Massachusetts sold for $8 million. And five stations in Texas sold for a combined $105 million. Remember, all of those broadcast licenses were handed out for free.[26] I mean, even my *driving* license costs money, and I'm not expecting to make any profit off of it! (The FCC does now hold auctions for radio station *construction permits,* with bids starting at $2,500.)

In that random sample, the average price is over $19 million per radio station. (Some of that goes for electronic equipment and the like, but the license—the right to broadcast on a particular band of the radio spectrum—makes up about 80% of the value.)

Let's be conservative and use the value of the radio spectrum back in 1996, at the start of this bidding war: $17 billion. So, if we'd have forced radio broadcasters to pay for what they've been using for free, we'd have at least an extra $17 billion in the Treasury. Not having to issue 7% bonds for that amount would save us $1.19 billion a year. (Since this is such a loose estimate, and almost certainly way too low, let's just call it an even $1.2 billion.) And remember, again, this doesn't count the costs of supporting a bureaucracy that regulates something it gives out for free.

REDUCING THE ADVERTISING DEDUCTION

The unlimited deductibility of advertising as a business expense is an indirect subsidy to the media (print as well as broadcast). Why, you ask, is that a form of wealthfare? Well, for one thing, it's only available to businesses; ordinary taxpayers can't deduct the cost of running an ad in the paper to sell their car or to find a babysitter for the kids.

Second, like any deduction, it's worth more to corporations and other higher-bracket taxpayers than it is to the average person. Third, it subsidizes ads we also regulate because of their potential harm—such as those for liquor or cigarettes, or ones aimed at children—which means we're paying these companies with our right hand to do something we're trying to get them to stop doing with our left hand. The tobacco industry alone spends $6 billion a year on advertising, which is 100% deductible. Meanwhile, we taxpayers scrounge up $250 million a year to pay the media for *anti-tobacco* advertising.[27]

Finally, the ad deduction allows the broadcast media to sell something—access to the airwaves—that we gave them for free. (Sure, their programming has increased the value of those airwaves, but that can't be the whole story, since, as we've seen, buying a station costs a lot of money, and the programming doesn't come with it.)

When running for president in 2000, Senator John McCain (R-AZ) called for scaling back the deductibility of advertising from 100% to 80%, as was done with business meals and entertainment in 1986 (see Chapter 8), and for allowing the remaining 20% to be amortized over four years. According to the Congressional Budget Office, that modest plan would reduce the federal deficit by about $5.6 billion a year.[28]

To that let's add the $7.4 billion a year it costs us not to auction off the existing TV spectra, and the $1.2 billion it costs us for the free radio spectra. This gives us a total for media handouts of $14.2 billion a year.

But let's keep our eye on the ball. It's been estimated that the total value of the electromagnetic spectrum in the United States is as high as $367 billion.[29] That's more than a third of a trillion dollars. With the importance of the telecommunications industry to the US economy, that number could be well over a trillion in ten years. Maybe we should be a little bit more careful about giving that away.

ACTIVIST'S TOOLKIT

Adbusters **Magazine**

1243 W. 7th Avenue, Vancouver, BC V6H 1B7, Canada • phone: (604) 736-9401 • fax: (604) 737-6021 • email: adbuster@wimsey.com • website: http://www.adbusters.org/home/

Alliance for Community Media

666 11th Street NW, Suite 806, Washington, DC 20001 • phone: (202) 393-2650 • fax: (202) 393-2653 • email: acm@alliancecm.org • website: http://www.alliancecm.org/

FAIR (Fairness and Accuracy in Reporting)

130 W. 25th Street, New York, NY 10001 • phone: (212) 633-6700 • fax: (212) 727-7668 • email: fair@igc.apc.org • website: http://www.fair.org/fair/

Institute for Alternative Journalism

77 Federal Street, San Francisco, CA 94107 • phone: (415) 284-1420 • fax: (415) 284-1414 • email: alternet@igc.apc.org • website: http://www.alternet.org/an/

mediareform.net

c/o Free Press • 26 Center Street, Second Floor, Northampton, MA 01060 • phone: (413) 585-1533 • fax: (413) 585-8904 • email: info@mediareform.net • website: http://www.mediareform.net/

Chapter 15

Nuclear Subsidies
($10 billion a year)

According to Noam Chomsky, most US industries wouldn't be competitive internationally if the federal government hadn't developed their basic technology with your tax dollars, then given it away to private companies. Computers, biotech, and commercial aviation are examples, and so—preeminently—is nuclear power.

Nuclear power is subsidized every step of the way. The US Geological Survey helps with uranium exploration. The Department of Energy (DoE) underwrites research. Federal law subsidizes insurance for the transportation of raw materials and for plant operations. The DoE helps to refine nuclear fuel at a loss to taxpayers. The tax code helps to subsidize the capitalization of new plants. The DoE helps out with marketing. The government helps to find new uses for nuclear by-products. And Uncle Sam has now taken responsibility for storing the industry's lethal waste for the next few hundred centuries.

And even with all that help, nuclear power is more expensive than electricity generated by coal-, oil-, gas-, or hydro-powered plants. After 50 years, nuclear power still can't stand on its own two feet. But with a sugar daddy like the federal government, it doesn't need to. Between 1948 and 1998, the government spent more than $66 billion (in 1999 dollars) on nuclear power research—almost two-thirds of all federal support for energy research and development.[1]

In 1998, we somehow managed to completely avoid direct nuclear research subsidies—the first year since 1950 in which we were so lucky. But Congress started them up again in 1999 and budgeted $50.5 million for them in fiscal year 2002.[2] And when the Bush-Cheney ticket took the White House in 2001, the nuclear industry suddenly had powerful friends in the West Wing. (The research budget alone quadrupled in 2003.)[3]

Even with all the nuclear welfare handed out over the years, nuclear power is still so risky and so controversial that there hasn't been a new plant built in this country in 30 years. But if the White House gets its way, that's about to change. Funding has already begun for the administration's Nuclear Power 2010 plan. This calls for throwing still more money at the nuclear industry in hopes of getting some new plants built by the end of the decade—with a goal of 50 new reactors by 2020.[4]

The government and the industry argue that we "need" nuclear power. But there are better ways of filling that need; we could gain much more energy capacity simply through better conservation. It's also true that if solar or wind power were subsidized as much as nuclear has been, these sources would be cost competitive as well as better for the environment.

THE INSURANCE SUBSIDY

Since 1959, the government has also limited the liability of nuclear utilities for damage caused by accidents. (Like so many other subsidies, it was originally intended to be temporary.) Until 1988, the utilities were only responsible for the first $560 million per accident; the limit is now $9.3 billion.[5]

But $9.3 billion wouldn't begin to cover the costs of a core meltdown or even a near meltdown like Chernobyl, whose total costs are estimated at $358 billion.[6] That's not to mention the 125,000 deaths it caused (according to Ukrainian government figures) or the damage to the health of people in neighboring countries. If anything like that happened in this country, we taxpayers would pick up all the costs after that $9.3 billion was used up.

The Energy Information Administration calculates that if nuclear utilities were required to buy insurance coverage above that $9.3 billion on the open market, it would cost almost $28 million per reactor, for a total annual subsidy of $3 billion.[7] (Even if nuclear power could pay its own way, its risks far outweigh its benefits. But that's a subject for another book.)

REPROCESSING FUEL RODS

Nuclear power plants create radioactive waste. Naturally, the government feels that it's our responsibility as taxpayers to take this waste and either reprocess it into new fuel rods or find some place to store it for the next 10,000 years or so.

Let's talk about reprocessing first. This involves separating the plutonium out of nuclear waste—which can then be used to make nuclear weapons. (That's why we get so upset when North Korea or Iran is suspected of reprocessing.) To do this, you have to cut up the spent fuel rods—the most radioactive things on the planet—and then dissolve them in powerful solvents (please don't try this at home). Then, instead of irradiated fuel rods, you have radioactive gases, liquids, and solid waste to deal with. Leakage of this nasty stuff has created cleanup problems that will cost hundreds of billions of dollars, and nobody really knows exactly how to do it in any case.

Argonne National Laboratory (outside of Chicago) used to operate an enormously expensive facility in Idaho for separating plutonium, uranium, and the like from spent nuclear fuel rods so that these elements could be used in new fuel rods or nuclear weapons. In 1994, Congress killed funding for that and started paying Argonne $25 million a year to terminate the program.[8] Meanwhile, the same sort of reprocessing is taking place at the Savannah River site in South Carolina.

Originally used for weapons production, the Savannah River site contaminated several square miles of land so badly that human beings will probably never be able to use it again. Reprocessing fuel rods may not cause quite the same amount of environmental damage, but it will cost us an average of $720 million a year through 2004.[9]

There's also a new reprocessing project called ATW (advanced transmutation of nuclear waste). Housed at Los Alamos National Laboratories near Santa Fe, and championed by New Mexico's powerful senator, Pete Domenici, friend of all things nuclear, the ATW is budgeted for $281 billion over the next 118 years.[10] (At that point, the taxpayers of 2121 will have to decide whether to throw good money after bad.) But so far, we're only on the hook for $76 million a year.[11]

Another reprocessing boondoggle is MOX, the Mixed-Oxide Power Reactors, which mix weapons-grade plutonium 239 with uranium oxide to be used as fuel for commercial reactors. Congress cut funding for a cheaper way of dealing with our surplus plutonium; according to Friends of the Earth, "vitrification," or immobilizing the plutonium in glass blocks for storage, would save $600 million compared to MOX over the life of the program. MOX amounts to a subsidy to the nuclear industry that the Bush administration has budgeted at $400 million for 2004.[12]

Finally, there's the Fast Flux Test Facility at the highly radioactive Hanford Nuclear Reservation in Washington State. (Hanford is the most contaminated site in the United States, where for years deadly nuclear materials were handled as recklessly as if by drunken teenagers.) Uncle Sam can't exactly decide what to do with it—though reprocessing would be a safe bet. So rather than shut it down (as the Energy Department agreed to do in 1992), we spent $28 million a year to keep it on "hot standby," just in case we needed it. Then, in a rare victory for common sense, the project was killed.[13] But there are no final victories in Washington, DC, and pro-nuclear advocates are keen to fire Hanford up again.

THEIR WASTE, OUR RESPONSIBILITY

A place like Hanford naturally brings the subject of waste to mind. Nobody wants nuclear waste stored in their state, so Congress picked a place in Nevada, a state with little congressional clout. Called Yucca

Mountain, it's the least stable site of any considered to date, with 33 known earthquake faults in the area. It's also subject to periodic lava flows and groundwater seepage.[14] Plus, it may actually belong to the Western Shoshone tribe, depending on whether they can prove in court that they were screwed out of it.[15]

Despite these problems, Congress and the White House agreed in 2002 that Yucca Mountain was the perfect place for 50 tons of highly radioactive nuclear waste.[16] However, work on Yucca Mountain can't proceed until the Supreme Court rules on a Nevada law that prohibits the storage of nuclear waste in the state. In the meantime, the Nuclear Regulatory Commission (NRC) would like the DoE to clear up 293 unresolved technical issues before it grants a license for the facility.[17] Yucca Mountain's planned opening has been moved back from 1998 to 2015, but we're still being charged $460 million a year just to study the situation.[18]

If Yucca Mountain does go ahead, it will cost us at least $58 billion to build the facility, transport radioactive waste to it from all over the country, and seal the waste into thousands of containers.[19] In the meantime, there are no long-term storage sites for nuclear waste (and Yucca may never be one either). The nuclear industry was pushing for a temporary storage site in Utah—its eagerness explained by the fact that once it turns the waste over to Uncle Sam, it's our problem, not the industry's. But the NRC had to turn the nuclear industry down because of fears that fighter jets from a nearby Air Force base might crash into the containers of nuclear waste.[20]

Yucca Mountain is supposed to be financed by the Nuclear Waste Fund, generated by charging utility customers a fee of 0.1 cents per kilowatt hour for nuclear-generated power. But in its 20 years of existence, the fund has never been adjusted for inflation, which has cut its purchasing power by 45%.[21] Indexing would have saved taxpayers $315 million just between 1996 and 2000.[22]

There's another catch: The funds come from existing reactors, and no new ones are on order in the United States (so far). As the old reactors are retired, the fund's revenues will decline and ultimately disappear, leaving taxpayers holding the bag. But not to worry—the White House is hoping to restart some of the old reactors that have already exceeded their normal life. Two of the three reactors at the Tennessee Valley Authority (which were shut down in 1985) have already been brought back online. It hopes to start up the third one as well, costing us taxpayers $2.1 billion.[23]

And there's another problem: Money in the Nuclear Waste Fund is currently being used to pay for interim storage, which depletes the amount available for Yucca Mountain (or whatever long-term storage site is eventually decided on). If everything remains unchanged, the Nuclear Waste Fund will fall $12 billion to $17 billion short (in 1996 dollars) of the money it needs.[24]

But here's the ultimate in nuclear waste recycling: For several years, the nuclear industry has been melting radioactive metal together with regular metal to dilute it down to supposedly "safe" levels. This "radscrap" is used in common household items like tableware, frying pans, and baby carriages.[25] So bring your Geiger counter when you go shopping.

THE COST OF CLOSING THEM DOWN

Nuclear reactors are licensed to operate for 40 years, but they average just 16 years, and only one has lasted past 30. Of the 104 reactors in the United States, only nine have begun to be "decommissioned" (cleaned up), but 20 others will need to be soon.[26]

The Yankee Rowe plant in Massachusetts, the nation's first commercial reactor, was the first to begin the process (except for the Shoreham plant on Long Island, which only operated for 300 hours). How much will decommissioning Yankee Rowe cost? The figure continues to rise; the owner's latest guess is $375 million—ten times what it cost to build the plant. Other estimates go as high as $500 million.[27]

Let's say it costs about $400 million, on average, to decommission a nuclear reactor. Decommissioning the 29 plants that need to be closed soon will cost about $12 billion. Closing down all the plants would cost almost $52 billion.

The utilities are supposed to maintain an adequate trust fund for decommissioning each plant. But they don't. Chicago's Commonwealth Edison owns six elderly nukes, which will cost about $2 billion to decommission. It has set aside about $542 million for that purpose—27% of what's needed. When the Trojan reactor in Oregon was shut down in 1992, it had only 22% of its estimated decommissioning costs set aside.[28] A 1999 General Accounting Office report stated that as many as 66 of the 76 nuke owners are failing to contribute sufficient amounts to their decommissioning funds.[29] According to the Critical Mass Energy Project, the public's eventual share of the cost of closing all nuclear power plants could run as high as $46.5 billion.[30]

To help bail the industry out, Congress dropped the corporate tax rate on the industry's decommissioning trust funds from 34% to 20%. This has cost taxpayers over $76 million already, and it's projected to cost another $800 million from 2000 through 2004. (In 1999, Congress sought unsuccessfully to expand this by another billion dollars over the next decade).[31]

The nuclear industry is lobbying for relaxed restrictions on what it can put the trust funds' money into, hoping that riskier investments will make up some of the shortfall. The industry's also asking the NRC for relaxed standards on decommissioning, so it can clean up its nukes on the cheap.[32]

A sympathetic federal appeals court has ruled that instead of decommissioning them, the utilities could turn their nuclear power plants into "sealed waste sites" for some unspecified period of time. Doing so will probably make the eventual decommissioning even more expensive, since these reactors weren't designed to be used as storage facilities.[33]

Besides, because nuclear power plants need some place to discharge the water that cools the reactor, they're all situated near large bodies of water—usually rivers. Rivers flood frequently, and even lakes do sometimes. If ocean levels rise significantly over the next century, as is predicted, seaside plants would also be threatened by high tides. And nuclear waste stays radioactive for a long, long time.

One way or another, the decommissioning of all these reactors will have to be paid for. It's not likely the utilities will cover the costs themselves. They'll probably leave the government to pick up the tab, along the lines of the S&L bailout. Keep an eye on your state government, too, if you're lucky enough to host some reactors. The nuke industry has lately been looking to recover its "stranded costs" by including them in various deregulation schemes.[34]

FUSION RESEARCH

Compared to fission (the process used by all commercial nuclear reactors to date), fusion—the way the sun makes power—is much cleaner, safer, and cheaper. Theoretically, that is. A few practical design problems crop up when you try to build a fusion reactor smaller than the sun.

Fusion research has been going on for more than 40 years, but even its most optimistic proponents admit that commercial applications can't be expected until at least the middle of the 21st century. While commercially viable reactors would theoretically—there's that word again—generate no waste, the currently existing experimental ones use radioactive tritium as a fuel and generate large amounts of waste.[35]

A 1991 DoE memo that evaluated energy options in terms of economics and environmental risk ranked fusion 22 out of 23.[36] In 1999 Congress killed funding for the International Thermonuclear Experimental Reactor (ITER), the main fusion project.[37] But a funny thing happened—the overall fusion budget was increased. Now, ITER funding has been restored as well, along with a billion dollars a year for the National Ignition Facility (NIF) in Livermore, California.[38]

The NIF is expected to spend $32 billion in an effort to fire lasers at radioactive pellets in hopes of starting a fusion reaction someday. So far, it's years behind schedule and billions over budget. The Energy Department is planning for fusion research until at least 2040. Since that research began in 1948, Scott Denman of the Safe Energy Communication Council says, "They're basically asking for a century of funding with no return."[39]

ADDING IT ALL UP

- The government will spend $127 million on basic nuclear research in 2004.
- The nuclear industry's insurance subsidy runs $3 billion a year.
- Reprocessing spent fuel rods costs us $1 billion a year.
- Just planning for long-term storage of nuclear waste costs us $375 million a year.
- Estimates of the shortfall in the Nuclear Waste Fund range up to $17 billion, and will go on virtually forever. If we issue 7% bonds, interest on them will run $882 million a year.
- Closing nuclear power plants is costing us $160 million each year in lost taxes.
- But the real cost will come when the utilities admit they haven't set enough money aside to do the job. If we have

to pay for the estimated $46 billion–plus shortfall with 7% bonds, the yearly interest will run about $3.25 billion.

• Fusion research costs us about $250 million a year, plus a billion for the NIF.

Put all these numbers together and you get a total annual subsidy for nuclear power of over $10 billion.

ACTIVIST'S TOOLKIT

Bulletin of the Atomic Scientists
6042 S. Kimbark Avenue, Chicago, IL 60637-2806 • phone: (773) 702-2555 • fax: (773) 702-0725 • website: http://www.thebulletin.org/

Critical Mass Energy Project
c/o Public Citizen • 1600 20th Street NW, Washington, DC 20009 • phone: (202) 588-1000 • email: CMEP@citizen.org • website: http://www.citizen.org/

Greenpeace USA
PO Box 7939, Fredericksburg, VA 22404-9917 • nuclear campaign website: http://archive.greenpeace.org/nuclear/

Institute for Energy and Environmental Research
6935 Laurel Avenue, Suite 204, Takoma Park, MD 20912 • phone: (301) 270-5500 • fax: (301) 270-3029 • email: ieer@ieer.org • website: http://www.citizen.org/CMEP/

Natural Resources Defense Council
40 W. 20th Street, New York, NY 10011 • phone: (212) 727-2700 • fax: (212) 727-1773 • email: nrdcinfo@nrdc.org • nuclear issues website: http://www.nrdc.org/nuclear/default.asp

The Nuclear Control Institute
1000 Connecticut Avenue NW, Suite 410, Washington, DC 20036 • phone: (202) 822-8444 • fax: (202) 452-0892 • email: nci@nci.org • website: http://www.nci.org/index.htm

Nuclear Information and Resource Service
1424 16th Street NW, #404, Washington, DC 20036 • phone: (202) 328-0002 • fax: (202) 462-2183 • email: nirsnet@nirs.org • website: http://www.nirs.org/

US Nuclear Weapons Cost Study Project
c/o The Brookings Institution • 1775 Massachusetts Avenue NW, Washington, DC 20036 • phone: (202) 797-6000 • fax: (202) 797-6004 • email: atomicaudit@earthlink.net • website: http://www.brook.edu/fp/projects/nucwcost/weapons.htm

Yucca Mountain Information Office
PO Box 714, Eureka, NV 89316 • phone: (775) 237-5372 • email: ecsharon@eurekanv.org • website: http://www.yuccamountain.org

Chapter 16

Aviation Subsidies
($5 billion a year)

The Seattle aerospace giant Boeing is being pinched by competition from Airbus, a European manufacturer that's supported, to the tune of about $300 million a year, by the governments of Germany, France, Britain, and Spain. Boeing argues that these subsidies amount to an unfair trade practice—conveniently forgetting that US aerospace firms get about $1 billion a year in military research and development assistance from our government.[1] (Not to mention the Pentagon's new sweetheart deal with Boeing, described in the first chapter.)

If there's an argument for government subsidies, it's that they help infant industries to get on their feet. Commercial aviation is hardly an infant industry anymore, yet the government still pays for the air traffic control system, hands out grants for airport construction, and provides reports from the National Weather Service. The Commerce Department lobbies aggressively for foreign purchases of US-built aircraft, and the airlines are exempted from the 4.3 cents per gallon fuel tax.

The Congressional Black Caucus says we can save $1.7 billion a year by cutting FAA (Federal Aviation Administration) airport grants and raise $357 million a year by charging fees for landing rights at just four airports (O'Hare, JFK, La Guardia, and DC National). The Caucus also advocates eliminating the Essential Air Service program, which subsidizes 82 small airports around the country, mostly in wealthy communities.[2] Yes, some of the airports are in nonwealthy areas. But taxpayers are footing the bill to fly mostly empty airplanes in and out of those communities. And as one economist puts it, "What is being subsidized is business and tourist travel. This program is not giving aid to the destitute. It is not feeding starving children. It is simply utilizing taxpayers' money to allow businessmen and tourists to pay less than the full cost of their transportation."[3]

Likewise, about $300 million a year could be raised by imposing a modest fee on the use of business jets. Private planes use more than 20% of the air traffic control system, but cover only 3% of the costs through fuel taxes. The difference is made up by a ticket tax on airline passengers. Of those private planes, 40% are corporate-owned jets—more than 5,000 of them—and you're helping to pay their costs every time you fly.[4]

Overall, including the handouts described above, the aviation industry gets an estimated $4.5 billion a year in government subsidies—and that's above and beyond the $1 billion it receives in military research funds.[5] And then there's the post-9/11 bailout.

Even though most of the airlines were leaking money before the attacks, it was decided that they were in need of special help in the aftermath. And it was special; industry-wide, the airlines lost $1.35 billion in the 9/11 shutdown and received three times as much in the bailout.[6] It didn't seem to matter that the main cause of their woes was that in the late '90s boom, they had built up huge amounts of over-capacity (that's too many planes and too many flights chasing too few passengers).

Congress granted the airline industry a $15 billion bailout ($5 billion in cash and the rest in loan guarantees). This turns out to be more than the combined total profits of the entire history of commercial aviation in the United States.[7] Of that $15 billion, 80% went to the nine largest airlines, which showed their gratitude to the taxpayers by laying off more than 70,000 workers. Smaller air carriers got the shaft, too. Larry's Flying Service lost $14,000 in the shutdown and received only $6,000 in compensation.[8]

Some have argued that a reasonable bailout would have been less than a tenth as large, while others maintained that the problems of the unprofitable airlines would have been better dealt with by restructuring in Chapter 11 bankruptcy courts—which is where some of them ended up anyway.[9] Two of the airlines went into bankruptcy, and four more teetered on the brink. Of the big nine, only Southwest remains profitable.

Business Week contended that the subsidies actually hurt the industry, by delaying the adjustment to new market conditions.[10] But none of these arguments stopped Congress from giving the airlines another $3 billion bailout to help them cope with the war against Iraq.[11]

While the first bailout froze CEO pay at unreasonably high levels, airlines used the occasion of the second one to pick their employees' pockets—even as they had their hands out for more from Uncle Sam. American Airlines used the threat of an impending bankruptcy to extract major concessions from its unions. Only after the employees had given up $600 million in pay and benefits was it revealed that top executives had created a special trust fund to protect their own pensions—even if the airline went out of business.

The story was much the same at other airlines. While Delta lost $1.3 billion, its CEO took a 104% raise, from $6.86 million to $13.8 million. He'd like his workers to get by with a little less. Continental's boss cut 1,200 jobs and gave himself a 172% raise. United, Northwest, and US Airways have shown similar sensitivity to their workers.[12]

Let's remember that the next time the airlines show up hat in hand. And if we'd have hung on to the $8 billion in handouts in the first place, Uncle Sam's interest payments would be lower by a half billion a year. So we'll just add that on to their $4.5 billion wealthfare tally for a total of $5 billion (remembering that this doesn't include the one-time expenditures for the bailouts).

ACTIVIST'S TOOLKIT

Aviation Conspiracy Newsletter
email: rockaway@prodigy.net • website: http://pages.prodigy.net/rockaway/ACNewsmenu.htm

National Association of Railroad Passengers
900 2nd Street NE, Suite 308, Washington, DC 20002 • phone: (202) 408-8362 • fax: (202) 408-8287 • email: narp@narprail.org • website: http://www.narprail.org/

Sane Aviation For Everyone (SAFE)
PO Box 183, Howard Beach, NY 11414 • phone: (718) 848-1800 • email: rockaway@prodigy.net • website: http://pages.prodigy.net/rockaway/safe.htm

US Citizens Aviation Watch Association (US-CAWA)
PO Box 1702, Arlington Heights, IL 60006-1702 • phone: (847) 506-0670 • fax: (847) 506-0202 • email: info@us-caw.org • website: http://www.us-caw.org/

Victoria Transport Policy Institute
1250 Rudlin Street, Victoria, BC V8V 3R7, Canada • phone and fax: (250) 360-1560 • email: info@vtpi.org • website: http://www.vtpi.org/

Chapter 17

Mining Subsidies
($4.7 billion a year)

Interior Secretary Bruce Babbitt was visibly angry. He was about to sign away federal land containing $68 million in gold for a total price of $540, but he had no choice. The best he could do was hold a news conference that featured a giant gift-wrapped box and call the deal "a massive rip-off of the taxpayers."[1]

Babbitt's hands were tied by a law that had been passed 123 years earlier, during the ultracorrupt administration of Ulysses S. Grant. Called the Mining Law of 1872, it was originally designed to encourage settlement of the West. The law allows anyone—including foreign corporations—to search for minerals on public lands and, if found, to "patent" the mineral rights at the 1872 price—which is never more than $5 an acre! (Patenting means the company gets to use the land as long as it's mining it.) More than 3.2 million acres—an area almost the size of Connecticut—have been given away at these ridiculous prices.[2]

A Canadian mining company called American Barrick patented the rights to more than $10 billion in gold from land in Nevada it paid $9,765 for. (Just coincidentally, one of the company directors is former President George H. W. Bush.)[3] The Chevron and Manville corporations hope to lay their hands on about $4 billion worth of platinum and palladium; to patent the Montana acreage where the minerals are found, they'll pay about $10,000.[4] The Summitville Mine in Colorado has provided $130 million in gold to its owners, who patented the land for the princely sum of $7,000.[5]

And yup, if you're wondering, individuals can take out patents, too, and you don't even need ten grand. One guy paid the government $155 and didn't even mine the claim. Instead, he put up a hotel that's now worth $6 million.[6]

ROYALTIES? WE DON'T PAY NO STINKIN' ROYALTIES

Since 1872, about $245 billion worth of minerals have been mined from public lands. How much has our government collected in royalties? Absolutely nothing. Royalties aren't mentioned in the Law of '72, nor in any mining law since. Coal, gas, and oil companies pay royalties of between 8% and 12.5% for exploiting our public lands, but the so-called hardrock mining industry (as opposed to coal mining) gets off scot-free.[7]

If a conservative 8% royalty rate had been charged on that $245 billion, we'd be almost $20 billion richer. And at that same 8% rate, the $3.75 billion in minerals that are currently being pulled out of public lands each year would earn the Treasury about $300 million annually.[8]

BUT WAIT—THERE'S LESS

It used to be that the worst thing about the Law of '72 was that it doesn't require companies to clean up after themselves when they're done mining and return the patented land. But believe it or not, Senator Larry Craig (R-ID) figured out a way to make the law even worse. His plan allowed mining companies to simply patent chunks of federal land and dump waste from other sites. It passed the Senate 56 to 33, but was subsequently modified in negotiations with the Clinton White House to apply only to mining patents after November 1997.[9] Right now, we're looking at cleanup costs of $70 billion for abandoned mines on public lands, according to the Mineral Policy Center. If the cleanup takes 20 years, that will amount to $3.5 billion a year.[10]

The Clinton administration also tried to institute a rule that would allow the Interior Department to deny a mining patent if it would cause "substantial and irreparable harm." But the Bush White House decided that irreparable harm was just fine, and so tossed the stricter rules out the window.

As if the Law of '72 weren't enough, mining companies enjoy a number of lucrative tax write-offs. The reclamation deduction allows them to begin deducting the eventual closing costs of a mine as soon as it's opened, instead of when those costs actually occur. Needless to say, there's no requirement that the money the reclamation deduction saves the mining companies be set aside in a trust fund for the eventual reclamation of the mine. Eliminating this deduction would earn the Treasury about $40 million a year.

Mining companies can deduct 85% of the projected costs of exploring for certain minerals (finding the site, determining the quantity and quality of the minerals there, and digging shafts and tunnels) in the first year of mining, rather than over the life of the mine. The "85% of costs up front" deal is just another accelerated depreciation scam (see Chapter 6), and no, most businesses can't do that. The mining industry can also treat the sale of coal and iron as capital gains rather than as ordinary income. These two tax loopholes cost us over $130 million a year.[11]

On top of that, the Energy Department subsidizes coal mining with the so-called Clean Coal Technology Program. This program has spent

RUNNiNG GOVERNMENT MORE LiKE a BUSiNESS

over $2 billion since 1984 to encourage coal companies to find cleaner methods of burning coal—even though they're already obligated to do so under the Clean Air Act. This handout is budgeted at $150 million for fiscal 2004,[12] and other subsidies for coal research and development run another $325 million.[13]

THE PERCENTAGE DEPLETION ALLOWANCE

Finally, there's the percentage depletion allowance, another ancient law that's still on the books. It lets mining companies take a set percentage of the gross income they derive from a mine off their taxable incomes, and continue to do that for as long as that mine is producing. (Presumably, this compensates them for the fact that they're depleting their source of income by mining it. Or did you think that the money they make selling the minerals was supposed to do that?)

The percentage depletion allowance varies depending on what's being mined; it ranges from 10% for clay, sand, and gravel, to 22% for uranium, sulfur, and lead. (Note that some of the most toxic substances have the highest allowances.)

Just as with its twin, the oil depletion allowance, this tax break can end up being worth many times what it cost to dig the mine. When mining companies end up making more money from a tax write-off than they've invested in the mine, that means we've invested more in their mine than they have. Eliminating this allowance would save us $322 million a year.[14]

Let's add things up. Royalty-free mining runs $300 million a year. Not requiring miners to clean up after themselves costs about $3.5 billion a year. The reclamation deduction runs $40 million each year and the percentage depletion allowance $290 million. The research subsidy for coal is $475 million. Other tax breaks add up to $130 million. That comes to a total of $4.7 billion a year. And if the White House and Congress get their way, that number will go up another $580 million a year, according to pending legislation. (Most of the increase is for the "clean coal" program, which industry flacks say is necessary to make coal a cleaner-burning fuel. Critics say coal will always be nasty for the environment. Either way, it ought not be something we subsidize through our taxes. It should be a regular cost of doing business.)

ACTIVIST'S TOOLKIT

Center for Environmental Equity
610 SW Alder, Suite 1021, Portland, OR 97205 • phone: (503) 221-1683 • fax: (503) 221-0599 • website: http://www.nevermined.org/

Environmental Media Services
1320 18th Street NW, Fifth Floor, Washington, DC 20036 • phone: (202) 463-6670 • email: ryan@ems.org • mining policy website: http://www.ems.org/mining/facts.html

Mineral Policy Center
1612 K Street NW, Suite 808, Washington, DC 20006 • phone: (202) 887-1872 • email: webmaster@mineralpolicy.org • website: http://www.mineralpolicy.org

The Mining of the West
Seattle Post-Intelligencer special report • 101 Elliott Avenue W, Seattle, WA 98119 • phone: (206) 448-8000 • website: http://seattlepi.nwsource.com/specials/mining/

Natural Resources Defense Council
40 W. 20th Street, New York, NY 10011 • phone: (212) 727-2700 • fax: (212) 727-1773 • email: nrdcinfo@nrdc.org • land-use web pages: http://www.nrdc.org/land/use/

Project Underground
1611 Telegraph Avenue, Suite 702, Oakland, CA 94612 • phone: (510) 271-8081 • fax: (510) 271-8083 • email: project_underground@moles.org • website: http://www.moles.org • *Drillbits & Tailings* newsletter: http://www.moles.org/ProjectUnderground/drillbits/index.html

Public Lands Foundation
PO Box 7226, Arlington, VA 22207 • email: leaplf@erols.com • website: http://www.publicland.org/

Chapter 18

Oil and Gas Tax Breaks
($1.7 billion a year)

Like the percentage depletion allowance for coal mining, the oil depletion allowance lets certain companies deduct 15% of the gross income they derive from oil and gas wells from their taxable incomes for as long as those wells are producing. Some smaller companies get to increase the deduction by 1% for every $1 the price of oil falls below $20 a barrel.[1]

This tax break, on which we lose about $660 million a year, can add up to many times the cost of the original exploration and drilling. In fact, it can sometimes amount to 100% of the company's profits—in which case the company paid no taxes, no matter how much money it made.[2]

The rationale for this loophole is that it encourages exploration for new oil—presumably something no oil company would do otherwise. Oil industry executives argue that other businesses are allowed to depreciate the costs of their manufacturing investments. That's true, but they're only allowed to take off the actual cost of those assets, not deduct 15% of their gross income virtually forever.

Introduced in 1926, the oil depletion allowance was restricted in 1975 to independent oil companies that don't refine or import oil. To make up for this, the larger, integrated companies were given the intangible drilling cost deduction, which in some ways is even better. It lets them deduct 70% of the cost of setting up a drilling operation in the year those expenses occur, rather than having to depreciate them over the expected life of the well. They can take off the other 30% over the next five years. This boondoggle costs us about $440 million a year.[3]

A third tax break is the enhanced oil recovery credit. It encourages oil companies to go after reserves that are more expensive to extract—like those that have nearly been depleted or that contain especially thick crude oil. The net effect of this credit, which costs us $656 million a year, is that we pay almost twice as much for gasoline made from domestic oil as we do for gas made from foreign oil.[4]

Together, these three loopholes sometimes exceed 100% of the value of the energy produced by that oil. In other words, it would be cheaper in some cases for the government to just buy gas from the companies and give it to taxpayers free of charge. (Of course, without the tax breaks, the oil companies would charge more for gas, bringing our prices closer to that of other countries. This would undoubtedly lower our per capita consumption of gas, which is currently the highest in the world.)

There's a fourth tax break I can't count because I can't estimate its size; for details on it, see the section on master limited partnerships in Chapter 23, "What's Been Left Out." But miscellaneous smaller tax breaks and subsidies add $300 million a year to the oil industry's wealthfare, which brings the total to $1.7 billion.[5]

Instead of throwing $1.7 billion a year at the oil companies, we could encourage them to cut down on waste during production and transport. Each year, the equivalent of a thousand Exxon Valdez spills is lost due to inefficient refining, leaking wells and storage tanks, spills at oil fields as well as from tankers and pipelines, evaporative losses, unrecycled motor oil, and the like.[6]

In addition, the oil companies have been underpaying Uncle Sam on royalties for oil extracted from public lands to the tune of about $66 million a year. Senator Kay Bailey Hutchison (R-TX) has worked since 1995 to prevent the Interior Department from enforcing new rules to collect these funds—that is, her efforts allow the oil companies to go on defrauding us.[7] Congress narrowly voted to allow enforcement to begin on March 15, 2000, but as of this writing, the Interior Department is dragging its feet on implementing the rules. Also at this writing, both the House and the Senate have passed bills giving oil companies $802 million in exemptions from royalty payments over the next five years—though the bills have yet to reach the President's desk.

But that's just scratching the surface, as far as proposals for new subsidies. When the Democrats controlled the Senate in 2001–2002, they managed to block the administration's energy bill from passing. Republicans simply waited until they controlled both houses, and as I write some hefty new handouts are working their way through the legislative process. The House and Senate bills were reconciled in one of those notorious backroom conference committees. The resulting legislation passed the House—and then failed by one vote to get past a Democratic filibuster in the Senate. But GOP leaders vow to try again in 2004.[8] If they succeed, the intangible drilling and enhanced recovery deductions would be expanded, and a variety of new tax dodges would be created. If all of them pass, they would add another $860 million to $1.4 billion a year in tax breaks to the oil and gas industries.[9]

These companies are immensely profitable, and need no help from you or me. ExxonMobil, the largest corporation on earth, took in $17.7 billion in profits in 2000. Even a small, independent oil company like Unocal made $760 million that year.[10]

In any case, the current oil and gas tax breaks encourage the use of fossil fuels at the expense of cleaner alternatives, reward drilling in environmentally sensitive areas like wetlands and estuaries, and artificially attract to the oil industry investment money that could be used more productively in other areas of the economy.

The handouts listed above don't count the costs of defending oil supplies in the Persian Gulf (in monetary, let alone human, terms), or export marketing assistance, or diplomatic efforts to secure pipeline routes. Many of those are covered in other sections of this book. But if you wanted to lump them all in this category, some experts estimate federal support for the oil industry at $30 billion a year or more.[11]

ACTIVIST'S TOOLKIT

Climate Solutions
610 4th Avenue E, Olympia, WA 98501-1113 • phone: (360) 352-1763 • fax: (360) 943-4977 • email: info@climatesolutions.org • website: http://climatesolutions.org/ • energy and transportation subsidies website: http://www.endgame.org/energy.html

Greenpeace USA
PO Box 7939, Fredericksburg, VA 22404-9917 • oil subsidies web pages: http://archive.greenpeace.org/climate/oil/fdsub.html

Institute for Local Self-Reliance
1313 5th Street SE, Minneapolis, MN 55414-1546 • phone: (612) 379-3815 • fax: (612) 379-3920 • email: info@ilsr.org • Carbohydrate Economy Clearinghouse website: http://www.carbohydrateeconomy.org/

Project Underground
1611 Telegraph Avenue, Suite 702, Oakland, CA 94612 • phone: (510) 271-8081 • fax: (510) 271-8083 • email: project_underground@moles.org • website: http://www.moles.org • *Drillbits & Tailings* newsletter: http://www.moles.org/ProjectUnderground/drillbits/index.html

Taxpayers for Common $ense
651 Pennsylvania Avenue SE, Second Floor, Washington, DC 20003 • phone: (202) 546-8500 • fax: (202) 546-8511 • email: staff@taxpayer.net • fossil fuel subsidies website: http://www.taxpayer.net/TCS/fuelsubfact.htm

Union of Concerned Scientists
2 Brattle Square, Cambridge, MA 02238-9105 • phone: (617) 547-5552 • fax: (617) 864-9405 • email: ucs@ucsusa.org • clean energy web pages: http://www.ucsusa.org/clean_energy/index.cfm

Chapter 19

Timber Subsidies

($976 million a year)

Here's a trivia question for you: What federal agency is responsible for the most miles of road in the United States? The Department of Transportation? Nope. It's the US Forest Service, with 360,000 miles of logging roads—eight times more than the entire interstate highway system. The Forest Service continues to pay for thousands of miles more each year, at an annual cost of $173 million.[1]

The Forest Service doesn't physically build the roads. Logging companies do, and the Forest Service pays for them by letting the companies cut down a certain number of trees.[2] To barter like that, the Forest Service needs to decide how much each tree is worth. Until recently, the prices were decided at secret meetings between Forest Service officials and timber industry executives. Although the Clinton administration did away with the secret meetings, the Forest Service remained stocked with big timber's cronies, and it continues to shamelessly undervalue our trees. In 1996, it came up with a value of $2.85—the price of a cheeseburger—for 1,000 board-feet of lumber (about 1% of the normal commercial rate).[3]

JUST GIVING IT AWAY

Despite prices like that, the Forest Service would like you to think it's making a profit managing our natural resources. It claims it made $214 million on timber sales in 1994, and $412 million in 1993. But that's only because it didn't subtract a lot of its costs.[4]

For example, it never counts what it pays the logging companies for new roads, which it says "add to the capital value of the forest." (Actually, logging roads contribute to soil erosion and water pollution, and to the loss of wildlife habitat and recreational value.) Even though the Forest Service admits to a $10 billion backlog in maintaining these logging roads, it's taking an extra $405 million from 2000 through 2004 to start paving some of them over.[5] The Clinton administration tried to end the road-building program with an executive order known as the Roadless Rule, but the order remains tied up in court, and the current administration is not too keen on defending the rule.

The Forest Service also amortizes certain reforestation costs over extremely long time spans—sometimes as much as 400 years. When you look at the bottom line, you find that in 1994, the Forest Service lost $309 million; in 1993, $442 million; and between 1985 and 1997, more than $7.6 billion.[6] Another $407 million was lost in 1998 alone, and after that the Forest Service says it has no idea.[7]

Government officials rationalize these huge losses because they think (or they'd like us to think) the subsidies help create jobs; the problem is that the timber industry is sending many of these jobs overseas. The current administration also believes that the market is the best way to preserve the environment, but it has to ignore the market distortions of these subsidies in order to make that assertion.

In 1999, the House, by a margin of 211 to 210, passed an amendment to cut timber subsidies by $48.5 million. That was a great victory—which was reversed when timber industry supporters forced a second vote on a parliamentary technicality. The second vote was a 211 to 211 tie, which meant that the amendment was defeated.[8]

As one economist has pointed out, "In terms of assets, the [Forest Service] would rank in the top five in *Fortune* magazine's list of the nation's 500 largest corporations. In terms of operating revenues, however, [it] would only be number 290. In terms of net income, [it] would be classified as bankrupt."[9]

Of the 120 forests the Forest Service managed in 1994, 87% lost money. Nine lost money even before subtracting the Service's costs![10] How is that possible? To answer that question, let's look at the biggest money loser of all: the Tongass National Forest in Alaska.

PLUNDERING THE TONGASS

The Tongass is the nation's largest forest and the largest remaining temperate rain forest on earth. A subsidiary of the giant conglomerate Louisiana Pacific (LP) has a contract with the Forest Service that guarantees it a 50-year monopoly on logging the Tongass at noncompetitive prices.[11] Recently, the value of the trees cut down by LP's subsidiary has been less than the cost of the roads it built, so we've been paying it millions of dollars a year—actually giving it checks—to cut down our trees![12]

In addition to being extremely beautiful, the Tongass hosts all five species of Pacific salmon and the world's largest concentrations of grizzly bears and bald eagles. This didn't impress Alaska's Republican senators, Ted Stevens and Frank Murkowski; they cosponsored legislation to increase logging operations in the Tongass by 48%.[13]

That bill didn't pass, so Stevens and Murkowski tried again. Their next bill would extend LP's lease to 2019 and guarantee that the company makes a profit in the Tongass for all that time. (Dave Katz of the Southeast Alaska Conservation Council called it "the most egregious piece of corporate welfare I can imagine.")[14]

Fortunately, that one was also killed, and LP shut down its pulp mill soon after, in 1997. But then it cut a deal with the Clinton administration that allowed it another three years to extract a last 300 million board feet of lumber, just for old times' sake. When that deal ran out at the end of 1999, LP got a year's extension, because it wasn't quite finished. But the Southeast Alaska Conservation Council says that LP is really interested in transferring ownership of the lumber to a new company—founded by former LP execs—that would set up a wood-veneer plant in the Tongass and sell its products back to LP. Now the plan calls for logging more than 85,000 acres of old growth through 2007.[15]

The General Accounting Office estimates that Uncle Sam has spent more than half a billion dollars on industrial logging in the Tongass since 1992. We're still spending an average of $30 million a year, and in 2002 Congress dropped an extra $10 million on top of the Bush administration's budget request. That same year, the Forest Service decided to open up another nine million acres in the Tongass for logging and development.[16]

This kind of thing is nothing new, unfortunately. Between 1987 and 1992, the timber industry contributed $6.9 million to congressional campaigns—and the Forest Service lost $1.5 billion on timber deals.

SPECIAL TAX BREAKS

In addition to ripping off the Forest Service, the timber industry gets a bunch of lavish tax breaks. Since 1944, its income has been treated as capital gains, which is virtually always taxed at a lower rate than other types of income (see Chapter 5).[17]

Timber companies are also allowed to deduct many capital costs up front (something other businesses can't do). A third tax loophole—the use of master limited partnerships—is discussed in Chapter 23.

Because of these tax breaks, timber companies were deeply involved in the acquisitions, mergers, and leveraged buyouts of the 1980s. This left many of them with huge debts; to pay the interest on them, they've been logging their own trees far faster than they can replace them. Now they have a huge appetite for more taxpayer-subsidized trees and a crop of pliant politicians who are all too happy to give them what they want.

The timber industry's tax loopholes cost us about $500 million a year. Add to that the $116 million we pay for new logging roads each year, the $330 million we lose by selling trees for less than they're worth, and another $30 million annually for despoiling the Tongass, and you get a total subsidy to the timber barons of over $976 million a year.

In December 2003 President Bush signed the Orwellian Healthy Forests Initiative, which will, you guessed it, make our forests a lot less healthy. Using the anxiety created by rising forest fires—ironically exacerbated by commercial logging practices[18]—the plan will allow "fuel reduction" by authorizing the removal of the largest, most fire-resistant trees. Not coincidentally, these are also the most valuable trees.[19] The plan will also permanently abolish the right of citizens to challenge logging plans in the courts.[20]

And not surprisingly, the White House plan will also increase subsidies to the timber industry by another $125 million a year.[21] This is not surprising because the administration appointed Mark Rey, a timber industry lobbyist, to be undersecretary of the Department of Natural Resources and Environment. And that's not surprising because the logging industry donated $6.7 million to the Republicans in the 2000 election cycle.[22]

ACTIVIST'S TOOLKIT

American Lands Alliance
726 7th Street SE, Washington, DC 20003 • phone: (202) 547-9400 • fax: (202) 547-9213 • email: ldix@americanlands.org • website: http://www.americanlands.org

Forest Service Employees for Environmental Ethics
PO Box 11615, Eugene, OR 97440 • phone: (541) 484-2692 • fax: (541) 484-3004 • email: andy@fseee.org • website: http://www.fseee.org

National Forest Protection Alliance
PO Box 8264, Missoula, MT 59807 • phone: (406) 542-7565 • fax: (406) 542-7347 • email: nfpa@forestadvocate.org • website: http://www.forestadvocate.org/

Natural Resources Defense Council
40 W. 20th Street, New York, NY 10011 • phone: (212) 727-2700 • fax: (212) 727-1773 • email: nrdcinfo@nrdc.org • forest policy web pages: http://www.nrdc.org/land/forests/default.asp

Thoreau Institute
PO Box 1590, Bandon, OR 97411 • phone: (541) 347-1517 • fax: (413) 778-2476 • email: rot@ti.org • public lands web pages: http://www.ti.org/publiclands.html

Wildlands Center for Preventing Roads
PO Box 7516, Missoula, MT 59807 • phone: (406) 543-9551 • email: kiffin@wildlandscpr.org • website: http://www.wildlandscpr.org

Chapter 20

Synfuel Tax Credits

($600 million a year)

President Jimmy Carter's synthetic fuels (synfuel) program, which aims to reduce dependence on imported oil, offers a tax credit for the production of synfuel from methane gas, shale, tar sands, coal, and other fossil sources.[1]

In the case of methane gas, this makes sense—to some extent. An undisturbed coal deposit is normally laced with veins of methane; unless this methane is extracted beforehand, it escapes into the atmosphere while the coal is being mined. It also makes sense to tap methane escaping from old garbage dumps and the like; it's a greenhouse gas, after all, and capturing it not only provides fuel but helps reduce global warming. (All synfuels—not just methane—come from fossil sources and contribute to the greenhouse effect.)

But it makes no sense to create artificial incentives to go after methane in risky areas where it would otherwise stay put, like old oil and gas fields. The new drilling fractures the earth and opens up new passageways; gas escapes through all kinds of holes besides the one just drilled (including old wells that weren't plugged properly); and drilling through a contaminated aquifer down into a pristine one contaminates the lower one.

This tax credit has encouraged synfuel production over conventional natural gas sources, which would otherwise be a much cheaper alternative. With oil prices relatively low, it hasn't saved consumers any money. What it has done—at a cost to us of almost $600 million a year—is increase pollution, diminish interest in renewable energy solutions, and enrich a few companies.

ACTIVIST'S TOOLKIT

Project Underground

1611 Telegraph Avenue, Suite 702, Oakland, CA 94612 • phone: (510) 271-8081 • fax: (510) 271-8083 • email: project_underground@moles.org • website: http://www.moles.org • *Drillbits & Tailings* newsletter: http://www.moles.org/ProjectUnderground/drillbits/index.html

Taxpayers for Common $ense
651 Pennsylvania Avenue SE, Second Floor, Washington, DC 20003 • phone: (202) 546-8500 • fax: (202) 546-8511 • email: staff@taxpayer.net • synfuels web page: http://www.taxpayer.net/TCS/wastebasket/environment/ 03-08-02synfuels.htm

The Great Energy Scam
by Donald L. Barlett and James B. Steele • *Time* magazine report • October 13, 2003 issue • website: http://www.time.com/time/magazine/article/ 0,9171,1101031013-493241,00.html

Chapter 21

Ozone Tax Exemptions

($320 million a year)

In 1985, a hole in the earth's ozone layer was discovered over Antarctica, and it has been growing rapidly ever since.[1] The ozone filters solar radiation, removing its most dangerous wavelengths; take the ozone away and skin cancer rates skyrocket, as do many other ailments.

But the direct effects on human beings are the least of the problem. Most plant life evolved on earth under conditions of ozone-filtered solar radiation. If enough of that filtration is removed, you're looking at the death of virtually all plants—followed rapidly by the death of virtually all animals. It would be back to the drawing board—4.5 billion years back.

Alarmed by this threat, more than 120 nations agreed in 1987 to phase out the use of chlorofluorocarbons (CFCs) and several other ozone-destroying chemicals. In keeping with this international agreement—which is called the Montreal Protocol—Congress passed a tax on those chemicals in 1989. The tax has successfully discouraged their use and has encouraged the development of safer substitutes.[2]

Unfortunately, the story doesn't end there. A fumigant (gaseous pesticide) called methyl bromide was added to the Montreal Protocol in 1992. In addition to shredding the ozone layer, methyl bromide is a deadly poison. Farmworkers exposed to even tiny amounts of it often suffer seizures, cancer, and respiratory ailments, and their children are born with birth defects. Larger doses damage the nervous system, often fatally.

Despite all that, methyl bromide still hasn't been added to the list of chemicals that require payment of the ozone-depletion tax. Why not? Because the Clinton administration agreed to leave it out in exchange for the support of 20 House members from California and Florida on the NAFTA treaty vote.[3]

But wait—it gets worse. The 1990 Clean Air Act amendments required US companies to phase out production of methyl bromide by 2001, but the Clinton administration worked hard to delay this ban until 2010, and to exempt "essential uses"—fumigation of strawberries, tomatoes, and timber—even after that. Since these essential uses are just about all methyl bromide is used for, the exemptions have provoked angry opposition from Germany, Canada, and the Netherlands, and from environmental activists in the United States.

A class of chemicals called hydrochlorofluorocarbons (HCFCs) were also left out of the initial Montreal Protocol, so that they could provide a transition from the even more dangerous CFCs to safer substitutes. Alternatives have now been found for nearly every use of HCFCs (as well as CFCs), and HCFCs were added to the Montreal Protocol in 1992. But our government still exempts them from the tax on ozone-depleting chemicals.[4]

Right now, methyl bromide is scheduled to be phased out in 2005, so we can still count the tax exemption as lost revenue. But the Bush administration is now pushing for "scores" of exceptions to this requirement, so stay tuned. Aside from costing $320 million a year, this policy endangers every living thing on earth. Or as Dr. Joe Farman, the scientist who discovered the ozone hole, put it, "This is madness. We do not need this chemical. We do need the ozone layer. How stupid can people be?"[5]

ACTIVIST'S TOOLKIT

Greenpeace USA
PO Box 7939, Fredericksburg, VA 22404-9917 • website on ozone action: http://archive.greenpeace.org/ozone/index.html

Intergovernmental Panel on Climate Change
c/o World Meteorological Organization • 7bis Avenue de la Paix, C.P. 2300, CH-1211 Geneva 2, Switzerland • phone: +41-22-730-8208 • fax: +41-22-730-8025 • email: ipcc_sec@gateway.wmo.ch • website: http://www.ipcc.ch/

Pesticide Action Network North America
49 Powell Street, Suite 500, San Francisco, CA 94102 • phone: (415) 981-1771 • fax: (415) 981-1991 • email: panna@panna.org • website: http://www.panna.org

Union of Concerned Scientists
2 Brattle Square, Cambridge, MA 02238-9105 • phone: (617) 547-5552 • fax: (617) 864-9405 • email: ucs@ucsusa.org • website: http://www.ucsusa.org/

Chapter 22

A Bouquet of Miscellaneous Ripoffs
($16.4 billion a year)

ASSORTED TAX BREAKS • $8.5 BILLION A YEAR

Littered throughout the federal tax code are all sorts of tax breaks for business I haven't included in earlier chapters, with arcane names like "expensing of research expenditures" ($3.3 billion over five years), "exclusion from NOL limits" ($2.5 billion), "credit for increasing research activities" ($1.6 billion), "completed contract rules" ($1.1 billion), "permanent exception from imputed interest rules" ($1.2 billion), and "cash accounting other than agriculture" ($0.6 billion). Add in a handful of other miscellaneous loopholes, and the latest Office of Management and Budget report estimates these breaks will total $42.7 billion from 2000 through 2004—or $8.5 billion a year.[1]

CORPORATE TAX BRACKETS • $6.2 BILLION A YEAR

You've heard of the flat tax and the graduated tax; how about the staggered tax? For reasons no one can explain, some small corporations are taxed at higher rates than the giant ones. There are eight different corporate income tax brackets, starting at 15% for the first $50,000 of taxable income, rising to 25% on the next $25,000, 34% on the next $25,000, and the top rate of 39% on the next $235,000. But then corporate income up to $10 million is taxed at the lower rate of 34%. Between $10 million and $15 million is taxed at the 35% rate, from $15 million to $18.33 million at 38%, and then above $18.33 million the rate goes back down again to 35%.

Of course, this invites all kinds of shell games with corporate income. By shifting $500,000 in income from one's own salary to the corporation's books, a business owner can save $16,400 on the lower rates. According to the Office of Management and Budget , this chicanery costs us $6.2 billion a year in lost taxes.[2]

COMMERCIAL SHIP SUBSIDIES • $1 BILLION A YEAR

For agreeing to make their ships available to the US military in the event of a war, commercial shipowners are given an average annual subsidy of $3.5 million per ship. The Pentagon, which has more than enough ships of its own, admits this program serves no earthly purpose, but we still pay a billion dollars a year for it. Perhaps the maritime industry's $17 million in PAC contributions over the past decade have something to do with it.[3]

"CLEAN CAR" SUBSIDIES • $158 MILLION A YEAR

The government used to give General Motors, Ford, and Chrysler—whose combined 1994 profits were almost $14 billion—$264 million each year to develop more fuel-efficient cars. At the same time, the Big Three propagandized widely in favor of watered-down fuel-efficiency standards. Well, the Bush administration quickly got rid of that Clintonian boondoggle—and replaced it with one of its own. The FreedomCAR Initiative aims to develop a fuel cell vehicle to be unveiled sometime around 2020. Meanwhile, Japanese and German automakers are already producing prototypes. But for Detroit, the main value of this program is that it takes the heat off of automakers to improve fuel efficiency in their existing fleets. That's what Clinton's program did, too. That one cost us more than $1.25 billion and never met its goal of producing an 80-mile-per-gallon car. Of course, the Japanese already have one.[4]

THE POLLUTION DEDUCTION • $300 MILLION A YEAR

If you haven't completely boiled over by now, try this: companies are allowed to deduct the costs arising from illegally polluting the environment. After dumping 11 million gallons of oil on the Alaskan coastline,

Exxon settled out of court for about $1 billion. It was able to deduct around a third of that, $300 million, along with the costs of cleanup, studies, public relations, and court costs. This hardly amounts to a deterrent. Friends of the Earth estimates that disallowing the pollution deduction could save $1.5 billion over five years.[5]

ADVANCED TECH SUBSIDIES • $143 MILLION A YEAR

In fiscal year 1999, the Commerce Department's Advanced Technology Program handed out $143 million in grants to the likes of GE, IBM, United Airlines, Xerox, and Du Pont "to enhance the competitiveness" of these poor, hapless giants.[6] For FY2004, the White House requested severe cuts to the Advanced Technology Program, the House voted to eliminate it, and the Senate voted to double funding. At this writing, the House and Senate versions have yet to be reconciled. FY2003 funding was $180 million.

TAXOL • $38 MILLION A YEAR

After the federal government spent 15 years and $32 million discovering, developing, and testing the anticancer drug Taxol, it gave Bristol-Myers Squibb (BMS) exclusive rights to market it, royalty free. It costs BMS $52.50 to produce each shot of Taxol, which it then sells for $1,023! (That's wholesale, not retail.) In 1995, BMS made $480 million on the drug. (That's profits, not sales.) If the government charged a conservative 8% royalty rate, it would be making more than $38 million on Taxol each year instead of nothing. Why doesn't it? Because it never does.

Instead, it relies on the "reasonable pricing" rule, which requires pharmaceutical firms not to overcharge for drugs developed with government assistance. Unfortunately, the Department of Health and Human Services dropped the pricing rule in April 1995 (under heavy lobbying), leaving BMS and other pharmaceutical companies free to charge whatever they want for government-developed drugs.

There are hundreds of such drugs, and the $38 million we lose on Taxol is a tiny fraction of what this no-royalty policy costs us each year. (What I don't understand is, where do they get the nerve to call themselves "ethical" drug companies?)[7]

ACTIVIST'S TOOLKIT

Health Care Industry

Public Citizen Health Research Group
1600 20th Street NW, Washington, DC 20009 • phone: (202) 588-1000 • website: http://www.citizen.org/hrg/

Chapter 23

What's Been Left Out

(untold billions every year)

As I mentioned in the introduction, there are many types of wealth-fare I couldn't list above. Although they're obviously treasure troves of welfare for the rich, getting good figures on which portion of them is actually wealthfare wasn't feasible (in some cases, it's virtually impossible, no matter how much time you have). In this chapter, I discuss a few of these areas, in no particular order.

STATE AND LOCAL CORPORATE WELFARE

Virtually all the wealthfare I've discussed so far operates at the federal level, but state and local governments also slather benefits on companies within their borders, and many desperately compete for new corporate business—relocating factories, say—by handing out tax breaks and waiving environmental regulations. This is called "the race to the bottom."

You can probably think of an example in your area—maybe a sports team that threatened to leave town unless the city built it a new stadium. In my hometown of Tucson, Arizona, giant defense contractor Raytheon has been exempted from paying property taxes, though it's located in one of the poorest school districts in town. The local "empowerment district," which gives employers federal tax breaks in economically challenged areas, was also amended to drop three poor neighborhoods so that Raytheon's holdings could be substituted for them.

Here are some of the worst state and local deals, courtesy of Greg LeRoy's "No More Candy Store" report:[1]

- Willamette Industries pulled in $132.2 million for a lumber mill expansion that created a total of 15 new jobs. That works out to $8.8 million per job.
- The New York Stock Exchange agreed not to move out of New York, perhaps because New Jersey Stock Exchange just doesn't have the same ring to it. Or perhaps it was the $600 million in incentives from the City of New York?
- The state of Alabama lured a small steel mill into opening thereby canceling its income taxes for the next 20 years—a deal worth between $166,000 and $187,000.

- Hyundai sued the city of Eugene, Oregon, to get a 100% property tax abatement on its microchip plant. Apparently it found the original 85% offer simply too insulting.
- One North Carolina citizen was so outraged by the wasteful expenditure of city and county funds for 24 separate "economic incentive projects" that he sued, arguing that the law authorizing such grants violated the state's constitution. The superior court ruled in his favor, but in March 1996 the North Carolina Supreme Court overruled the decision.

EASY TREATMENT OF WHITE-COLLAR CRIMINALS

Although much of what I've already discussed in this book can be considered white-collar crime, there's also a lot of it I haven't covered. That's what this section is about.

The easy treatment white-collar criminals get in this country isn't a spending program or a tax break, but it is a major form of welfare for the rich. When the fines imposed by the Environmental Protection Agency, for example, are so low that polluting companies consider them a normal cost of doing business (along with the tax-deductible cost of the lawyers they use to defend themselves against the charges), we end up paying, both in higher health care costs and higher cleanup costs.

All the burglaries, robberies, and muggings in the United States cost us about $4 billion in 1995. That same year, crime in the suites, perpetrated by corporate officers, lawyers, accountants, doctors, and the like, cost us $200 billion—50 times as much. This figure, which comes from W. Steve Albrecht, a professor of accountancy at Brigham Young University, includes the costs of fraud, defective products, monopolistic practices, and so on, but it doesn't include pollution costs, government corruption, or preventable on-the-job deaths due to negligence.[2]

No one knows how much money is stolen from the medical system each year, but estimates range up to $250 billion—25% of the trillion dollars spent each year.[3] But that's just money. While there are 24,000 murders in the United States each year, medical negligence kills an estimated 120,000 of us—five times as many.[4]

On-the-job accidents and occupational diseases like black lung or asbestosis kill 66,800 people each year—more than twice as many as are murdered. And it's estimated that nearly a third of all cancer deaths are due to carcinogens in the workplace. Another 28,000 people die and 130,000 are injured each year because of dangerous or defective products.[5]

Air-bag technology has been around since the early 1970s, but for 20 years the automakers fought efforts to enact a federal law requiring air bags as standard equipment on new cars. Now they tout them in their advertising. In the meantime, an estimated 140,000 of the people who lost their lives in accidents during those 20 years would still be alive if their cars had been equipped with air bags.

Asbestos, banned since 1975, is still killing 8,000 Americans a year.[6] The list goes on and on and on. Yet virtually all we hear about in the media is the supposedly heavy regulatory burden imposed on US industry. Some burden. Of all the cases the Justice Department prosecutes, those involving product safety, occupational diseases, and environmental crimes together amount to half of 1%.[7]

UNLIMITED INTEREST DEDUCTIONS

If you have to borrow money, either to make ends meet or to start a business, the interest you pay on that loan shouldn't be counted as part of your taxable income. That fair-minded principle was the basis for the deduction for interest payments. But by making the deduction virtually unlimited for corporations, Congress has subsidized a mountain of debt that's paid for by the average taxpayer.

In the 1950s, US corporations paid $185 billion in federal income tax; in the 1980s, they paid $675 billion—more than 3.5 times as much. In contrast, corporate interest payments rose from $44 billion in the 1950s to $2.2 trillion ($2,200 billion!) in the 1980s—50 times as much. Thus in those 30 years, corporate interest grew almost 14 times faster than corporate taxes.

The interest deduction on corporate debt currently costs us over $200 billion a year. Once this deduction subsidized the replacement of plants and equipment or the hiring of new workers, but it increasingly underwrites the shuffling of paper assets.

The absence of limits on this write-off helped fuel the great financial scams of the 1980s, like the S&L scandal, the rise of junk bonds, and the mania for mergers and acquisitions. Between 1980 and 1988, US companies spent over two-thirds of a trillion dollars buying each other in mergers and acquisitions. In the case of leveraged buyouts—which are financed by borrowing large sums of money—the resulting debt-ridden companies were forced to lay off workers and sell productive assets to pay off their creditors.[8]

None of this created a single additional product, but it did create staggeringly huge fortunes. The unlimited interest deduction helped, by subsidizing the borrowing that made the layoffs and selloffs necessary.

It still seems fair to keep interest payments deductible for most taxpayers. But I don't think any company should be allowed to deduct interest payments that exceed its income.

CUT-RATE ELECTRICITY

In 1935, the government set out to bring electricity—and later, telephone service—to rural America. This mission was largely completed 40 years ago; nearly 100% of rural America now has electricity, and 98% has telephone service—better numbers than the nation as a whole.

Despite that, various government agencies continue to provide about $2 billion a year in grants, subsidized loans, and below-market electricity to profitable utilities—some with sales in the billions. Some of the areas these utilities service, like Las Vegas, can hardly be considered rural anymore.

The Northeast is the only region of the country not served by these programs; not coincidentally, it has the highest power costs in the nation. This accounts for a great deal of job flight, as manufacturing firms relocate to areas with subsidized power. In effect, northeastern taxpayers shell out tax money so their jobs can be moved to Tennessee or Idaho.

Some electricity subsidies provide low-cost power to schools, hospitals, and Indian reservations. But they also subsidize businesses like casinos and ski resorts. So the next time you find yourself bathed in the ghastly glare of Las Vegas, you can tell yourself proudly, "I paid for that."

In 1995, Senator John McCain (R-AZ) introduced legislation to means test the recipients of these programs, but it was defeated. As a result, we can't estimate how much of these subsidies amount to welfare for the rich.

MASTER LIMITED PARTNERSHIPS

Another corporate tax break is the master limited partnership (MLP), which allowed even large corporations like Burger King and Days Inn to restructure as partnerships. Why would they want to do that? Because profits parceled out to the partners are taxed just on their individual income tax returns. So by restructuring as an MLP, a corporation can pay the same dividends as always to its investors, but avoid paying taxes on those dividends at the corporate level.

From 1981 to 1987, there was nothing limited about these master limited partnerships; they cost the Treasury more than $500 million a year. This loophole was plugged in 1987, with an exception—MLPs are still allowed in the oil, gas, and timber industries. So Burlington Industries was able to take a timber corporation that paid corporate taxes of $33 million in 1988 and turn it into an MLP that paid no taxes at all in 1989.[9]

LOW-COST LABOR

In 1968, one person working full-time at the minimum wage would come pretty close to the federal poverty level for a family of four (so if someone else in the family worked just part-time, that family would be over the poverty line). Today that same full-time, minimum-wage job takes a worker up to just 56% of the poverty line.

Who makes up the difference? We do, through food stamps, the Earned Income Tax Credit, and other programs designed to help the working poor. In effect, we're subsidizing employers so that they can pay less than a living wage.

Until the mid-'90s, the Federal Reserve Board tried to keep the pool of unemployed workers above the so-called natural rate of 6%, on the theory that anything lower would fuel inflation. (The Fed does that by raising or lowering interest rates to slow down or speed up the economy.) As unemployment dipped below 4% with no corresponding rise in inflation, that theory became discredited. The Fed refrained from raising rates only because worker productivity went up while wages remained stagnant (that is, people were working harder for the same pay).[10]

But as the '90s drew to a close, the Fed again began to raise interest rates to slow down the economy. Higher unemployment guaranteed that there would be plenty of competition for jobs at below-subsistence wages. Still, there's a steadily growing pool of even cheaper labor—the nation's prison population.

PRISON LABOR

Since 1990, 30 states have legalized contracting prison labor out to private firms. Inmates were once employed booking reservations for TWA, and still enter data for the Bank of America and restock shelves for Toys"R"Us. Prisoners not only work for much lower wages than people on the outside, but they have virtually no way to organize or strike. For an employer, it's the best of all possible worlds.

The United States imprisons more of its citizens than any other nation on earth, and prison construction is growing by leaps and bounds. This great boon to the construction industry results from mandatory minimums for nonviolent drug offenders, the tough new "three-strikes" laws—the California version alone is costing $5.5 billion a year, five times what was estimated—and the roundup of undocumented workers.[11]

In fact, as of 1995, the largest employer of undocumented immigrants in the United States was UNICOR, a $500-million-a-year company that pays prison laborers between 23 cents and $1.15 an hour to make clothing and furniture for the US government. UNICOR is a US government corporation, set up by the Department of Justice. Its main customer is the federal government, and it uses federal prisons as its workplace. But much of the stock is held by Department of Justice employees as well as

the Welfare Line

by investment banks and Wall Street firms, and dividends are skimmed off without much congressional oversight.[12]

AUTOMOBILE SUBSIDIES

Automobiles kill about 50,000 of us each year, nearly as many as died during the entire Vietnam War. Respiratory diseases caused by auto exhaust kill another 120,000 Americans prematurely every year; their medical bills run more than $100 billion. Traffic injuries and deaths cost $400 billion a year.

Crop losses and property damage from car pollution (like damage to buildings caused by acid rain) cost another $100 billion a year. Motor vehicle fees and US gasoline taxes—the lowest in the industrialized world—don't begin to cover these costs; the costs are paid by drivers and nondrivers alike, and by future generations of taxpayers.[13]

Cars offer convenience, privacy, and safety. These are important benefits, but if the true costs of using a car were reflected in vehicle prices, registration fees, gas prices, etc., a lot more people would choose public transportation, bicycling, and walking than do today.

Federal, state, and local governments spend over $300 billion a year—nearly 100 times what they spend on public transportation—on car-related costs such as road construction and maintenance, enforcement of traffic laws, and the like. Riders on Amtrak and local mass transit systems pay much more toward the cost of their own transportation than auto users do—and at much less cost to society.

Meanwhile, the trucking industry tears up our roads far in excess of what it pays in fees. To wit: the trucking industry pays about 40% of the costs imposed on the rest of us—but trucks cause 20 times as much damage to the roads as cars do. The costs of more frequent maintenance, higher overpasses, thicker roadbeds, and more heavily reinforced pillars, as well as the price of regulating the industry, inspecting vehicle loads, and policing the roadways, are all indirect subsidies to trucking interests.

According to one estimate (which adds things like work time lost because of traffic jams), the true social cost of automobiles to US society is $1.4 trillion a year—and that's beyond what we pay, as individuals and businesses, to buy and use them. If none of these costs were subsidized, hidden away, or ignored, cars would cost more than $200,000 apiece.

Now, most people own cars, and some of these subsidies benefit as well as harm us. But $1.4 trillion is a lot of money, and it includes huge handouts to the oil companies, the car manufacturers, the mining companies (who supply the raw materials that are turned into a new car every second), and the road construction industry (which has paved over 38 million acres of our meadows, forests, and plains). Automobile subsidies have also been a great boon to the real estate industry, as the interstate highway system and other roads made vast tracts of land more accessible.[14]

The extent to which automobiles dominate our lives didn't just happen by accident—at least part of it was the result of a criminal conspiracy. Back in the early 1930s, most people living in cities got around on electric streetcars. Concerned that this wasn't the kind of environment in which they could sell a lot of buses, General Motors (GM), using a series of front companies, began buying up streetcar systems, tearing out the tracks, buying buses from itself, and then selling the new, polluting bus systems back to the cities—usually with contracts that prohibited the purchase of "any new equipment using fuel or means of propulsion other than gas." Sometimes the contracts required that the new owners buy all their replacement buses from GM.

GM was soon joined by Greyhound, Firestone Tire and Rubber, Standard Oil of California (also called Chevron), and Mack Trucks. In 1949—after these companies had destroyed more than 100 streetcar systems in over 40 cities, including New York, Los Angeles, Philadelphia, San Francisco, Oakland, Baltimore, St. Louis, and Salt Lake City—GM, Chevron, and Firestone were convicted of a criminal conspiracy to restrain trade. They were fined $5,000 each, and the executives who organized the scheme were fined $1 each. (Ouch! They'll certainly never do anything like that again.)[15]

The legacy of this conspiracy lives on. If you seek a monument to it, look above you. In the 1930s, when Los Angeles had the world's largest interurban electric railway system, the air over the city was clean every day of the year.

OTHER CATEGORIES

Here are some other scams and tax breaks you can't get good wealth-fare figures for: Medicare waste and fraud; the effects of Federal Reserve policies; the NAFTA and GATT treaties; the deregulation of various industries; import restrictions against Asian computer parts (which are said to add enormously to what US consumers pay for personal computers); fraudulent charitable deductions; and the depreciation of real property (which, since it tends to increase in value, not decrease, shouldn't be depreciated at all).

There are many other types of wealthfare, but by now you've surely gotten the point: our federal, state, and local governments have become so corrupt that dispensing welfare to corporations and wealthy individuals has become their major activity. The only time they do anything for average citizens is when we force them to.

ACTIVIST'S TOOLKIT

State and Local Wealthfare

An Act to End Business Extortion of Local Tax Giveaways

Robert W. Benson, Loyola Law School, Los Angeles, CA 90015 • website: http://www.greens.org/s-r/10/10-20.html

Business Incentives Reform Clearinghouse

c/o Corporation for Enterprise Development • 777 N. Capitol Street NE, Suite 800, Washington, DC 20002 • phone: (202) 408-9788 • fax: (202) 408-9793 • email: bi@cfed.org • website: http://www.cfed.org/sustainable_economies/business_incentives/research/bookshelf.html

Field of Schemes

by Joanna Cagan and Neil DeMouse (Monroe, ME: Common Courage Press, 1998).

Good Jobs First

1311 L Street NW, Washington, DC 20005 • phone: (202) 737-4315 • fax: (202) 638-3486 • email: info@goodjobsfirst.org • website: http://www.goodjobsfirst.org/gjf.htm

White-Collar Crime

Corporate Crime and Violence

by Russell Mokhiber (San Francisco, CA: Sierra Club Books, 1989).

Corporate Crime Reporter

1209 National Press Building, Washington, DC 20045 • phone: (202) 737-1680 • website: http://www.corporatecrimereporter.com/

Crackers, the Corporate Crime Chicken

website: http://www.dogeatdogfilms.com/tv/cracker.html

National White Collar Crime Center
7401 Beaufont Springs Drive, Suite 300, Richmond, VA 23225-5504 • website: http://www.nw3c.org/index.html

Prison Labor

Coalition Against the American Correctional Association
c/o PDAG • PO Box 40683, Philadelphia, PA 19107 • phone: (215) 724-6120, ext. 3 • email: prisons@stoptheaca.net • website: www.stoptheaca.net

Critical Resistance: Struggling to End the Prison Industrial Complex
1904 Franklin Street, Suite 504, Oakland, CA 94612 • phone: (510) 444-0484 • fax: (510) 444-2177 • email: crnational@criticalresistance.org • website: http://www.criticalresistance.org

Prison Activist Resource Center
PO Box 339, Berkeley, CA 94701 • phone: (510) 893-4648 • fax: (510) 893-4607 • email:parc@prisonactivist.org • website: http://www.prisonactivist.org/index.shtml • prison labor page: http://www.prisonactivist.org/prison-labor/

PrisonSucks.com
Research on the crime control industry • c/o Prison Policy Initiative • PO Box 20038, Cincinnati, OH 45220 • email: staff@prisonpolicy.org • website: http://www.prisonsucks.com/

Automobile Subsidies

America's Autos on Welfare
http://www.sierraclub.org/sprawl/articles/subsidies.asp

Asphalt Nation: How the Automobile Took Over America and How We Can Take It Back
by Jane Holtz Kay (New York: Crown Publishers, 1997; pbk., Berkeley: University of California Press, 1998).

Auto-Free Ottawa
797 Somerset Street West, Suite 103, Ottawa, K1R 6R3, Canada • phone: +1 (613) 237-1549 • email: afo-info@flora.org • "The Full Costs Of The Car I –V," a collection of excerpts and articles • website: http://www.flora.org/afo/cc0.html

Car Busters Magazine
Kratka 26, 100 00 Praha 10, Czech Republic • email: info@carbusters.org • website: http://www.carbusters.org/

Carfree Cities
by J.H. Crawford (Utrecht, Netherlands: International Books, 2000) • email: mailbox@carfree.com • website: http://www.carfree.com/

Appendix A

Welfare for the Poor
($193 billion a year)

Federal expenditures on welfare for the poor total about $193 billion for fiscal year 2004. There are two basic categories of benefits: those that go exclusively to the poor (or are supposed to) and those that go partially to the poor. The following programs fall into the first group.

FOOD STAMPS • $27.7 BILLION

This program was severely cut back by the 1996 welfare "reform" bill, and was whacked again in 1999 to help pay for the war in Kosovo. In constant dollars, it's now 10% lower than it was eight years ago, when we were in the middle of an economic boom.

TANF (TEMPORARY AID TO NEEDY FAMILIES) • $16.8 BILLION

(The same as 1999 funding, though three million jobs have since been lost.) This program replaced the core welfare program AFDC (Aid to Families with Dependent Children), which was essentially abolished by the 1996 welfare "reform" bill. Welfare money now goes from Washington to the states in block grants. During the late '90s boom, states moved so many families off the program (many because of "technicalities" like being late for an appointment) that there was over $7.4 billion in unspent funds. Both Congress and the states were creative in finding ways to transfer this money to other programs. During the recession, of course, unspent funds dwindled, and 35 states have cut various TANF-funded programs.

HOUSING ASSISTANCE • $17.2 BILLION

Section 8 helps families living in private housing keep their rent below 30% of their income (at a cost of $12.5 billion a year), but the White House is proposing to transfer this program to the states as well. (That is, it will allocate the money as block grants and generally loosen regulations on how the money can be spent. Also, the grants are for specified amounts, whereas a federal entitlement is funded on the basis of need, or in other words, how many people apply for it.) Another program subsidizes rents for people living in public housing projects (at $4.7 billion a year). Between them, the programs cost about half of the $32 billion in wealthfare rich homeowners receive (as described in Chapter 2), and end up benefiting the landlords and developers who get the money as well as the tenants who get the housing.

WIC (SPECIAL SUPPLEMENTAL NUTRITION PROGRAM FOR WOMEN, INFANTS, AND CHILDREN) • $4.7 BILLION (down from $8 billion in 1996)

WIC provides poor women and children with vouchers for nutritional counseling, referrals to other programs, and some food items. WIC isn't an entitlement program; it's offered only if funds are available. Many states have waiting lists of people who want to get on WIC.

HEAD START • $6.8 BILLION

Since 1965, Head Start has provided preschool readiness programs along with health and nutrition services to children whose families live below the poverty line. Head Start has never been funded well enough to serve everyone who qualifies for it; currently, it serves only about 60%. The 2004 allocation will drop 28,000 children from the rolls. Though it is regarded as one of the most successful federal programs in history, the White House would like to convert Head Start into a block grant program for the states to administer. As the experience with TANF shows, this can lead to various parts of the program being dismantled.

LOW-INCOME ENERGY ASSISTANCE • $1.7 BILLION

This program provides funds for heating, cooling, and other weather-related and emergency needs for families at or below 110% of the poverty line. (Some states provide funding beyond the federal government's.)

LEGAL SERVICES CORPORATION • $352 MILLION

Legal Services helps poor people deal with civil—not criminal—matters like divorces, consumer fraud, housing, jobs, education, and entitlement benefits.

These programs total about $75.2 billion (again, 10% below 1996 levels, adjusted for inflation), and we can count that entire amount as welfare for the poor. For five other programs, things are more complicated.

The largest of these is Medicaid, which cost $176 billion in FY2004—more than double the 1996 figure of $82 billion, due to soaring medical costs. (I don't count Medicare because it provides medical care for the elderly regardless of income.)

Medicaid pays medical bills for poor people and for blind, disabled, or elderly people whose medical costs exceed their income, no matter what that income is. (With nursing homes now costing $40,000 a year or more, you don't have to be poor not to be able to afford medical care.)

In theory, you're not eligible for Medicaid if you have more than $4,000 in assets, but your house doesn't count; nor do your spouse's assets or income. You can even transfer up to $70,000 of your assets to your spouse, as well as $1,800 a month ($21,600 a year) of your own income. These loopholes led *Consumers' Research* magazine to call Medicaid "one of the largest middle-class entitlement programs on the books."

Even millionaires can receive Medicaid benefits, simply by transferring assets to their children three years before applying (although this could cost a lot in gift taxes). An entire industry has sprung up to run seminars that teach people how to mine Medicaid.

According to the Coalition on Human Needs, Medicaid does not cover many poor Americans: "Medicaid is no longer an automatic service for low-income people. In particular, the 1996 TANF reforms severed the automatic link between cash assistance and Medicaid eligibility for parents of eligible children." In particular, poor people without children often fall between the cracks of the system.[1]

In addition, a lot of Medicaid money goes to pharmaceutical companies, makers of medical equipment, hospital owners, doctors, and other wealthy people who are famous for overcharging for their products and services (and that's not even considering Medicaid fraud). So even when Medicaid recipients are actually poor, a large part of the program's funding ends up going to wealthy price gougers.

Then there's SSI (Supplemental Security Income), which comes to $34.2 billion in FY2004. SSI is supposed to provide a guaranteed income to blind, disabled, or elderly people with limited assets and low incomes, but the means testing is similar to that under Medicaid. (Your spouse's income does count, but not unearned income from investments; your house doesn't count, regardless of what it's worth.)

Pell grants, a federally funded scholarship program, cost $11.4 billion in FY2000. These funds are available to undergraduate students whose families make $30,000 a year or less and have a net worth of up to $85,000. This doesn't make them well-to-do, but since the median net worth of US households is $37,587—or was, in 1993—even households that are quite a bit richer than average qualify for Pell grants.

The Earned Income Tax Credit (EITC) is a $4.9 billion tax break that applies only to the working poor who make enough money to pay taxes. As such, it's also wealthfare, because it allows some companies to get away with paying their employees less than a living wage (since the EITC supplements that wage). And it does nothing for the chronically unemployed.

Finally, there are the School Lunch and School Breakfast Programs, which run to $8.5 billion in FY2004. Started in 1946, they serve about half of all school-aged children; in 1993, 48% of the households participating were below the poverty line. (Thirty-three million Americans, or 11.7%— including 16.3% of all children—live at or below the poverty line. That threshold is currently set at an annual income of $14,255 for a family of three, or $17,960 for a family of four. The average income of a poor family is about half of the poverty threshold.)

So, how are we going to figure out what portion of Medicaid, SSI, Pell grants, EITC, and school lunches should count as welfare for the poor? There isn't a clear answer for any of these programs, and of course there's also the question of where to draw the line for what we call "poor."

If the focus of this book were welfare for the poor, rather than welfare for the rich, I would have analyzed this issue more thoroughly, but since it isn't, my best estimate is that half the money spent on this second category of programs should be counted.

If that seems too low to you, feel free to pick another percentage. But one thing is clear: 100% is too high. There's no way these programs serve the poor exclusively.

These five programs cost a total of about $235 billion a year, and half of that is $117.5 billion. Add the $75.2 billion spent on programs that serve the poor exclusively, and you get $192.7 billion as a total for welfare for the poor (let's call it an even $193 billion).[2]

And just to remind you, we're shelling out at least $815 billion a year in welfare for the rich, more than four times as much as welfare for the poor.

ACTIVIST'S TOOLKIT

Center for Community Change
1000 Wisconsin Avenue NW, Washington, DC 20007 • phone: (202) 342-0519 • email: info@communitychange.org • website: http://www.communitychange.org/default.asp

Center on Hunger and Poverty
The Heller School for Social Policy and Management, Brandeis University • Mailstop 077, Waltham, MA 02454-9110 • phone: (781) 736-8885 • fax: (781) 736-3925 • email: hunger@brandeis.edu • website: http://www.centeronhunger.org/

Economic Apartheid in America: A Primer on Economic Inequality & Insecurity
by Chuck Collins, Felice Veskel, and United for a Fair Economy (New York: the New Press, 2000).

Inequality.org
phone: (212) 894-3704, ext. 2487 • email: info@inequality.org • website: http://www.inequality.org/

Institute for Research on Poverty

University of Wisconsin-Madison, 1180 Observatory Drive, 3412 Social Science Building, Madison, WI 53706-1393 • phone: (608) 262-6358 • fax: (608) 265-3119 • website: http://www.ssc.wisc.edu/irp/

National Center on Poverty Law

111 N. Wabash, Suite 500, Chicago, IL 60602 • phone: (312) 263-3830 • fax: (312) 263-3846 • website: http://www.povertylaw.org/

Northwestern University Institute for Policy Research

2046 Sheridan Road, Evanston, IL 60208 • phone: (847) 491-3395 • fax: (847) 467-2459 • email: ipr@northwestern.edu • website: http://www.jcpr.org/

The Politics of Rich and Poor

by Kevin Phillips (New York: Random House, 1990).

Poverty & Race Research Action Council

3000 Connecticut Avenue NW, Suite 200, Washington, DC 20008 • phone: (202) 387-9887 • fax: (202) 387-0764 • email: info@prrac.org • website: http://www.prrac.org/abtprrac.htm

University of Chicago Harris Graduate School of Public Policy Studies

1155 E. 60th Street, Chicago, IL 60637 • phone: (773) 702-0472 • fax: (773) 702-0926 • email: jcpr@uchicago.edu • website: http://www.jcpr.org/

The War on the Poor: A Defense Manual

by Randy Albelda, Nancy Folbre, and the Center for Popular Economics (New York: The New Press, 1996).

Wealth and Democracy

by Kevin Phillips (New York: Broadway Books, 2002).

Welfare Information Network

A project of the Finance Project • 1401 New York Avenue NW, Suite 800, Washington, DC 20005 • phone: (202) 587-1000 • fax: (202) 628-4205 • website: http://www.financeprojectinfo.org/win/

Appendix B
Glossary

amortization

When you amortize something, you spread the cost of it over time—either in reality or in your calculations. Say you're thinking of installing a solar water-heating system. You might amortize the cost by dividing it by the monthly savings you expect to get on your utility bill. This would give you the number of months until payback—the point at which the system would begin saving you money. (To be accurate, you'd also have to figure in the interest you'd lose on the money you spent on the system, and that therefore couldn't be invested somewhere else.)

With mortgages, the cost of a house (or whatever) plus interest on the loan are amortized into a series of monthly payments. *Depreciation* is another form of amortization.

averages

When you use the word average in everyday speech, you're usually talking about the mean, which you get by adding up all the numbers and dividing by how many numbers there are. But there are two other kinds of averages—the median and the mode—and they sometimes give a more accurate picture of what we're actually thinking of when we say "average."

Let's say we're doing a survey of incomes in Brunei (a little oil-producing enclave carved out of Borneo Island by the British). To make things simple, let's say that Brunei only has 11 inhabitants: the sultan, who makes $1 billion a year; two counselors to the sultan, who make $100,000 a year; three merchants, who make $10,000 a year; and five laborers, who make $1,000 a year.

To get the mean, we add up everyone's annual income ($1 billion + $200,000 + $30,000 + $5,000) and divide by 11; this comes to an average annual income of about $91 million. But it's obviously misleading to say that the average person in our hypothetical Brunei makes $91 million a year, since nobody makes anything like that amount—the sultan makes much more, and everybody else makes much less. That's where the median and the mode come in.

The median is the middle value in the distribution, the one halfway between the top and the bottom. Since there are 11 inhabitants, we're looking for the sixth income counting from either the top or the bottom, the one with five incomes above it and five below it. As you can see from the chart below, this makes the median income $10,000.

In this case, the median obviously gives a much better idea of the average income than the mean does. (It does the same when we're talking about incomes in the United States. If you use the mean instead of the median, huge incomes at the top skew it upward and give a misleadingly optimistic picture of what the average American actually makes.)

The mode is the value that occurs the most frequently. In this distribution, it's $1,000, since five laborers make that amount and no more than three people make any other amount. The mode is the value you'd get most often if you picked inhabitants at random and asked them to tell you their incomes. (In fact, $1,000 is the answer you'd get 45% of the time.)

So in this example, the mode also provides a much better idea of the average than the mean does. (The mode isn't typically at the bottom of the distribution, by the way; often it's near the median.)

Here's our example in chart form:

Income	Mean, Median, and Mode Values
$1,000,000,000	
	←mean ($90,930,455)
$100,000	
$100,000	
$10,000	
$10,000	
$10,000	←median
$1,000	
$1,000	
$1,000	} ←mode
$1,000	
$1,000	

billion

Numbers in the billions contain three commas. A billion dollars is a thousand times more than a *million* dollars. It's equal to a stack of crisp, new dollar bills 12 times as high as the Empire State Building.

If you laid those dollar bills end to end, they'd stretch from New York to Los Angeles and back 16 times, and you'd still have enough left over to go from New York to Mexico City and back.

Let's say you took a road trip. If you really pushed it, you might be able to drive an average of 12 hours a day (not counting gas stops, meals, sleep, etc.). If you drove seven days a week and averaged 65 miles per hour while moving, it would take you almost four months to drive past a billion dollar bills. A billion dollars would buy two months of health insurance for every uninsured child in the United States.

But a billion dollars is nothing compared to a *trillion* dollars.

black budgets

Both the Pentagon and the various intelligence agencies have secret "black budgets" that are completely off the books. Despite a Supreme Court ruling to the contrary, black budgets clearly violate the US Constitution, which states that "no money shall be drawn from the Treasury, but in consequence of appropriations made by law," and requires that the government publish a "regular statement… of the receipts and expenditures of all public money."

bonds

Bonds are basically IOUs—promises to pay back funds with interest. Unlike *stocks,* they don't give you a piece of the company, but they're much less risky. If the bond issuer defaults, you are guaranteed a place in line at the bankruptcy court before any stockholders. When you "float a bond," you're borrowing money to finance some incredibly expensive undertaking like a bridge or a hospital or a bunch of huge tax breaks for your campaign contributors.

COLA

COLA is an acronym for "cost of living adjustment"—typically an increase in pensions or salaries to account for inflation.

Congressional Black Caucus

This policy-planning group consists of the African American members of Congress.

constant dollars

Due to *inflation* (or rarely, *deflation*), the value of a dollar is always changing. So if you contrast how much something cost in, say, 1980 with how much it costs today, you're not going to get an accurate comparison. The way around that is to pick what the dollar was worth in a given year and make that the standard. Then you can say, "The project was expected to cost $2.3 billion in 1980, but ended up costing $7.8 billion (in 1980 dollars)."

consumer price index
According to the US government's Bureau of Labor Statistics, "The Consumer Price Indexes (CPI) program produces monthly data on changes in the prices paid by urban consumers for a representative basket of goods and services." There is no explanation for what might constitute a "basket of services."

cost overruns
This is Pentagon speak for "cheating." It means that Boeing or Lockheed is charging you a whole lot more for their airplanes than they originally said they would. But hey, close enough for government work!

credit — see *tax credit*

debt
The federal debt is the cumulative figure for how much the government owes at a given point in time (in other words, it's the total of all the *deficits,* minus any surpluses). On the last day of 2003, the national debt stood at approximately $6.96 trillion, increasing at a rate of $1.91 billion per day. You can get the current figure at the National Debt Clock, http://www.brillig.com/debt_clock/. Compare *deficit.*

deduction — see *tax deduction*

deficit
The federal budget deficit is the amount that expenditures exceed revenues in a given fiscal year. The federal budget deficit for FY2003 was a record $374.2 billion, projected to rise to about half a trillion for FY2004. Compare *debt.*

deflation
Deflation occurs when, over time, a given amount of money is able to buy more and more things. Compare *inflation.*

depreciation
Depreciation allows you to deduct a certain part of the cost of an asset from your taxable income each year, supposedly to allow for the decrease in that asset's value as it ages. (Thus, it's a kind of *amortization.*) Depreciation schedules tell you how much you can take off each year; they vary with the type of property and with changes in the tax code.

depression

A depression is simply a really bad *recession*. (There isn't a generally agreed on benchmark for when a recession becomes a depression, but some people say it's when unemployment reaches 20 %.)

earned income

This is the money you make by the sweat of your brow, so to speak. If you receive a paycheck, whether it's for wages or a salary, that counts as earned income. Enjoy it! Compare *unearned income*.

entitlement

An *entitlement* is a federal program (like Social Security) whose funding rises and falls with need. Its budget level does not have to be appropriated by Congress. It is simply spent every year, based on how many retired people (or unemployed people, or so on) there happen to be that year. Welfare used to be an entitlement, but since 1996, it's been part of the *discretionary budget*, which means that Congress decides every year how much money to spend on it.

family — see *household*

federal debt or deficit — see *debt* or *deficit*

fiscal year

A fiscal year is any 12-month period an organization (a corporation, governmental entity, or whatever) uses for its budgets. It can be the same as a calendar year (January 1 to December 31) but often isn't.

The federal government's fiscal years begin on October 1 and are named after the calendar year in which they end. Thus, fiscal year 1996 (typically abbreviated FY96) began October 1, 1995, and ended September 30, 1996.

GDP — see *gross domestic product*

general fund revenues

These include all federal revenues except for entitlement programs like Social Security and Medicare, which aren't discretionary and are provided for by separate trust funds (at least they were separate before greedy politicians got their hands on them). Combining entitlements with general fund revenues is a trick politicians play to hide how much money they're spending on discretionary items like the military budget.

GNP — see *gross national product*

gross domestic product
The gross domestic product (GDP) is the total market value of the goods and services brought into final use in a nation in a certain period of time (usually a year). It became the official measure of the US economy in 1991, replacing the *gross national product.*

This change brought us in line with the way most other industrialized nations figure it, thus making comparisons easier. (For the United States, the GDP and the GNP are very similar.)

gross national product
The gross national product (GNP) is the *gross domestic product* plus income earned by the nation's residents from foreign investments, minus income earned by foreign investors in the domestic market. In other words, the GNP measures what's produced by a nation's citizens, regardless of where they're located.

household
The Census Bureau distinguishes between a household (any group of people living together) and a family (an "economic unit" joined by marriage). That's why figures for median household income (or net worth) are different from those for family income (or net worth).

House Progressive Caucus
This policy-planning group consists of the most left-wing or liberal members of the House of Representatives.

income disparity
As the term implies, this is a measure of how evenly or unevenly income is distributed among people in a particular group (usually a nation). Of course, there can be different kinds of income disparity. In Saudi Arabia, for example, few people are really poor and a relatively small group makes tons of money.

In the United States, many more people are poor and many more are rich (although few make as much as the richest Saudis). These varieties of income distribution complicate the question of how to measure income disparity, but if you just want to know if a nation has a lot of income disparity or a little, it usually isn't hard to tell.

income taxes
Unlike payroll taxes, income taxes are theoretically *progressive,* meaning that the wealthier you get, the higher percentage you have to pay. But if

you've read this whole book, you know it doesn't always work out that way. Compare *payroll taxes.*

inflation

Inflation occurs when, over time, a given amount of money is able to buy fewer and fewer things. Compare *deflation.*

mean — see *averages*

means testing

Means testing is figuring out how much money someone has to determine eligibility for a welfare program that's only supposed to be open to people with low incomes and few assets.

median — see *averages*

million

Numbers in the millions contain two commas. A million dollars is a thousand times more than a thousand dollars. Laid end to end, a million dollar bills would stretch almost 95 miles. Imagine yourself driving by them. You're doing 65 miles per hour, so they're just a blur by the side of the road. Still, it takes you almost an hour and a half to get past all those bills. A million dollars would buy one day of school for 53,000 students.

But a million dollars is nothing compared to a *billion* dollars.

mode — see *averages*

multinational — see *transnational*

negative tax rate

When your company (or your personage) is more profitable after taxes than before, congratulations, you're enjoying a negative tax rate.

PAC

A PAC (political action committee) is just a way to get around limits on campaign contributions. Also, by bundling many small-to-medium-sized donations, PACs have more influence. A politician may not know—or care—what industry you're associated with if you send in a $100 donation, but that's never the case when $5,000 or $10,000 comes from a PAC.

payroll taxes

These are the taxes withheld from your paycheck under the category of "FICA." They pay for your Social Security and Medicare benefits. Unlike *income taxes,* poor people pay a higher percentage of their income in payroll taxes than rich people do. Go figure.

perk
A perk—short for perquisite—is an extra benefit, beyond a salary, that someone gets by virtue of being in a certain job (or unpaid position). For example, a company pays for a business flight, but the employee who makes the flight gets the frequent flyer miles. (Fringe benefit means almost the same thing as perk, but a perk is much more likely to be an unofficial benefit that isn't explicitly stated anywhere.)

prime rate
Theoretically, the prime rate is the lowest interest a bank charges (on money it lends to its best customers). More typically, it's an arbitrary benchmark to which other interest rates are pegged.

progressive tax
With a progressive tax, the more money you make, the higher the percentage of it you pay in taxes. US *income taxes* are supposed to be progressive. Compare *regressive tax*.

recession
A recession is usually defined as a decline in general business activity (as measured by the GDP) that goes on for at least two or three quarters (that is, for six to nine months). When a recession is really bad, it's called a *depression*.

regressive tax
With a regressive tax, the less money you make, the higher the percentage of it you pay in taxes. Many new tax proposals—as well as many existing provisions—are in fact regressive (the Social Security tax is a good example). Compare *progressive tax*.

revenues
Money coming in to the government. See also *general fund revenues*.

stocks
Stocks are sort of like IOUs where you never really know what you're going to be paid back—if anything. Their value rises and falls depending on how many investors are buying or selling them. Unlike *bonds,* they do allow you to own piece of the company, but they're much riskier. Of course, that risk also entails the possibility of huge capital gains. But if the company goes belly up, you don't have a great deal of protection (unless its executives have defrauded their shareholders, in which case, have fun in the legal system). Compare *bonds*.

tax credit

A tax credit lets you subtract an expense from the taxes you owe, not merely from your taxable income (as a *tax deduction* does). Depending on your tax bracket, a credit is currently worth about two to seven times more than a deduction of the same size. Compare *tax deduction.*

tax deduction

A tax deduction lets you subtract an expense from the income you report on your tax return. Compare *tax credit.*

transnational

A transnational—or multinational—is simply a corporation that operates in more than one country. Typically, however, the term is used to refer to the larger corporations, which are richer than many countries and more powerful than most. (I prefer the term transnationals to multinationals because it's better at giving the flavor of how these corporations soar over and subsume mere nations.)

trillion

Numbers in the trillions contain four commas. A trillion dollars is a thousand times more than a *billion* dollars and a million times more than a *million* dollars.

A trillion dollars is equal to a stack of crisp, new dollar bills almost 3,000 miles high. If you laid that pile down on its side, packed tightly together, it would stretch from New York to Los Angeles.

If you took that same trillion dollars in dollar bills and laid it down end to end, it would stretch from New York to Los Angeles and back about 17,000 times—or from the earth to the sun and then around it.

If President George W. Bush were laid end to end 2 trillion times, he would stretch to the sun and back 13 times. He might choose to do this at night, when it's cooler (thanks to collegenews.org for that one).

If you started a business the day Christ was born and it lost a million dollars a day, you'd still have more than 700 years to go before you lost a trillion dollars. A trillion dollars would buy 454 B-2 stealth bombers—which is pretty pathetic, when you think about it.

unearned income

This is the money you get by living off of your investments. If you collect a capital gain or a dividend (no matter how much work you had to do to be a smart investor), that counts as unearned. Nothing personal. Compare *earned income.*

Endnotes

INTRODUCTION

1 Office of Management and Budget, *Fiscal Year 2004 Budget of the United States* (Washington, DC: GPO, 2003).

2 Wait, the federal debt just got higher while you read this. For an update, see the National Debt Clock, http://www.brillig.com/debt_clock/.

3 Mark Zepezauer and Arthur Naiman, *Take the Rich off Welfare* (Tucson, AZ: Odonian Press, 1996).

4 You can always do this for yourself at http://data.bls.gov/cgi-bin/cpicalc.pl.

5 Stop Corporate Welfare, press release, January 28, 1997.

6 Editorial, *Wall Street Journal,* "Highway Robbery," March 31, 1998.

7 See Zepezauer and Naiman, *Take the Rich,* 1996 ed., table of contents.

8 Jim Riccio, telephone interview, January 2000.

9 Jonathan Chait, "Manservant," *The New Republic Online,* December 5, 2003, http://www.tnr.com/doc.mhtml?i=20031 215&s=trb121503.

10 Chuck Collins, Betsy Leonder-Wright, and Holly Sklar, *Shifting Fortunes: The Perils of the Growing American Wealth Gap* (Boston, MA: United for a Fair Economy, 1999).

11 Lois Stevens, "Speaking Out for Head Start," *Entry Point: The Quarterly Newsletter of RESULTS,* Summer 1996, 1.

12 Donald L. Barlett and James B. Steele, *America: Who Really Pays the Taxes* (New York: Touchstone Books, 1994), 140.

13 Citizens for Tax Justice, "Corporate Tax Payments Near Record Low This Year," March 15, 2002, http://www.ctj.org/html/corp0302.htm; see also David R. Francis, "Bye-Bye Corporate Tax Revenues," *Christian Science Monitor,* November 3, 1999.

14 Joel Friedman, "The Decline of Corporate Income Tax Revenues," Center on Budget and Policy Priorities Report, October 24, 2003, http://www.cbpp.org/10-16-03tax.htm.

15 William Greider, *Who Will Tell the People* (New York: Touchstone Books, 1992), 80.

16 Edward N. Wolff, "Time for a Wealth Tax?" *Boston Review*, February/March 1996, http://www.bostonreview.net/BR21.1/wolff.html.

17 Collins, Leonder-Wright, and Sklar, *Shifting Fortunes.*

18 Paul Krugman, "What the Public Doesn't Know Can't Hurt Us," *Washington Monthly,* October 1995, 8–12.

19 See interactive chart, "The Richest Americans," *Forbes.com,* http://www.forbes.com/2002/09/13/rich400land.html.

20 Economic Policy Institute, "Datazone," http://www.epinet.org/content.cfm/datazone_index.

21 Children's Defense Fund, press release, August 22, 1999.

22 Barlett and Steele, *America,* 216–19.

23 American Horse Council, "Tax Bill Includes Provisions Beneficial to Horse Industry," press release, June 2002.

24 Barlett and Steele, *America,* 140.

25 US Census Bureau, *Statistical Abstract of the US, 2002,* (Washington, DC: GPO, 2003).

26 The economic "boom" of the 1990s essentially returned wages back to 1964 levels—that is, $277.54 a week in January 1964, and $277.55 a week in April 2003 (both figures in constant dollars). See US Bureau of Labor Statistics, http://146.142.4.24/cgi-bin/dsrv?ee (choose "seasonally adjusted," "average weekly earnings, 1982 dollars," "total private," and "all years").

27 Barlett and Steele, *America,* 53–55.

28 Billionaires for Bush (or Gore), "Attention Billionaires," http://www.billionairesforbushorgore.com.

29 Center on Budget and Policy Priorities, "Bearing Most of the Burden," research paper, November 26, 1996, http://www.cbpp.org/104TH.htm.

1—SOCIAL SECURITY

1   Ronnie Dugger, *On Reagan: The Man and His Presidency* (New York: McGraw Hill, 1983), 111.
2   Greider, *Who Will Tell,* 92 (see introduction, n. 15).
3   Barlett and Steele, *America,* 104 (see introduction, n. 12).
4   Jared Bernstein, Lawrence Mishel, and Chauna Brocht, "Any Way You Cut It: Income Inequality on the Rise Regardless of How It's Measured," Economic Policy Institute, briefing paper, September 2000, http://www.epinet.org/content.cfm/briefingpapers_inequality_inequality.
5   Barbara Ehrenreich, "Helping the Rich Stay That Way," *Time,* April 18, 1994, 86.
6   Harry Figgie Jr. and Gerald Swanson, *Bankruptcy 1995: The Coming Collapse of America and How to Stop It,* 3rd ed. (New York: Little, Brown and Company, 1993), 57.
7   Barlett and Steele, *America,* 100.
8   Gareth G. Davis and D. Mark Wilson, *The Impact of Removing Social Security's Tax Cap on Wages* (Washington, DC: Heritage Foundation, 1999).

2—HOMEOWNER TAX BREAKS

1   See Vicki Kemper, "Home Inequities," *Common Cause Magazine,* Summer 1994, 14.
2   Peter G. Peterson, *Facing Up* (New York: Simon & Schuster, 1993), 110.
3   Robert McIntyre, *Tax Expenditures: The Hidden Entitlements* (Washington, DC: Citizens for Tax Justice, 1996), 43.
4   Joint Committee on Taxation, *Estimates of Federal Tax Expenditures for Fiscal Years 2000–2004* (Washington, DC: GPO, 1999).
5   Robert J. Shapiro, *Cut-and-Invest, Vol. II, A Budget Strategy for the New Economy* (Washington, DC: Progressive Policy Institute, 1995).

3—RUNAWAY PENSIONS

1   Gareth G. Cook, "The Pension Time Bomb," *Washington Monthly*, January/February 1995, 17–20.

2   Cook, "Pension Time Bomb."
3   Cook, "Pension Time Bomb."
4   National Center for Policy Analysis, "Federal Spending and the Budget: Excessive Cost-of-Living Increases," http://www.ncpa.org/pd/budget/jan97d.html.
5   Cook, "Pension Time Bomb."
6   John Crawley, "Pension Shortfalls at US Firms Double," *truthout issues,* September 4, 2003, http://www.truthout.org/docs_03/090503J.shtml.
7   *Associated Press*, "Deficit at Pension Insurance Agency Soars," *New York Times,* October 14, 2003, http://www.afponline.org/ohc/102203/228_article_5/228_article_5.html.
8   Robert J. Samuelson, "The Pension Time Bomb," *Washington Post,* July 16, 2002.
9   Crawley, "Pension Shortfalls."
10 Samuelson, "Pension Time Bomb."
11 Albert B. Crenshaw, "Business Pushing Pension Change," *Washington Post,* September 2, 2003.
12 See Robert Kuttner, "The Great American Pension-Fund Robbery," *Business Week,* September 8, 2003, 24.
13 Editorial, *Madison Capital Times,* "Corporate America: Too Lean, Too Mean,", August 3, 2003.
14 Samuelson, "Pension Time Bomb."

4—TRANSNATIONAL TAX

1   William Shakespeare, *Julius Caesar,* 1.2.135–38.
2   Jim Hightower, "Corporate Tax Cheats," *Texas Observer,* March 28, 2003, http:// www.alternet.org/story.html?StoryID =15299.
3   Byron Dorgan, "Global Shell Game: How Corporations Operate Tax Free," *Washington Monthly,* July/August 2000, 33–36.
4   McIntyre, *Tax Expenditures,* 23 (see chap. 2, n. 3).
5   Barlett and Steele, *America,* 190 (see introduction, n. 12).
6   McIntyre, *Tax Expenditures,* 24; Office of Management and Budget, *Fiscal Year 2000 Budget of the United States* (Washington, DC: GPO, 1999); and Joint Committee on Taxation, *Tax Expenditures* (see chap. 2, n. 4).

7 Office of Management and Budget, *Fiscal Year 2004 Budget* (see introduction, n. 1).

8 Eni F. H. Faleomavaega, "Faleomavaega Cosponsors Legislation to Provide Federal Tax Preference for Businesses in American Samoa," press release, July 19, 2001, http://www.house.gov/apps/list/press/as00_faleomavaega/TaxPref.html.

9 Barlett and Steele, *America,* 183–89.

10 McIntyre, *Tax Expenditures,* 23.

11 Ralph Estes, *Who Pays? Who Profits? The Truth About the American Tax System* (Washington, DC: Institute for Policy Studies, 1993), 40.

12 Robert McIntyre, "Reality Check: Why the Bush Treasury Department's Line on Corporate Taxes Doesn't Track," *The American Prospect* 13, no. 23 (December 30, 2002): 19.

13 US Senate Permanent Subcommittee on Investigations, *What Is the U.S. Position on Offshore Tax Havens?* opening statement by Subcommittee Chair Carl Levin, 107th Cong., 1st sess., July 18, 2001, 1–4.

14 Senate Subcommittee, *Offshore Tax Havens,* testimony of Robert Morgenthau.

15 Colin Woodard, "Clean Beaches, Dirty Money," *The Bulletin of the Atomic Scientists* 56, no. 3 (May–June 2000): 18–20.

16 Arianna Huffington, "Tax Avoidance and a Tan," *Campaign for America's Future,* May 15, 2002, http://www.ourfuture.org/readarticle/.asp?ID=1385.

17 US House Democratic Policy Committee, "Offshore Corporate Tax Havens," press release, May 21, 2002.

18 Dan Ackman, "IRS Targets Offshore Chargers," *Forbes.com,* October 31, 2000, http://www.solami.com/IRSaccess.htm.

19 Roma Khanna, "Enron's Tax Records Lead Experts to Call for Change in Laws," *Houston Chronicle,* January 17, 2002, http://www.chron.com/cs/CDA/story.hts/special/enron/1216617.

20 Victor Cruz, "Miami Bankers Join Fight to Curtail Law Hurting US Deposits," *Miami Today,* August 23, 2001, http://www.miamitodaynews.com/news/010823/story3.shtml.

21 Chris Floyd, "Global Eye: Follow the Money," *Moscow Times* (Russia), September 28, 2001, http://www.blacksamba.com/articles/GlobalEyeFollowtheMoney.html.

22 Huffington, "Tax Avoidance."

23 House Committee, "Tax Havens."

24 McIntyre, *Tax Expenditures,* 56; and Office of Management and Budget, *Fiscal Year 2000 Budget.*

5—CAPITAL GAINS TAX

1 General discussion of this topic indebted to Robert McIntyre, *Tax Expenditures,* 14–21 (see chap. 2, n. 3).

2 Edward N. Wolff, cited in Mishal Lawrence, Jared Bernstein, and Heather Boushey, *The State of Working America, 2002–03* (Washington, DC: Economic Policy Institute, 2002), 286–89.

3 Barlett and Steele, *America* (see introduction, n. 12); Donald L. Barlett and James B. Steele, *America: What Went Wrong?* (Kansas City, MO: Andrews and McMeel, 1992), 216.

4 Citizens for Tax Justice, "Who Pays Capital Gains Taxes?" http://www.ctj.org/html/cgwp698.htm.

5 McIntyre, *Tax Expenditures,* 23.

6 Citizens for Tax Justice, "Top Federal Tax Rates since 1916," press release, June 1996.

7 Congressional Research Service, "Capital Gains Taxes: An Overview," report no. 96-769, August 30, 1999.

8 Joint Committee on Taxation, *Summary of Conference Agreement on HR 2,* document no. JCX-54-03, 108th Cong., 1st sess., May 22, 2003, 3, http:// www.depreciationbonus.org/pdf/JCT_Summary.pdf.

9 Office of Management and Budget, "Table 22–4: Tax Expenditures by Function," *Budget of the United States Government, 2002,* (Washington, DC: GPO, 2002), http://www.whitehouse.gov/omb/budget/fy2002/bud22_4.html.

10 McIntyre, *Tax Expenditures,* 20.

11 McIntyre, 19.

12 McIntyre, 20.

13 McIntyre, 20.

14 McIntyre, 18.
15 For the record, two years after the cut, employment had risen by 0.7% and economic growth by 0.2%—hardly a ringing endorsement of the stimulus theory.
16 Joint Committee on Taxation, "Table 1: Tax Expenditure Estimates by Budget Function, Fiscal Year 2003–2007," *Estimates of Federal Tax Expenditures for Fiscal Years 2003–2007* (Washington, DC: GPO, 2002), http:// www.nptaxpolicy.org/tax_expenditures/ jct_03-07.pdf.
17 Joint Committee on Taxation, *Estimated Budget Effects of the Conference Agreement for HR 2*, document no. JCX-55-03, 108ᵗʰ Cong., 1ˢᵗ sess., May 22, 2003, 1, http://www.house.gov/jct/ x-55-03.pdf.

6—ACCELERATED DEPRECIATION

1 General discussion of this topic indebted to McIntyre, *Tax Expenditures*, 11–14 (see chap. 2, n. 3).
2 Robert J. Shapiro, *Paying for Progress* (Washington, DC: Progressive Policy Institute, 1991).
3 McIntyre, *Tax Expenditures*, 12.
4 Cited in McIntyre, *Tax Expenditures*, 12–13.
5 McIntyre, *Tax Expenditures*, 12–13.
6 Ralph Nader, "Take U.S. Job Exporters off Corporate Welfare," press release, September 4, 1995.
7 Ralph Nader, "CEOs Demand Balanced Budget but Won't Give Up Corporate Welfare," press release, June 7, 1996.
8 McIntyre, *Tax Expenditures*, 13.
9 North Carolina Budget and Tax Center, "New Federal Bonus Depreciation Rules," fact sheet, http:// www.ncjustice.org/btc/ Fact_Sheet_2002_03.htm.
10 Joint Committee on Taxation, *Summary of Conference Agreement* (see chap 5. n. 8).
11 Robert Greenstein, Richard Kogan, and Andrew Lee, "Tax Policy Center and CBPP Analyses Show That House Tax Plan Would Be More Tilted toward the Very Wealthy—and More Expensive—

Than Bush Plan," Center on Budget and Policy Priorities, press release, May 21, 2003.

7—INSURANCE LOOPHOLES

1 Allan Sloan, "Deal of a Lifetime," *Newsweek,* October 23, 1995, 46–47.
2 Ellen E. Schultz and Theo Francis, "Worker Dies, Firm Profits," *Wall Street Journal,* April 19, 2002.
3 Lee A. Sheppard, "'Janitor' Insurance as a Tax Shelter," *Tax Notes,* September 25, 1995, 1526.
4 Tom Herman, "Tax Report," *Wall Street Journal,* February 21, 2001.
5 Thomas Kostigen, "IRS Curbs Corporate Life-Insurance," *CBS MarketWatch.com,* October 8, 2002, http://tearsheet.marketwatch.com/ mastercard/sophisticated_investor.asp.
6 L. M. Sixel, "Profiting from Death?" *Houston Chronicle,* April 16, 2002, A1.
7 L. M. Sixel, "Wal-Mart Lawsuit Blames Insurers," *Houston Chronicle,* September 11, 2002, business sec., 1.
8 Rahm Emanuel, press release, March 12, 2003, http://www.house.gov/ emanuel/pr_031203b.htm.
9 Gene Green, "Green Reintroduces Bill Forcing Corporate Disclosure of Life Insurance Policies," press release, http:// www.house.gov/green/nr020703.htm.
10 McIntyre, *Tax Expenditures*, 33–34 (see chap. 2, n. 3); and Office of Management and Budget, *Fiscal Year 2004 Budget* (see introduction, n. 1).
11 Center for Responsive Politics, cited in *Ouch! A Regular Bulletin on How Money in Politics Hurts,* no. 89, December 18, 2001.
12 J. Robert Hunter and Travis Plunkett, "The Truth about Terrorism Insurance: Wild Claims by Business Lobbyists Don't Hold Up Under Scrutiny," Consumer Federation of America, press release, April 17, 2003, http: //www.consumerfed.org/TRIA_report_ release.pdf.
13 Daniel Gross, "Bush's 300,000 Phony Construction Jobs," *Slate,* October 17, 2002, http://www.slate.msn.com/id/ 2072722/.
14 Michael Dugan, cited in Steven Rosenfeld, "The Selling of Terrorism

Insurance," *TomPaine.com,* November 20, 2002, http://www.tompaine.com/feature2.cfm/ID/6777/view/print.

15 *Associated Press*, "Congress Overwhelmingly Passes Terrorism Insurance Bill," *Concord Monitor,* November 20, 2002, http://www.concordmonitor.com/stories/market/bizstori2002/terrorism insurance_21y46y02_2002.shtml.

16 Ji H. Chong, "Terrorism Insurance Giveaway," Taxpayers for Common Sense, June 28, 2002, http://www.taxpayer.net/bailoutwatch/terrorisminsurance.htm.

8—MEALS/ENTERTAINMENT

1 Robert S. McIntyre, testimony before the Committee on the Budget, US House of Representatives, hearings on "Unnecessary Business Subsidies," 106th Cong., 2nd sess., June 30, 1999, http://frwebgate.access.gpo.gov/cgi-bin/getdoc.cgi?dbname=106_house_hearings&docid=f:57748.wais.

2 McIntyre, *Tax Expenditures,* 28 (see chap. 2, n. 3).

3 Joint Committee on Taxation, *General Explanation of Tax Legislation Enacted in the 107th Congress* (Washington, DC: GPO, 2003), http://www.nptaxpolicy.org/Tax%20Legislation/107th%20Congress/JCT-Summary-All107thCongressTax Legislation.pdf.

9—TAX-FREE MUNI BONDS

1 General discussion of this topic indebted to McIntyre, *Tax Expenditures,* 25–27 (see chap. 2, n. 3).

2 Joint Committee on Taxation, "Table 1" (see chap. 5, n. 16).

10—EXPORT SUBSIDIES

1 Office of Management and Budget, *Fiscal Year 2004 Budget* (see introduction, n. 1).

2 Ralph Nader, "Washington's Holiday Gift Exchange," press release, December 25, 1995.

3 Bruce Hamnes, "Trade Policy Statement: The Future of U.S.

Agricultural Export Programs," testimony of the US Wheat Associates before the Senate Subcommittee on Production and Price Competitiveness of the Committee on Agriculture, Nutrition, and Forestry, July 18, 2000, http://www.uswheat.org/marketnews.nsf/0/45ba2548a2b3b0118525691f00707de9?OpenDocument.

4 Janice Shields, *Aid for Foreign and US Corporations* (Washington, DC: Center for Study of Responsive Law, 1995); see also Stephen Moore and Dean Stansel, *Ending Corporate Welfare as We Know It* (Washington, DC: Cato Institute, 1995).

5 Philip Merrill, testimony before the Subcommittee on Foreign Operations, Committee on Appropriations, US House of Representatives, March 26, 2003, http://www.exim.gov/news/speeches/mar2603.html.

6 Bernie Sanders, "The Export-Import Bank: Corporate Welfare at Its Worst," *Common Dreams,* May 15, 2002, http://www.commondreams.org/views02/0515-09.htm.

7 Sanders, "Export-Import Bank."

8 Daphne Eviatar, "Public Money in the Pipeline," *Mother Jones* (January–February 2003), http://www.motherjones.com/news/outfront/2003/01/ma_216_01.html.

9 Office of Management and Budget, *Fiscal Year 2004 Budget.*

10 Moore and Stansel, *Ending Corporate Welfare;* Nader, "Washington's Holiday Gift Exchange"; and Ralph Nader, "Take US Job Exporters off Corporate Welfare," press release, September 4, 1995.

11 Janice Shields, "Overseas Private Investment Corporation," *Foreign Policy in Focus* 2, no. 17 (January 1997), http://www.fpif.org/briefs/vol2/v2n17opi_body.html.

12 Office of Management and Budget, *Fiscal Year 2004 Budget.*

11—MILITARY WASTE & FRAUD

1 Office of Management and Budget, *Fiscal Year 2003 Budget of the United States* (Washington, DC: GPO, 2002).

2 Center for Defense Information, "Last of the Big Time Spenders: US Military Budget Still the World's Largest, and Growing," http://www.cdi.org/budget/2004/world-military-spending.cfm.

3 CDI, "Big Time Spenders."

4 Federation of American Scientists, "Fast Facts," http://www.fas.org/asmp/fast_facts.htm.

5 War Resisters League, "The Federal Pie Chart," http://www.warresisters.org/piechart.htm.

6 War Resisters League "Pie Chart," (current military, $459 billion, plus veterans' benefits, $63 billion).

7 Center for Defense Information, *2001–2002 Military Almanac* (Washington, DC: Center for Defense Information, 2002), 34. Also at http://www.cdi.org/products/almanac0102.pdf.

8 Colman McCarthy, "Military Has Real Money, Fake Enemy," *National Catholic Reporter,* June 30, 1995, 20.

9 Keith Ashdown, "Military Spending: Everything and the Kitchen Sink," Taxpayers for Common Sense, http://www.progress.org/archive/tcs26.htm.

10 Anthony Lewis, "The Defense Anomaly," *New York Times,* January 22, 1996.

11 McCarthy, "Military Has Real Money."

12 Joel Brinkley, "Auditors Say U.S. Agencies Lose Track of Billions," *New York Times,* October 13, 2002.

13 Colleen O'Connor, "The Waste Goes On—And On and On," *Nation,* October 4, 1993, 350–51.

14 Christopher Cerf and Henry Beard, *The Pentagon Catalog* (New York: Workman, 1986) 5, 8, 9, 11-15, 18, 22, 24-27, 44, 46.

15 Project on Government Oversight, "Defense Contractor Spare Parts Ripoffs Make Comeback," press release, November 17, 2000, http://www.pogo.org/p/defense/da-001122-reform.htm.

16 Project on Government Oversight, "Pentagon Parts Prices Balloon," press release, September 2, 1999.

17 Donald H. Rumsfeld, "Defense for the 21st Century," *Washington Post,* May 22, 2003; see also Project on Government Oversight, "Concern over Rumsfeld Transformation Grows," press release, May 13, 2003, http://www.pogo.org/p/defense/da-030502-defense.html.

18 Linda Rothstein, Lauren Spain, and Danielle Gordon, "A Sense of Proportion," *Bulletin of the Atomic Scientists* 51, no. 5 (September–October 1995): 32–33, http://www.thebulletin.org/issues/1995/so95/so95.mil-spending.html#anchor1566271.

19 Project on Government Oversight, "Federal Contractor Misconduct: Failures of the Suspension and Debarment System," http://www.pogo.org/p/contracts/co-020505-contractors.html.

20 On GE procurement and mail fraud, see General Accounting Office, *Defense Procurement Fraud, Information on Plea Agreements and Settlements* (Washington, DC: GPO, September 1992). On 1961 GE case, see Russell Mokhiber, *Corporate Crime and Violence* (San Francisco: Sierra Club Books, 1989), 219. On 1977 to first 1985 case, see Greider, *Who Will Tell,* 350–52 (see introduction, n. 15). On the second 1985 case, see Andy Pasztor, *When the Pentagon Was for Sale* (New York: Simon & Schuster, 1995), 31. On the 1989 and 1990 cases, see Greider, *Who Will Tell.* On the 1992 to 2001 cases, see CleanUpGE.org, "GE Misdeeds," http://www.cleanupge.org/gemisdeeds.html.

21 John Holusha, "Delay in Martin Marietta's Purchase of GE Unit," *New York Times,* January 23, 1993.

22 Project on Government Oversight, "Federal Contractor Misconduct."

23 Nathan Newman, "Three Strikes and You're Rich," *Progressive Populist,* http://www.populist.com/02.3.newman.html.

24 Pasztor, *When the Pentagon,* 37–38.

25 Pasztor, *When the Pentagon,* 366.

26 Howard Banks, "Aerospace and Defense," *Forbes,* January 2, 1995, 126–27, and January 1, 1996, 80–81.

27 Steven Aftergood, Federation of American Scientists, telephone interview, January 2000.

28 John Pike, telephone interviews, June 1996, January 2000.

29 Project on Government Oversight, "Fighting with Failures Series: B-2 Bomber," http://www.pogo.org/p/defense/do-020515-failures-b2bomber.html.

30 Dave Barry, "Go Jets," *Miami Herald,* October 24, 1997, http://www.qis.net/~jimjr/misc63.htm.

31 Tim Weiner, *Blank Check: The Pentagon's Black Budget* (New York: Warner Books, 1990), 46–47.

32 Todd Halvorson, "New MILSTAR Set for Launch on Friday but Report Says Satellite Isn't up to the Job," *Florida Today,* April 29, 1999, http://www.floridatoday.com/space/explore/stories/1999/042999b.htm.

33 J. Whitfield Larrabee, "Black Holes," *Humanist,* May–June 1996, 13–14.

34 US Const. art. I, sec. 9, cl. 7.

35 Center for Responsive Politics, "Defense: Long-Term Contribution Trends," *Opensecrets.org,* http://www.opensecrets.org/industries/indus.asp?Ind=d&Format=Print.

36 Rothstein and others, "A Sense of Proportion," 33.

37 Citizens Against Government Waste, "Pork Alert," press release, November 9, 1999.

38 Larrabee, "Black Holes"; see also Center for Responsive Politics, "The Best Defense: The Money," *opensecrets.org,* http://www.opensecrets.org/pubs/cashingin_defense/defense1.html.

39 William D. Hartung, "An Indefensible Budget," *Harper's,* November 1995, 27.

40 ABC News, "The Bush-Gore Race is a Battle of the Hawks," http://abcnews.go.com.

41 Chris Hellman, "The Bush Administration: What Can We Expect for the Pentagon?" *Foreign Policy in Focus,* http://www.fpif.org/commentary/2000/0012pentagon.html; see also John Isaacs and Dan Koslovsky, "Trim Pentagon Fat," *Bulletin of the Atomic Scientists* 57, no. 1 (January–February 2001): 26–28.

42 Nightline, "The Plan: Were Neo-Conservatives' 1998 Memos a Blueprint for Iraq War?" *ABC News,* March 5, 2003, http://www.abcnews.go.com/sections/nightline/DailyNews/pnac_030310.html.

43 CNN, "Fact Sheet: The Debate over the Crusader," *CNN.com,* May 10, 2002, http://www.cnn.com/2002/ALLPOLITICS/05/10/crusader.fact.sheet.

44 Walter Pincus, "Crusader a Boon to Carlyle Group Even If Pentagon Scraps Project," *Washington Post,* May 14, 2002, http://www.commondreams.org/headlines02/0514-05.htm.

45 Lauren Spain, "Chasing the Phantom Fleet," *Bulletin of the Atomic Scientists* 51, no. 5 (September–October 1995): 45.

46 John Isaacs, "Not in My District," *Bulletin of the Atomic Scientists* 50, no. 5 (September–October 1994): 13–15.

47 Center for Defense Information, "FY04 Request for Selected Weapons Systems," http://www.cdi.org/budget/2004/weapons.cfm.

48 "The V-22 Continues to Fail," *G2mil: The Magazine of Future Warfare,* http://www.g2mil.com/V-22struggles.htm.

49 Center for Defense Information, "Selected Weapons Systems."

50 Robert L. Borosage, "All Dollars, No Sense," *Mother Jones,* September–October 1993, 41.

51 "Two Jobs for One," *Roanoke Times,* January 25, 1993.

52 "Why We Overfeed the Sacred Cow," *Defense Monitor,* February 1996, 4.

53 Mike Moore, "More Security, Less Money," *Bulletin of the Atomic Scientists* 51, no. 5 (September–October 1995): 37.

54 Knut Royce and Nathaniel Heller, "Cheney Led Halliburton to Feast at Federal Trough," Center for Public Integrity, http://www.public-i.org/story_01_080200.htm.

55 James McCartney, *Friends in High Places* (New York: Ballantine, 1989), 169–74.

56 Center for Responsive Politics "Rebuilding Iraq: The Contractors," *opensecrets.org,* http://www.opensecrets.org/news/rebuilding_iraq/index.asp.

57 Pasztor, *When the Pentagon,* 74, 96.

58 William D. Hartung, "Stormin' Norman," *Washington Post,* July 28, 1996.

59 Dan Briody, "Carlyle's Way: Making a Mint inside the 'Iron Triangle' of Defense, Government, and Industry," *Red Herring,* January 8, 2002, http://www.redherring.com/Article.aspx?f=Articles/Archive/vc/2002/0111/947.xml&hed=Carlyle's %20way.

60 Pasztor, *When the Pentagon,* 36.

61 William D. Hartung, "Welfare Kings," *Nation,* June 19, 1995, 873–74.

62 Eyal Press, "Prez Pampers Peddlers of Pain," *Nation,* October 3, 1994, 340.

63 Ramsey Clark, *The Fire This Time* (New York: Thunder's Mouth Press, 1993), 155.

64 Rachel Stohl, "Post Sept. 11 Arms Sales and Military Aid Demonstrate Dangerous Trend," Center for Defense Information, http://www.cdi.org/program/document.cfm?documentid=454&programID=73&from_page=../friendlyversion/printversion.cfm.

65 Center for Responsive Politics, "Defense: Long-Term Contribution Trends."

66 Federation of American Scientists, "Fast Facts."

67 Benjamin Schwarz, "Why America Thinks It Has to Rule the World," *Atlantic Monthly,* June 1996, 94.

68 Tom Gervasi, *The Myth of Soviet Military Superiority* (New York: Harper & Row, 1986).

69 Seymour Melman, "Military State Capitalism," *Nation,* May 20, 1991, 649; see also Sherwood Ross, "The Progressive Interview: Seymour Melman," *Progressive,* February 1992, 34–36; and http://www.aftercapitalism.com/archive.html.

70 Robert H. Johnson, "Reconsiderations: Periods of Peril: The Window of Vulnerability and Other Myths," *Foreign Affairs* 61, no. 4 (Spring 1983): 950–70.

71 See the Reagan Years website, "Budgets and Deficits," http://www.aliveness.com/kangaroo/5Debt.htm.

72 Lauren Spain, "The Dream of Missile Defense," *Bulletin of the Atomic Scientists* 51, no. 5 (September–October 1995): 49–50.

73 John Pike, telephone interview, June 1996.

74 Tim Weiner, "Lies and Rigged 'Star Wars' Tests Fooled the Kremlin—and Congress," *New York Times*, August 18, 1993.

75 Spain, "Missile Defense."

76 William D. Hartung, "Star Wars Revisited: Still Dangerous, Costly, and Unworkable," *Foreign Policy in Focus Brief* 4, no. 24 (September 1999), http://www.fpif.org/briefs/vol4/v4n24star.html.

77 Larry Margasak, "GAO: Pentagon Fudged Missile Test," *Washington Post,* March 4, 2002, http://www.nucnews.net/nucnews/2002nn/0203nn/020304nn.htm#055; see also David Abel, "MIT Faces Criticism on Missile Test Study," *Boston Globe,* November 29, 2002, http://www.nucnews.net/nucnews/2002nn/0211nn/021129nn.htm#040; and Fred Kaplan, "The Pentagon's Laughable Weapons Test," Council for a Livable World, http://www.clw.org/nmd/laughtest.html.

78 Council for a Livable World, "Synopsis of the 2004–2005 Deployment," http://64.177.207.201/pages/8_273.html.

79 Center for Arms Control and Non-Proliferation, "The Full Costs of Ballistic Missile Defense," http://www.armscontrolcenter.org/nmd/fullcost.pdf.

80 Lauren Spain, "The Competition Has Bowed Out," *Bulletin of the Atomic Scientists* 51, no. 5 (September–October 1995): 39.

81 Center for Defense Information "FY04 Budget Request," http://www.cdi.org/budget/2004/.

82 Danielle Gordon, "More Missiles, Fewer Targets," *Bulletin of the Atomic Scientists* 51, no. 5 (September–October 1995): 47; see also Center for Defense Information, "Selected Weapons Systems."

83 Project on Government Oversight, "Fighting with Failures Series: Comanche Helicopter," http://www.pogo.org/p/defense/do-020517-failures-comanche.htm.

84 Lauren Spain, "A Stealthy $72 Billion," *Bulletin of the Atomic Scientists* 51, no. 5 (September–October 1995): 46; see also Center for Defense Information, "Selected Weapons Systems."

85 Brendan Matthews, "Plane Crazy: The Joint Strike Fighter Story," *Bulletin of the Atomic Scientists* 54, no. 3 (May–June 1998): 26–33; see also "An Idea That Won't Fly," *Waste Basket* 7, no. 14 (April 5, 2002), http://www.taxpayer.net/TCS/wastebasket/nationalsecurity/04-05-02jsf.htm.

86 John Isaacs, "Pentagon Clings to Costly Lifestyle," *Bulletin of the Atomic Scientists* 49, no. 3 (April 1993): 3.

87 Borosage, "All Dollars," 41.

88 Lauren Spain, "The C-17: A $340 Million Ugly Duckling," *Bulletin of the Atomic Scientists* 51, no. 5 (September–October 1995): 46–47; see also Center for Defense Information, "Selected Weapons Systems."

89 Russell Mokhiber and Robert Weissman, "The Boeing Boondoggle," *Common Dreams,* January 6, 2002, http://www.commondreams.org/views02/0101-07.htm; see also Juliet Eilperin, "Plane Lease Deal to Cost US Extra," *Washington Post,* December 26, 2002.

90 Project on Government Oversight, "DoD Delays Boeing Tanker Lease; Inspector General to Investigate," press release, December 2, 2003.

91 Lawrence J. Korb, testimony before the House Budget Committee, 107th Cong., 2nd sess., February 12, 2002, http://www.sensiblepriorities.org/KorbTestimony.pdf; see also Council for a Livable World, "Military Spending Briefing Book, 1999," http://www.clw.org/milspend/bbook/alternative.html. In the latter, Korb argued for a $225 billion Pentagon budget, $45 billion below the Clinton administration's proposal for FY2000.

92 Council for a Livable World, "Briefing Book." The Cato plan, authored by Earl Ravenal, called for a five-year reduction in military spending from 1998 through 2002, reaching $154 billion in the latter year. It focused on defense of the American homeland and a disengagement from overseas military conflicts.

93 Council for a Livable World, "Briefing Book." This plan called for savings of $1 trillion from projected spending levels from 2000 to 2010 by restructuring US forces away from the Cold War model and cooperating closely with our allies.

94 Council for a Livable World, "Briefing Book." Pike's plan, which he acknowledged was unlikely to be adopted, would essentially have demobilized the US military for the first time since Pearl Harbor. It assumed that active duty forces could hold off any potential adversary while large numbers of reserve forces could be mobilized. The plan also called for maintaining the existing B-52 program for another 40 years, and eliminating redundancy in the roles and missions of the various armed services. At the time it was proposed, the so-called One Percent Solution would have cost about $75 billion to $80 billion a year.

95 Let me just acknowledge that this number is necessarily more arbitrary than figures used elsewhere in this book—for good reason. Nobody knows exactly how much money the Pentagon is really wasting, including the people who run it. Remember, they have trillions of dollars in accounting errors. The four alternative budgets presented here are all a few years old, but two of them projected specific budget figures for FY2004; Pike's was updated as a percentage of the GDP, and Korb confirmed his general figure in a telephone interview. If you think the 9/11 attacks make these numbers obsolete, please see the sidebar "What about the War on Terror?"

12—S&L BAILOUT

1 Robert Sherrill, "The Looting Decade: S&Ls, Big Banks, and Other Triumphs of Capitalism," *Nation,* November 19, 1990, 592–93.

2 Robert Sherrill, "The Inflation of Alan Greenspan," *Nation,* March 11, 1996, 11–15; see also William Greider, *Secrets of the Temple* (New York: Simon & Schuster, 1987).

3 US Census Bureau, *Statistical Abstract of the United States* (Washington, DC: GPO, 1995).

4 Greider, *Secrets*, 76–77.

5 Sherrill, "Looting Decade," 592.

6 Sherrill, "Looting Decade," 592.

7 Sherrill, "Looting Decade," 593.

8 Brooks Jackson, *Honest Graft* (New York: Knopf, 1988), 203.

9 Sherrill, "Looting Decade," 594–95.

10 Stephen Pizzo, Mary Fricker, and Paul Muolo, *Inside Job: The Looting of America's Savings and Loans* (New York: Harper Perennial, 1991), 26.

11 Pizzo, Fricker, and Muolo, *Inside Job,* 236–37, 251–55, 436.

12 Sherrill, "Looting Decade," 609–10.

13 Pete Brewton, *The Mafia, CIA & George Bush* (New York: SPI Books, 1992).

14 Sherrill, "Looting Decade," 609.

15 Sherrill, "Looting Decade," 608.

16 Brewton, *The Mafia,* 4.

17 Sherrill, "Looting Decade," 593.

18 Sherrill, "Looting Decade," 610–11.

19 Sherrill, "Looting Decade," 620.

20 Sherrill, "Looting Decade," 618.

21 Pizzo, Fricker, and Muolo, *Inside Job,* 20.

13—AGRIBUSINESS SUBSIDIES

1 Dave Aftandilian, "Farm Bill 2002: Corporate Welfare or Farmer's Friend?" *Conscious Choice,* July 2002, http://www.consciouschoice.com/note/note1507.html.

2 Brian M. Riedl, "Top 10 Reasons to Veto the Farm Bill," *Heritage Foundation Backgrounder* 1538, April 17, 2002, http://www.heritage.org/library/backgrounder/bg1538.html.

3 Richard J. Dennis, "Privilege and Poverty," *Reason,* April 1993, 29.

4 C. Ford Runge, John A. Schnittker, and Timothy J. Penny, "Ending Agricultural Entitlements: How to Fix Farm Policy," (Washington, DC: Progressive Foundation, May 1995).

5 United States Department of Agriculture, *FY 2002 Budget Summary* (Washington, DC: USDA, 2002), http://www.usda.gov/agency/obpa/Budget-Summary/2002/2002budsum.htm.

6 Environmental Working Group, "Where Can I Learn More about Farm Subsidies?" http://www.ewg.org/farm/help/faq.php#learnmore.

7 Environmental News Service, "Farm Subsidies Pay for Handful of States," Stewardship America, December 13, 2001, http://www.privatelands.org/articles/farm_bill_ENS_12-13-2001.htm.

8 Anuradha Mittal, "Giving Away the Farm: The 2002 Farm Bill," *Food First Backgrounder* 8, no. 3 (Summer 2002): 2–3, http://www.foodfirst.org/pubs/backgrdrs/2002/s02v8n3.html.

9 Environmental News Service, "Farm Subsidies."

10 Charles Schumer, "New York Dairy and Apple Farmers Win Big in the Farm Bill," press release, May 1, 2002, http://www.senate.gov/~schumer/SchumerWebsite/pressroom/press_releases/PR00951.html.

11 Mittal, "Giving Away the Farm," 3.

12 Gay Alcorn, "Congress Helps Out down on the Farm," *Age* (Australia), September 3, 2001, http://www.theage.com.au/news/world/2001/09/03/FFKBIU5Q3RC.html. On Lugar, see John Lancaster, "Farm Subsidy Website Sows Discord," *Washington Post,* December 19, 2001.

13 Environmental Working Group, "City Slickers: Location of Farm Subsidy Recipient in Major Cities," http://www.ewg.org/farm/cityslickers/.

14 Brian M. Riedl, "Still at the Federal Trough: Farm Subsidies for the Rich and Famous Shattered Records in 2001," *Heritage Foundation Backgrounder* 1542, April 30, 2002, http://www.heritage.org/library/backgrounder/bg1542.html.

15 Environmental Working Group, "Where Can I Learn More."

16 "Few Agricultural Subsidies Go to Struggling Family Farms," http://

www.awitness.org/news/june_2002/agricultural_subsidies.html.

17 Environmental Working Group, "Where Can I Learn More."

18 Riedl, "Still at the Federal Trough."

19 Brian M. Riedl, "The Cost of America's Farm Subsidy Binge: An Average of $1 Million Per Farm," *Heritage Foundation Backgrounder* 1510, December 10, 2001, http://www.heritage.org/Research/Agriculture/BG1510.cfm.

20 On sugar prices, see Shannon Collier, Navin Nyak, Erich Pica, and others, *Green Scissors 2003* (Washington, DC: Friends of the Earth, 2003), 15. On peanut prices, see Taxpayers for Common Sense, "Taxpayer Scorecard," http://scorecard.taxpayer.net. On dairy prices, see Citizens Against Government Waste, "Milk Marketing Order Reform," 1999.

21 Environmental Working Group, "Where Can I Learn More."

22 Mittal, "Giving Away the Farm."

23 Dawn Erlandson, Jessica Few, and Gawain Kripke, *Dirty Little Secrets* (Washington, DC: Friends of the Earth, 1995).

24 National Public Lands Grazing Campaign, "Estimating the $500 Million Cost of the Federal Livestock Grazing Program," http://www.publiclandsranching.org.

25 Thomas M. Powers, "Taking Stock of Public Lands Grazing: An Economic Analysis," National Public Lands Grazing Campaign, http://www.publiclandsranching.org.

26 K. Moskowitz and C. Romaniello, *Assessing the Full Cost of the Federal Grazing Program* (Tucson, AZ: Center for Biological Diversity, 2002).

27 Forest Guardians, "Wing-Tipped Welfare Cowboys Ride the Range," http://www.fguardians.org/cowboy.htm.

28 National Public Lands Grazing Campaign, "Economic Facts of Public Lands Grazing," http://www.publiclandsranching.org.

29 National Public Lands Grazing Campaign, "Welfare Ranching: The Subsidized Destruction of the American West," http://www.publiclandsranching.org.

30 National Public Lands Grazing Campaign, "Economic Facts."

31 Taxpayers for Common Sense, "Cut Cowboy Welfare II," in *Taxpayer Scorecard, Second Session of the 105ᵗʰ Congress*, originally posted at http://scorecard.taxpayer.net/docs/house.cfm.

32 United States Department of Agriculture, "USDA Fact Sheet: Questions and Answers Related to the Livestock Compensation Program," http://www.usda.gov/news/releases/2002/09/0392fs2.htm; see also Office of Management and Budget, *Fiscal Year 2003 Budget of the US* (see chap.11, n. 1).

33 American Cancer Society, "Tobacco Use," http://www.cancer.org/tobacco.html.

34 David Hosansky, "Under Fire from All Sides, Tobacco Program Thrives," *Congressional Quarterly Weekly Report,* December 2, 1995, 3648.

35 Joseph Califano, "In Reply," *Journal of the American Medical Association* 273, no. 12 (March 22–29, 1995): 919.

36 National Center for Tobacco-Free Kids, "Federal Tax Burdens on US Households Caused by Tobacco Use," press release, June 29, 2000, http://www.tobaccofreekids.org.

37 National Center for Tobacco-Free Kids, "Tobacco Industry Gave More Than $9.4 Million in Federal Political Contributions in 2001–2002 Election Cycle," press release, May 12, 2003, http://www.tobaccofreekids.org.

38 Ed Mierzwinski, "Tobacco PAC Contributions to Congress," Public Interest Research Group, press release, March 14, 1996.

39 American Cancer Society, "Tobacco Use."

40 Editors, "Tobacco Imperialism," *Multinational Monitor,* January–February 1992, http://www.multinationalmonitor.org/hyper/mm0192.html#ed.

41 Green Scissors, "Up In Smoke: Tobacco Program," http://www.greenscissors.org/agriculture/tobacco.htm.

42 United States Department of Agriculture, "USDA Fact Sheet:

Tobacco Payment Program," http://www.fsa.usda.gov/pas/publications/facts/html/topp03.htm.

43 Environmental Working Group, "Summary Analysis of USDA Subsidy Payments, 1985–1994," press release, July 1996.

44 Kenneth Cook, "Freedom to Farm," Environmental Working Group, press release, February 27, 1996.

45 Concord Coalition, press release, December 9, 1999.

46 Concord Coalition, press release.

47 "Congress Approves $7.1 Billion Farm Bailout," *Insurance Journal,* May 26, 2000, http://www.insurancejournal.com/news/newswire/national/2000/05/26/11057.htm.

48 Environmental Working Group, "Congress to Approve Emergency Farm Aid for Fourth Year: $5.5 Billion Added to Subsidies," press release, http://www.ewg.org/reports/farmfairness.

49 National Center for Policy Analysis, "The Gravy Train That Is Farm Welfare," August 23, 2001, http://www.ncpa.org/pd/budget/pd082301d.html.

50 Chris Edwards and Tad DeHaven, "Farm Reform Reversal," *Cato Institute Bulletin,* March 2002, 1, http://www.cato.org/pubs/tbb/tbb-0203-2.pdf.

51 Taxpayers for Common Sense, "Agriculture," June 7, 2002, http://www.taxpayer.net/bailoutwatch/agriculture.htm.

52 Brian M. Riedl, "Agriculture Lobby Wins Big in New Farm Bill," *Heritage Foundation Backgrounder* 1534, April 9, 2002, http://www.heritage.org/library/backgrounder/bg1342.html.

53 Taxpayers for Common Sense, "Agriculture."

54 Charles Abbot, "Myriad Ways to Avoid US Limits on Crop Subsidies," *Forbes.com,* May 29, 2003, originally posted at http://www.forbes.com.

55 Environmental Working Group, "About the 2002 Farm Bill: A Missed Opportunity," http://www.ewg.org/farm/farmbill/stake.php.

56 Riedl, "The Cost of America's Farm Subsidy Binge."

57 Sarah Newport and others, *Green Scissors 2001*(Washington, DC: Friends of the Earth, 2001), 21.

58 Edward A. Chadd, "Manifest Subsidy," *Common Cause Magazine,* Fall 1995, 18–21.

59 Collier and others, *Green Scissors 2003,* 25.

60 E. Robert Scrofani, "The Greening of the California Desert," *Understanding Economics,* Henry George Institute, http://www.henrygeorge.org/caldes.htm.

61 Chadd, "Manifest Subsidy."

62 Chris Edwards and Tad DeHaven, "Farm Subsidies at Record Level as Congress Considers New Farm Bill," Cato Institute, briefing paper 70, October 18, 2001.

63 Stephen Moore and Dean Stansel, "How Corporate Welfare Won," Cato Institute, May 15, 1996; and "Principal Federal Statistical Agencies," http://www.members.aol.com/copafs/20table.htm.

64 Sarah Newport and others, *Green Scissors 2001* (Washington, DC: Friends of the Earth, 2001), 21; and Office of Management and Budget, *Fiscal Year 2004 Budget* (see introduction, n. 1); see also ; Ross Davidson, statement before the Subcommittee on Agriculture, Rural Development, and Related Agencies, 108th Cong., 1st sess., March 5, 2003.

65 Edwards and DeHaven, "Farm Subsidies."

66 James Bovard, "Archer Daniels Midland: A Case Study in Corporate Welfare," Cato Institute, policy analysis 241, September 26, 1995.

67 Dan Carney, "Dwayne's World," *Mother Jones,* July–August 1995, 44.

68 Charles Lewis, *The Buying of the President* (New York: Avon, 1996), 10.

69 Carney, "Dwayne's World."

70 Common Cause, "ADM's A-maize-ing Subsidy," http://www.fueltracker.com/NewsStories/ADMstories/CommonCause.html.

71 Bovard, "Archer Daniels Midland."

72 Paul A. Gigot, "Guess Who's Trying To Save Corporate Welfare," *Wall Street Journal,* June 6, 1997, http://www.s-t.com/daily/06-97/06-07-97/a04op022.htm.

73 Bovard, "Archer Daniels Midland."

74 Bovard, "Archer Daniels Midland."

75 Common Cause, "Fuel's Gold," http://www.commoncause.org/publications/fuelsgold-toc.htm.

76 Bob Sherman, "PAC Money, Soft Money, Allegiance of Congress," http://www.flash.net/~bob001/pacmoney.htm.

77 Ken Bentsen, "Bentsen Introduces Legislation to End Ethanol Subsidies," press release, February 5, 1999.

78 Gloria Lee, "Ethanol Continues to Reap Subsidy Windfall," Taxpayers for Common Sense, June 28, 2002, http://www.taxpayer.net/bailoutwatch/ethanol.htm.

79 Bovard, "Archer Daniels Midland."

80 Carney, "Dwayne's World."

81 Carney, "Dwayne's World."

82 Julie Forster, "A Different Kind of Andreas at ADM," *Business Week,* July 9, 2001, 62–64.

14—MEDIA HANDOUTS

1 Steve McClellan, "Big 4 Improve," *Broadcast & Cable,* March 6, 2000, 11.

2 Henry Geller and Tim Watts, "The Five Percent Solution," New America Foundation, Spectrum Series working paper 3, May 2002, http://www.newamerica.net/Download_Docs/pdfs/Pub_File_844_1.pdf.

3 Editorial, "GOP Giveaway," *Wall Street Journal*, September 1, 1995.

4 "GOP Giveaway," *Wall Street Journal.*

5 Common Cause, "Channeling Influence," April 2, 1997, http://www.commoncause.org/publications/040297_rpt.htm.

6 BetterTv.org, "The Dangers of Digital Television," http://www.bettertv.org/dangers.html (site now discontinued).

7 Arthur E. Rowse, "Off the Spectrum," *Extra!* July–August 1996, 16–17.

8 Geller and Watts, "Five Percent Solution."

9 National Technology and Information Administration, *U.S. Spectrum Management Policy: Agenda for the Future,* Appendix F, http://www.ntia.doc.gov/osmhome/91specagen/appendix.html#apf.

10 Economics and Technology Inc., "Subsidizing the Bell Monopolies," tables 1, 7, http://www.teletruth.org/docs/corporatewelfare.pdf.

11 Editorial, "GOP Giveaway"; and Common Cause, "Channeling Influence."

12 Throughout, we calculate long-term costs as single-year budget items by figuring the annual cost of paying interest on 7% bonds. However, at this writing, the rate on 30-year bonds is around 5%. I've left the figures as they are because they are almost certain to rise again, and fairly soon, given the gigantic long-term debt created by the current administration. While nobody can predict the future, even 7% payouts are going to look like a bargain for the taxpayer if we don't get our fiscal house in order soon.

13 CNN, "FCC Adopts New Media Ownership Rules," *CNN/Money,* June 2, 2003, http://money.cnn.com/2003/06/02/news/companies/fcc_rules/index.htm.

14 Project for Excellence in Journalism, "Does Ownership Matter in Local Television News? A Five-Year Study of Ownership and Quality," http://www.journalism.org/resources/research/reports/ownership/network.asp#2.

15 Frank Ahrens, "Compromise Puts TV Ownership Cap at 39%," *Washington Post,* November 25, 2003.

16 John Nichols, "Mega Media Madness," *TomPaine.com,* June 2, 2003, http://www.tompaine.com/feature2.cfm/ID/7952/view/print.

17 Center for Public Integrity, "Well Connected: FCC and Industry Maintain Cozy Relationships on Many Levels," May 22, 2003, http://www.publicintegrity.org/dtaweb/report.asp?ReportID=524&L1=10&L2=10&L3=0&L4=0&L5=0.

18 Bill Moyers, "Big Media: Media Deregulation Timeline," NOW with Bill Moyers, PBS, http://www.pbs.org/now/politics/mediatimeline.html.

19 Eric Boehlert, "One Big Happy Channel?" *Salon,* June 28, 2001, http://dir.salon.com/tech/feature/2001/06/28/telecom_dereg/index.html.

20 Media Reform Network, "The Lesson from Radio," http://www.mediareform.org/why.php#corrupt.

21 Boehlert, "Happy Channel."

22 Media Reform Network, "Lesson from Radio."

23 Eric Boehlert, "Clear Channel's Big, Stinking Deregulation Mess," *Salon,* February 19, 2003, http://www.salon.com/tech/feature/2003/02/19/clear_channel_deregulation/index2.html.

24 Chuck Metalitz, "Licenses to Steal Are Expensive," Henry George School of Social Science (Chicago), research note 4, September 2001.

25 "A League of Their Own," *US News and World Report,* October 9, 1995, 62–65.

26 For all these figures, see http://www.broadcastingcable.com.

27 Corpwatch, "Tobacco's Impact on the Economy," http://www.corpwatch.org/issues/PrT.jsp?articleid=400.

28 Americans for Tax Reform, press release, February 15, 2000.

29 Geller and Watts, "Five Percent Solution."

15—NUCLEAR SUBSIDIES

1 Newport and others, *Green Scissors 2001,* 3 (see chap. 13 n. 57).

2 Erich Pica, Pierre Sadik, Cena Swisher, and others, *Green Scissors 2002* (Washington, DC: Friends of the Earth, 2002), 11.

3 Collier and others, *Green Scissors 2003,* 17 (see chap. 13, n. 20).

4 Critical Mass Energy and Environment Program, "Nuclear Power 2010 Unveiled," April 2003, http://www.citizen.org/documents/nuke2010analysis.pdf.

5 Jill Lancelot, "Price-Anderson Act: Special Subsidies and Protections for the Nuclear Industry," *Progress Report,* http://www.progress.org/nuclear04.htm.

6 "The Nuclear Power Industry Is at a Standstill," *USA Today Magazine,* May 1993, 66–67.

7 Energy Information Administration, "Federal Energy Subsidies," press release, December 11, 1995.

8 Newport and others, *Green Scissors 2001;* see also Green Scissors, "Nuclear Alchemy Accelerated Transmutation of Nuclear Waste and Pyroprocessing," http://www.greenscissors.org/energy/atw.htm.

9 Institute for Energy and Environment Research, "Reprocessing and Spent Nuclear Fuel Management at the Savannah River Site," http://www.ieer.org/fctsheet/srs-snf.html.

10 Taxpayers for Common Sense, "TCS Analysis of Nuke Power Giveaways in Senate Energy Bill," http://www.taxpayer.net/greenscissors/LearnMore/nukepowergiveaways.htm; see also Bill Mesler, "Senator Strangelove," *Mother Jones,* December 1999, 57–59.

11 Collier and others, *Green Scissors 2003,* 7.

12 Collier and others, *Green Scissors 2003,* 16–17.

13 Newport and others, *Green Scissors 2001,* 3.

14 Collier and others, *Green Scissors 2003,* 18.

15 Toby Eglund, "Yucca Mountain's Other Story," *Gully,* March 28, 2002, http://www.thegully.com/essays/US/politics/020327_yucca_mountain.html.

16 Eureka County Nuclear Waste Page, "Yucca Mountain Approved by Congress," http://www.yuccamountain.org/archive/legal.htm.

17 Associated Press, "Congressional Investigators Urge Delay in Nuclear Waste Dump," *Las Vegas Sun,* November 30, 2001, http://www.lasvegassun.com/sunbin/stories/text/2001/nov/30/113010835.html.

18 Collier and others, *Green Scissors 2003,* 18.

19 John Ensign, "Yucca Mountain & Nuclear Waste," http://www.ensign.senate.gov/issues/Yucca.htm.

20 Reuters, "NRC Panel Blocks Plan for Utah Nuclear-Waste Dump," March 11, 2003, http://biz.yahoo.com/rm/030311/utilities_utah_nuclear_2.html (site now discontinued).

21 Newport and others, *Green Scissors 2001;* see also supplemental material, http://www.greenscissors.org/energy/nuclearwastefundfee.htm.

22 Collier and others, *Green Scissors 2003*, 17.

23 Mark Holt and Carl E. Behrens, *Issue Brief for Congress: Nuclear Energy Policy,* report IB88090 (Washington, DC: Congressional Research Service, March 20, 2003), http://hutchison.senate.gov/Energy3.pdf.

24 Newport and others, *Green Scissors 2001,* see also supplemental material, http://www.greenscissors.org/energy/yuccamountain.htm.

25 Allyce Bess, "Nuclear Waste Recyclers Target Consumer Products," Reuters, September 3, 2001, http://mailman.mcmaster.ca/mailman/private/cdn-nucl-l/0109.gz/msg00002.html.

26 Sasha Abramsky, "Bracing for a Nuclear Bailout," *Nation,* September 25, 1995, 312–14; and Scott Denman, Safe Energy Communication Council, telephone interview, January 2000.

27 Greg Bourget, "The True Cost of Nuclear Power," Mendocino Environmental Center, http://www.mecgrassroots.org/NEWSL/ISS38/38.07CostNuclear.html; see also Abramsky, "Nuclear Bailout."

28 Abramsky, "Nuclear Bailout."

29 General Accounting Office, *Nuclear Regulation: Better Oversight Needed to Ensure Accumulation of Funds to Decommission Nuclear Power Plants,* report RCED-99-75 (Washington, DC: GPO, 1999), 5.

30 Public Citizen, press release, January 26, 1999.

31 Associated Press, "Nuke Plant Tax Break Criticized," *New York Times*, August 10, 2001, http://www.nucnews.net/nucnews/2001nn/0108nn/010810nn.htm#120/.

32 Abramsky, "Nuclear Bailout."

33 Abramsky, "Nuclear Bailout."

34 Critical Mass Energy Project, "Study Shows Electricity Deregulation Could Cause Unfunded Nuclear Waste Liabilities That May Exceed $50 Billion," press release, January 26, 1999.

35 Newport and others, *Green Scissors 2001;* see also supplemental material, http://www.greenscissors.org/energy/

nif.htm; and Collier and others, *Green Scissors 2003*, 16–18.

36 Friends of the Earth, *Paying for Pollution,* http://www.foe.org/camps/eco/payingforpollution/tokamak.html.

37 Gawain Kripke, Beth Moorman, Erich Pica, and others, *Green Scissors 1999* (Washington, DC: Friends of the Earth, 1999), 10.

38 Collier and others, *Green Scissors 2003*, 17–18.

39 Scott Denman, telephone interview, January 2000.

16—AVIATION SUBSIDIES

1 Bruce Bernard, "EU Suspects US of Violating Bilateral Aircraft Subsidy Accord," *Journal of Commerce and Commercial*, March 18, 1993, 3A.

2 Congressional Black Caucus, "The FY 1996 CBC Alternative Budget: A Budget for the Caring Majority," 1995.

3 John Semmens, "Essential Air Service Subsidies: Just Plane Foolish," *Freeman* (Foundation for Economic Education) 31, no. 3 (October 1981), http://www.libertyhaven.com/theoreticalorphilosophicalissues/protectionismpopulismandinterventionism/essentialair.html.

4 James K. Glassman, "Corporate Welfare in the Sky," *US News & World Report,* July 28, 1997.

5 Matthew Mitchell, "Amtrak Budget at a Glance," *Delaware Valley Rail Passenger* 13, no. 5A (May 1995), http://www.etext.org/Zines/ASCII/DelawareRail/DVRP95AM.TXT.

6 Taxpayers for Common Sense, "Big Airlines Benefit from Bailout Bill," *Waste Basket* 7, no. 23 (June 7, 2002), http://www.taxpayer.net/TCS/wastebasket/budget/06-07-02airline bailout.htm.

7 "Harper's Index," *Harper's*, March 2003, 11.

8 Taxpayers for Common Sense, "Big Airlines Benefit."

9 TCS, "Big Airlines Benefit."

10 Gary S. Becker, "The Airline Bailout Sets a Bad Precedent," *Business Week,* November 26, 2001, http://www.businessweek.com/magazine/content/01_48/b3759036.htm.

11 James L. Gattuso, "Airline Bailout II: This Approach Won't Fly," Heritage Foundation, May 5, 2003, http://www.heritage.org/Press/Commentary/ed050503.cfm.

12 Lee Sustar, "Greed Air: Airline Unions Agree to Pay Cuts While Bosses Stuff Their Pockets," *CounterPunch,* May 1, 2003, http://www.counterpunch.org/sustar05012003.html.

17—MINING SUBSIDIES

1 Jim Lyon, "Patenting Plunder Continues," Mineral Policy Center, press release, September 26, 1995.

2 Collier and others, *Green Scissors 2003* (see chap. 13, n. 20), 20.

3 Dan Hirschmann, "The Last American Dinosaur: The 1872 Mining Law," Mineral Policy Center, press release, October 17, 1995.

4 US House Subcommittee on Oversight and Investigations, Committee on Natural Resources, *Taking from the Taxpayer: Public Subsidies for Natural Resource Development*, Democratic staff report, 103rd Cong., 2nd sess., August 1994, http://www.house.gov/resources/105cong/democrat/subsidy.htm.

5 Editorial, "Corporate Welfare," *Arizona Daily Star,* October 20, 2001.

6 Charles Levendovsky, "Old Mining Law Gives Citizens the Shaft," *Arizona Daily Star,* May 31, 2002.

7 Newport and others, *Green Scissors 2001* (see chap. 13, n. 57) 7–8; and Collier and others, *Green Scissors 2003*, 20.

8 Robert J. Shapiro, "Cut-and-Invest: A Budget Strategy for the New Economy," Progressive Policy Institute, March 1995.

9 Newport and others, *Green Scissors 2001*, 7–8.

10 Hirschmann, "Last American Dinosaur."

11 Friends of the Earth, "Tax Breaks for Polluters Growing More Expensive," press release, December 15, 1998, http://www.commondreams.org/pressreleases/Dec98/121598d.htm.

12 Collier and others, *Green Scissors 2003*, 16.

13 Collier and others, *Green Scissors 2003*, 16.

14 McIntyre, *Tax Expenditures* (see chap. 2, n. 3), 36 ; Office of Management and Budget, "Table 22–4: Tax Expenditures" (see chap. 5, n. 9).

18—OIL & GAS TAX BREAKS

1 General discussion of this topic indebted to Taxpayers for Common Sense, "Fossil Fuel Subsidies: A Taxpayer Perspective," http://www.taxpayer.net/TCS/fuelsubfact.htm; Jenny B. Wahl, "Oil Slickers: How Petroleum Benefits at the Taxpayer's Expense," http://www.ilsr.org/carbo/costs/truecosts1.html; and to McIntyre, *Tax Expenditures,* 34–35 (see chap. 2, n. 3).

2 McIntyre, *Tax Expenditures,* 34–35.

3 Joint Committee on Taxation, "Table 1: Tax Expenditure Estimates," 18 (see chap. 5, n. 16).

4 Taxpayers for Common Sense, "Fossil Fuel Subsidies"; Office of Management and Budget, "Table 22–4: Tax Expenditures" (see chap. 5, n. 9).

5 McIntyre, *Tax Expenditures,* 34–35; Joint Committee on Taxation, "Table 1: Tax Expenditure Estimates," 18–19. (see chap. 5, n. 16).

6 Friends of the Earth, "The Big Waste: Adding up the Barrels," Fact Sheet, http://www.foe.org/new/releases/1102crude.html.

7 Taxpayers for Common Sense, "Senate to Vote on Oil Royalties This Week," press release, September 14, 1999.

8 Charles Abbott and Tom Doggett, "Energy Bill Blocked in Senate on Close Vote," Reuters, November 21, 2003, http://www.commondreams.org/headlines03/1121-12.htm; see also John McCain, "Objectionable Provisions And Policy Changes In The Energy Bill," http://www.straightalkamerica.com/cgi-data/news/files/143.shtml.

9 Aileen Roder, "An Overview of Senate Energy Bill Subsidies to the Fossil Fuel Industry," Capitol Hill briefing, May 12, 2003, http://www.taxpayer.net/greenscissors/LearnMore/senatefossilfuelsubsidies.htm.

10 Matt Bivens, "Introducing a Bill to Rob the Public, Because We Can," *Nation,* April 12, 2002, http://www.thenation.com/failsafe/index.mhtml?bid=2&pid=47.

11 See Jane Holtz Kay, "Infernal Combustion," *In These Times,* August 8, 1999; see also Wahl, "Oil Slickers."

19—TIMBER SUBSIDIES

1 Newport and others, *Green Scissors 2001,* 9 (see chap. 13, n. 57).

2 Randall O'Toole, Thoreau Institute, telephone interview, June 1996.

3 Michael Francis, Wilderness Society, telephone interview, June 1996.

4 Randall O'Toole, "Reinventing the Forest Service," Thoreau Institute, 1995.

5 Newport and others, *Green Scissors 2001,* 24.

6 O'Toole, "Reinventing."

7 Taxpayers for Common Sense, "Why Does Congress Subsidize Timber Corporations to Cut Down the Public's National Forests?" http://www.taxpayer.net/forest/learnmore/cost.htm.

8 Friends of the Earth, "House Votes to Pave Forests," press release, 1999.

9 Randall O'Toole, cited in Courtney Cuff and others, *Green Scissors 1996* (Washington, DC: Friends of the Earth, 1996).

10 Janice Shields, "Timber Sales Losses on Federal Lands," Center for Study of Responsive Law, press release, July 7, 1996, http://lists.essential.org/corporate-welfare/msg00008.html.

11 Alaska Rainforest Campaign, "Taxpayers Underwrite Tongass Timber Sales," http://www.akrain.org/rainforest/tongass/logexpense.asp; see also Pica and others, *Green Scissors 2002,* (see chap. 15, n. 2) supplemental material, http://www.greenscissors.org/publiclands/tongass.htm.

12 O'Toole, telephone interview.

13 Newport and others, *Green Scissors 2001,* 9.

14 Dave Katz, Southeast Alaska Conservation Council, telephone interview, June 1996.

15 Buck Lindekugel, Southeast Alaska Conservation Council, telephone interview, January 2000.

16 American Lands Alliance, "Administration Attacks on the National Forests," http://www.americanlands.org/attacks.htm.

17 Edward A. Chadd, "Manifest Subsidy," *Common Cause Magazine,* Fall 1995, 18–21.

18 Jonathan Oppenheimer, "Money to Burn: Wildfire Risks from Commercial Logging," Taxpayers for Common Sense, report, http://www.forestadvocate.org/resources/forestadvocate/1_01_money_burn.html.

19 J. A. Savage, "House Debates Orwellian Logging Bill," *AlterNet,* May 19, 2003, http://www.alternet.org/print.html?StoryID=15933.

20 American Lands Alliance, "Administration Attacks."

21 Savage, "Orwellian Logging Bill."

22 Native Forest Network, "By the Numbers: Facts about Wildfire and Logging," National Forest Protection Alliance, http://www.forestadvocate.org/news/btn_10_27_02.html.

20—SYNFUEL TAX CREDITS

1 General discussion of this topic indebted to Erlandson and others, *Dirty Little Secrets* (see chap. 13, n. 23); see also Joint Committee on Taxation, "Table 1: Tax Expenditure Estimates," 19 (see chap. 5, n. 16).

21—OZONE TAX EXEMPTIONS

1 R. Montaskersky, "Northern Hemisphere Ozone Hits Record Low," *Science News,* March 20, 1993, 180–81.

2 For the text of the Montreal Protocol, see http://www.unep.org/ozone/montreal.shtml.

3 Alexander Cockburn and Jeffrey St. Clair, "Slime Green," *Progressive,* May 1996, 18–21.

4 Gawain Kripke and Brian Dunkiel, "Taxing the Environment: Corporate Tax Breaks to Promote Environmental Destruction," *Multinational Monitor,* September 1998, http://www.

thirdworldtraveler.com/Corporations/
CorporateTaxBreaks.html.

5   Geoffrey Lean, "Bush OK of Methyl
Bromide Use by Agribusiness Will
Destroy Ozone Treaty," *Independent*
(London), July 20, 2003, http://www.
organicconsumers.org/corp/methyl_
bromide.cfm.

22—MISCELLANEOUS RIPOFFS

1   McIntyre, *Tax Expenditures,* 37–39
(see chap. 2, n. 3); see also Office of
Management and Budget, "Table 22-4:
Tax Expenditures" (see chap. 5, n. 9).

2   McIntyre, *Tax Expenditures,* 38; see
also Office of Management and Budget,
"Table 22-4: Tax Expenditures."

3   Common Cause, "Common Cause
Urges Senate to Act to End Corporate
Welfare Programs," press release, 1995.

4   Collier and others, *Green Scissors 2003,*
4 (see chap. 13, n. 20).

5   Newport and others, *Green Scissors
2001* (see chap. 13, n. 57).

6   Moore and Stansel, "How Corporate
Welfare Won," (see chap. 13, n. 63).

7   Janice Shields, "Ending (Corporate)
Welfare as We Know It," *Business and
Society Review,* Summer 1995, http:
//lists.essential.org/corporate-welfare/
msg00003.html.

23—WHAT'S BEEN LEFT OUT

1   Greg LeRoy, "Good Jobs First," press
release, April 15, 1999.

2   Russell Mokhiber, "Underworld USA,"
In These Times, April 1–13, 1996,
14–16.

3   L. J. Davis, "Medscam," *Mother Jones,*
March–April 1995, 26–29.

4   Ron Winslow, "Study Says Hospital
Errors May Kill Many Thousands of
Patients a Year," *Wall Street Journal
Interactive Edition*, November 30,
1999, http://www.productslaw.com/
medmal2.html.

5   Russell Mokhiber, *Corporate Crime and
Violence* (San Francisco: Sierra Club
Books, 1989), 16.

6   Mokhiber, "Underworld USA."

7   Daniel Burnham, "White-Collar Crime:
Whitewash at the Justice Department,"

Covert Action Quarterly, Summer 1996,
24–26.

8   Barlett and Steele, *America: What Went
Wrong?* 18–19 (see chap. 5, n. 3).

9   Barlett and Steele, *America,* 156–59
(see introduction, n. 12).

10 Randy Albelda, Nancy Folbre, and the
Center for Popular Economics, *The War
on the Poor: A Defense Manual* (New
York: New Press, 1996), 67.

11 Christian Parenti, "Making Prison Pay,"
Nation, January 29, 1996, 11–14.

12 Chris Cozzone, "Busted: Corruption
at UNICOR," *Prison Life,* January
1995; see also Michael Robinson, "The
Money Machine," *VOICES ELECTRIC:
An Online Journal of Student Writing,*
http://webs.ashlandctc.org/jnapora/
voices/michael_robinson.htm.

13 Media Foundation, "The End
of the Automotive Age," http:
//www.adbusters.org/~adbusters/
main.html.

14 Guerrilla Media, "Mo'slain Greedy
Sponsored by Slayer's Unltd.," press
release, September 2, 1995.

15 Mokhiber, *Corporate Crime,* 221–28.

APPENDIX A—WELFARE FOR THE POOR

1   Coalition on Human Needs, "CHN
Issue Brief on Medicaid," http://www.
chn.org/issuebriefs/medicaid.asp.

2   Updated figures from Office of
Management and Budget, *Fiscal Year
2004 Budget* (see introduction, n.
1); see also background from Randy
Albelda, Nancy Folbre, and the Center
for Popular Economics, *The War on the
Poor: A Defense Manual* (New York:
New Press, 1996); and Chuck Collins
and Felice Veskel, *Economic Apartheid
in America: A Primer on Economic
Inequality and Insecurity* (New York:
New Press, 2000).

Index

G

Gallo (corporation), 48

GAO (General Accounting Office), 56–57, 61, 72, 124

gas, 94–95, 104, 119–121, 139. *See also* oil

gasohol, 94–95

gasoline taxes, 138

Gates, Bill, 14

GATT (General Agreements on Tariffs and Trade), 1, 140

GDP (gross domestic product): 5, 36, 74; defined, 152

General Accounting Office (GAO), 56–57, 61, 72, 124

General Electric (GE): accelerated depreciation use, 38; advanced tech subsidies for, 132; Ex-Im loans to, 49; legal difficulties, 58–60; NBC and, 98

general fund revenues, defined, 151

General Mills, 48

General Motors (GM), 5: accelerated depreciation use, 39; destroys streetcar systems, 139; Ex-Im loans to, 49; fuel efficiency subsidy, 131

Gephardt, Dick, 62

Getty Oil, 91

Gigot, Paul, 94

Gingrich, Newt, 89

GlobalSecurity.org, 61, 74

glossary, 147–155

GNP (gross national product), 152

golden parachutes, 65

Goldwater, Barry, 73

Gore, Al, 57, 63

Gould Simulation System, 56

Government Accountability Project, 66

Grant, Ulysses S., 115

Grassley, Chuck, 83

grazing leases, 85–86, 96

Green, Gene, 42

Greenspan, Alan, 76, 81

Greyhound (corporation), 139

Grimes Manufacturing, 56

gross domestic product (GDP): 5, 36, 74; defined, 152

gross national product (GNP), defined, 152

Grumman Aerospace, 56

Grumman, 57

H

Halliburton, 26, 32, 49, 64–67

Hanford Nuclear Reservation, 106

Harkin, Tom, 82

Hazeltine, 60

HDTV (high definition television), 99

Head Start, 3, 143

Healthy Forests Initiative, 125

Heritage Foundation, 17, 90–91, 155, 163–165, 168

Hewlett, Bill, as a farmer, 86

home equity loans, interest deduction for, 21

Homeland Security Department, US, 54

homeowner tax breaks, 19–21

horse deductions, 7–8

House Progressive Caucus, 152

household, defined, 152

housing assistance, 142–143

Houston Post, 79

Hughes Aircraft, 49, 60

Hussein, Saddam, 66

Hutchinson, Kay Bailey, 120

hydrochlorofluorocarbons (HCFCs), 128–129

Hyundai, 134

I

IBM, accelerated depreciation use, 39; advanced tech subsidies to, 132; Ex-Im loans to, 49

Ill Wind. *See* Operation Ill Wind

import restrictions, 84, 87, 89, 95–96, 140

income disparity: 6; defined, 152

income taxes, 2, 14–15, 152–153

Infinity, 101

inflation, 36, 76–77, 137; adjustments for, 2, 14, 24, 70, 72, 108, 143; COLA as adjustment for, 149; constant dollars and, 149; defined, 153

Ingersoll-Rand, 32

inheritance taxes, 3

insurance: COLI, 41–42; companies, 83, 91; crop, 84, 93; FSLIC, 78–79; mortgage, 20; nuclear subsidy, 104–105; OASDI, 14–15; ordinary people and, 41–42, 85–88; pension, 14–15, 25; tax exemptions, 42; unemployment, 85; write-offs, 7

Intel, 31

About South End Press

South End Press is a nonprofit, collectively run book publisher with more than 250 titles in print. Since our founding in 1977, we have tried to meet the needs of readers who are exploring, or are already committed to, the politics of radical social change. Our goal is to publish books that encourage critical thinking and constructive action on the key political, cultural, social, economic, and ecological issues shaping life in the United States and in the world. In this way, we hope to provide a forum for a wide variety of democratic social movements, and provide an alternative to the products of corporate publishing.

From its inception, the Press has organized itself as an egalitarian collective with decision-making arranged to share the rewards and stresses of running the business as equitably as possible. Each collective member is responsible for core editorial and business tasks, and all collective members earn the same salary. The Press also has made a practice of inverting the pervasive racial and gender hierarchies in traditional publishing houses; our staff has had a female majority since the mid-1980s, and has included at least 50 percent people of color since the mid-1990s. This diversity is reflected in our author list, which includes Arundhati Roy, bell hooks, Noam Chomsky, Winona LaDuke, Holly Sklar, Ward Churchill, Cherrie Moraga, Manning Marable, Grace Chang, and Howard Zinn.

Through the Institute for Social and Cultural Change, South End Press works with other political media projects—Alternative Radio, Speakout, and *Z Magazine*—to expand access to information and critical analysis.

For current information on our books, please ask for a free catalog by sending your request by mail to South End Press, 7 Brookline Street, Cambridge, MA 02139, or by email to southend@southendpress.org. Our website, www.southendpress.org, also has a complete listing of our titles, as well as information on author events, important news, and other interesting links.